You are the Messiah, and I should know

You are the Messiah, and I should know

Why leadership is a myth (and probably a heresy)

Justin Lewis-Anthony

BLOOMSBURY

LONDON • NEW DELHI • NEW YORK • SYDNEY

A Continuum book

Bloomsbury Publishing Plc
50 Bedford Square
London WC1B 3DP

www.bloomsbury.com

Bloomsbury Publishing, London, New Delhi, New York and Sydney

A CIP record for this book is available from the British Library.

ISBN 9781441186188

10 9 8 7 6 5 4 3 2 1

Typeset by Fakenham Prepress Solutions, Fakenham, Norfolk NR21 8NN
Printed and bound in Great Britain by CPI Group (UK) Ltd, Croydon, CRO 4YY

For David, my father

Quod enim munus rei publicae adferre maius

meliusve possumus, quam si docemus atque

erudimus iuventutem?

Cicero, De Divinatione, II.4

'For what greater or better gift can we bring to

the republic, than if we teach and instruct the

youth?'

Contents

Foreword

It must surely seem odd for me, an American, to write a foreword to this book on leadership by Justin Lewis-Anthony. He is, after all, very English and I am not. Moreover the argument of the book draws from and depends on extremely sophisticated film criticism about which I know very little. When Lewis-Anthony asked me to consider writing a foreword, therefore, I could only speculate why he had approached me but, now that I have read and learned much from the book, I can only be grateful that he asked me to engage with what he has written.

As it turns out, however, America plays a central part in his account of the role movies play in determining our pictures of what leadership looks like. For, as Lewis-Anthony observes, the myths that shape the movies that shape us are American myths. It, therefore, makes some sense that an American should write the foreword to this book. I have after all been formed by the images of leadership Lewis-Anthony so skillfully helps us see portrayed in American movies.

That portrayal, Lewis-Anthony rightly argues, was at the heart of Emerson's vision of the new man, the "new Adam," that now determines how most of the world understands "leadership." That man (and the gender certainly mattered) was one that assumed the leader must be the "great man" who heroically kept the forces of anarchy and the abyss at bay. I am particularly gratified that Lewis-Anthony calls attention to the work of R. W. B. Lewis for understanding the role of the "new Adam" in American life.

As an American, and in particular an American shaped by the American West, I can certainly testify to the power of the "great man" image of leadership in America. Accordingly I think

Lewis-Anthony is quite right to suggest that war movies express the central motifs that give expression to the American under-standing of leadership. His account of the movie, *Patton*, is worth the price of the book. I simply had not seen, until I read Lewis-Antony's treatment, the connections between Patton, Hitler, and the Star War movies. Yet I take it one of the troubling strengths of Lewis-Anthony's "method" is to help us recognize the hold images have on our lives that we often fail to acknowledge.

That Lewis-Anthony's "method" forces us to recognize images that hold us captive suggests that, though this is a book about leadership, I suspect many readers of the book will discover the book has far- reaching implications beyond questions of leadership. In particular, Lewis-Anthony makes us consider how we are to understand what it means to be a faithful church in the world in which we now find ourselves. His account of what it means for the church to be a people who, by following Jesus, cannot avoid being open to the new, obviously has ecclesial implications that are immediate and demanding. Lewis-Anthony forces us to ask what kind of church we must be to raise up people who can recognize as determinative how we must live lives like the life of Dietrich Bonhoeffer.

Lewis-Anthony does not explicitly call attention to the use of lots in Acts to determine who would replace Judas among the disciples, but I think it an example commensurate with the way he is trying to have us rethink questions of leadership. Ask yourself what kind of community you need to be such that your leaders can be chosen by lot. Some churches in the Anabaptist tradition continue to choose their ministry in that fashion. I think it a fascinating question because it directs attention to the appropriate subject for consid-ering questions of leadership, that is, to the community rather than the individual. To assume that you must be the kind of community whose leaders may be chosen by lot defeats any presumption that a leader in the church must be "strong" if they are to be a leader.

The "strong-man" account of leadership unfortunately cannot but signal the death of the kind of community Lewis-Anthony suggests the Church must be. When it is assumed a "strong-man" is needed to make up for what is assumed to be the deficiency of the community, then calls for leadership cannot help but be disguised forms of coercion and even violence. By contrast, when "leaders" are chosen by lot it is not the deficiencies of the community that make leadership necessary, but rather a leader is needed to coordinate and give direction to the many gifts that constitute the life of the community. In such a community the "leader" does not impose order on the community but rather the leader is an agent of memory to help the community not lose what makes them who they are.

Lewis-Anthony begins the first chapter with this remark by Dr. Rowan Williams: "Often people demand 'moral leadership' from religious figures. Confession time: like others, I suspect, my heart sometimes sinks when I hear this, and I think, cynically, that it's just about people wanting religious leaders to tell them that they're right." I call attention to this comment because Lewis-Anthony's book cannot help but invite reflection on Rowan Williams' style of leadership as Archbishop of Canterbury. Williams, who was often criticized for failing to "provide strong leadership," refused to be "heroic" and, if Lewis-Anthony's account of the leadership constitutive of the Church is right, in the process Williams gave the Church a great gift. He did so because he acted as one who understood his task was to follow Jesus in such a manner that he was not on the radar screen of those whose image of leadership has been set by the movie screen.

It is, as Lewis-Anthony suggests, tempting to be cynical about leadership in our time. Cynicism is an attempt to avoid being manipulated by self-appointed leaders. It is, therefore, all the more remarkable that Lewis-Anthony has written such a hopeful book. He has refused to let secular models of leadership provide the norm for how Christians must discover how Jesus' intimate love of the church has transformed how we govern our common life. He has accomplished that task, moreover, in an entertaining way and in the process helped us better appreciate how wonderful it is to be part of a community that does not rely on the rule of "great men."

Professor Stanley Hauerwas

Introduction

In 2005 senior clergy and lay people within the Church of England launched an initiative designed to apply the insights of secular leadership studies to the situation of the church. At the introductory conference of the Foundation for Church Leadership, Bishop Michael Turnbull declared:

> A question never far from the mind of a church leader is 'How can I break out of institutional shackles and be the true, adventurous, uninhibited leader I want to be?'.[1]

This book is intended to question the two presumptions behind that 'true, adventurous and uninhibited' aspiration. First, why should we think that 'leadership' can be the universal solution to any number of social problems? Second, even if 'leadership' can work in that way in secular society, why should it be something encouraged and fostered within the Church?

We'll question the presumptions in three different stages, and, in doing so, we shall make a distinction between three different models of leadership.

First, in **Section One** I will look at the way in which leadership has been understood and practiced in the Church of England (*Chapter 1: Jesus, MBA*), and how the Church has attempted to define a specifically Christian form of leadership. This has been called *Missionary-Leadership* (*MissL*). Some are concerned that

---

[1] Michael Turnbull, 'Introduction', in *Focus on Leadership,* The Foundation for Church Leadership (2005), 4.

the Church is attempting to 'baptise' secular models of leadership, so I look at the ways in which 'leadership' has been presented to the secular business world (*Chapter 2: The panacea of leadership*). I will show that leadership is a problematic word with no agreed definition, but this hasn't prevented the overwhelming growth of what I call *Managerial-Leadership* (*ManL*). In *Chapter 3, The myths of the mighty,* I argue that 'leadership' is actually best understood as a 'myth', something more compelling and powerful than a 'fairy tale', and that our myths today are perpetuated, created even, through the medium of cinema. As the most powerful cinema in the world today is American, it is important to say something about the fundamental myths of American society: there are two dominant myths, which, when combined, can be fairly called the American religion (and Ralph Waldo Emerson is important in understanding this religion).

In **Section Two** I will show how cinema creates and sustains a third, powerful and unconscious, model of leadership, what I call *Mythological-Leadership* (*MythL*): here is the worship of the 'great man' model of leadership (*Chapter 4: The leadership principle*); attempts to reject the 'great man', which only succeed in reinforcing the power of the *MythL* (*Chapter 5: Leadership repudiated*); and the irrepressible source model for all depictions of leadership in Hollywood film, the character and roles of John Wayne (*Chapter 6: Leadership redux*). All this mythology has a moral consequence: at the base of both the American Religion and the myth of leadership is the promise and use of violence (*Chapter 7: The Duke of deception*).

In **Section Three** I propose a possible antidote. By being more aware of the real nature of Scripture often cited as justifying Christian leadership (*Chapter 8: Leading and leaving the dead),* we can see (in *Chapter 9: Mythos and anti-mythos*) how to resist the heresy and temptations of *MythL,* a myth fundamentally and fatally tainted by the threat, use and acceptance of violence. We find in the life, teaching and practice of Dietrich Bonhoeffer, an exemplification of how to repudiate 'great man' leadership, and shall see in his modelling of the true Christian pattern of social organization, discipleship, a way of living out this repudiation in the complicated and grief-stricken world in which we find ourselves.

In short, if you are interested in films, read Section Two and Chapter 9. If you are interested in secular managerial-leadership, read Chapter 2, and Chapter 3 for the mythological roots of that leadership. If you are interested in the way in which the Church organizes itself then read Chapter 1 and Chapter 9, and underpin that with the biblical record in Chapter 8. If, on the other hand, you are interested in the way in which mythology, anthropology, culture, capitalism and the threat of violence have been combined into something that can be sold to fearful people, within and without businesses, within and without the churches, then read the whole book. You don't have to read the secular business literature listed in the bibliography. I did that, so you don't have to.

Making a choice of movies

Writing theologically about cinema is a tricky thing to do. Some writers are able to assert that: 'there is no single person, entity, organization, institution, or power in our society today that even comes close to rivalling the power of film and television to shape our faith, values, and behaviour'.[2] Other writers ask: 'What has Jerusalem to do with Hollywood?'.[3] Mostly people tend to think that theologians writing about films is a 'lark'.[4] I hope I will show through Section Two that myths are expressed through culture, and that a proper understanding of myths shows that they are 'framing metaphors',[5] expressed through repetition, and their very power lies in that repetition. They are 'stories we never get tired of hearing'[6]— an excellent, intuitive, definition of popular cinema. But what stories to choose?

There are many different examples and genres of film which I might have chosen. Crime films, such as *The Godfather* series or *Chinatown;* political thrillers, such as *The Parallax View*, *Three*

---

[2] Bryan P. Stone, *Faith and Film* (2000), 7.

[3] James M. Wall, *Church and Cinema* (1971) — Wall's choice of title for chapter 1.

[4] Margaret R. Miles, *Seeing and Believing* (1996), ix.

[5] William G. Doty, *Mythography* (1986), 18. See p. 151.

[6] Kelton Cobb, *The Blackwell Guide to Theology and Popular Culture* (2005), 123.

Days of the Condor, and *All the President's Men;* even comedies, such as *M*A*S*H* and *Being There,* all depict leaders and those in authority (and the portrayal of leaders is usually to show them as amoral, corrupt, and self-serving).

However, I have chosen, chiefly, to look at the war-film. Stanley Kubrick, early in his career, argued that the war film as a genre 'provides an almost unique opportunity to contrast an individual of our contemporary society with a solid framework of accepted value'.[7] In other words, everyone knows where they stand in a war film, and the audience also knows where everybody stands. War films explore a society in which the expectations of authority and command are both explicit and implicit: explicit, in that protagonists have signifiers of their ranking and power within the society (four-star generals, double-bar captains, three-stripe sergeants, and so on); implicit, in that the signifiers point to modes of behaviour and relationship which are normative and imposed (saluting a senior officer, accepting orders, standing to attention), all of which are designed to reinforce the military chain of command and military effectiveness.

Related to war-pictures genre is a second, important, category of film, namely the Western. This group of films is largely represented by the work of John Ford and John Wayne in the so-called 'Cavalry Trilogy' of the late 1940s and early 1950s. The choice of these pictures was for three reasons: first, they are *cinematically* significant. John Ford is an acknowledged master of moviemaking, and the stories, motifs, techniques and tropes of the films have been duplicated in many subsequent films. Second, they are *morally* significant. John Wayne accumulated much of his later status as an ethical American icon through being in these films. Third, they are *mythically* significant. The films of the 'Cavalry Trilogy' fulfil a dual function: they are military-westerns: a clearly hierarchical society within the important mythological *milieu* of the American West.

But still, why movies, as opposed to all the other cultural artefacts which might be mythical? Just thinking briefly about

---

[7]Colin Young, 'The Hollywood War of Independence', *Film Quarterly* (Spring 1959): 10.

the question will throw up all kinds of other media: what about print (novels, short stories, poetry, polemics)? In what way is music-making mythic (opera, oratorios, musical theatre, popular music)? What about the visual arts? What about newspapers and television?

It is true that all these media have ways in which they can function mythologically. We repeat stories, within the news, which, when examined critically, show that they are more about myth (a story we tell to make sense of the world) than they are about fact (these things, and only these things happened). But how do the news media make these myths? Think about the way eye-witnesses describe what they see to journalists: 'It didn't feel real. It was just like a movie'. This has become such a common description that Susan Sontag, in reaction to the events of September 2001, noted 'After four decades of big-budget Hollywood disaster films, "It felt like a movie" seems to have displaced the way survivors of a catastrophe used to express the short-term unassimilability of what they had gone through: "It felt like a dream"'.[8] Most of our mythic media (news, novels, music, paintings) are subsets of our main myth-source, cinema:

> We pay our votive offerings at the box office. We buy our ritual corn. We hush in reverent anticipation as the lights go down and the celluloid magic begins. Throughout the filmic narrative we identify with the hero. We vilify the antihero. We vicariously exult in the victories of the drama. And we are spiritually inspired by the moral of the story, all while believing we are modern techno-secular people, devoid of religion.[9]

The religion being promulgated in these movie-temples, the 'common unconscious' and 'common memory' in Martin Scorsese's words,[10] is a thing of wonder, but it is not morally neutral

---

[8]Susan Sontag, *Regarding the Pain of Others* (2003), 19. See also chapter 3, 'Like a Movie', in Marc Redfield, *The Rhetoric of Terror* (2009).

[9]Geoffrey Hill, *Illuminating Shadows* (1992), 3.

[10]Martin Scorsese and Michael Henry Wilson, *A Personal Journey with Martin Scorsese Through American Movies* (1997), 166.

or morally necessary. The high priests of this religion might pretend to us that it is ('A man's gotta do what's a man's gotta do'), but we can only accept that as long as we are unaware of exactly what is being demanded of us, along with our votive popcorn.

SECTION ONE

Leadership is a myth

...Now the philosophers have engaged in a great deal of complicated debate about the supreme ends of good and evil; and by concentrating their attention on this question they have tried to discover what it is that makes a man happy. ...Although they have gone astray in different ways, the limits imposed by nature set bounds to their deviation from the path of truth, so that there were none who did not set the Supreme Good and Supreme Evil in one of three locations: in the soul, or in the body, or in both. On the basis of this threefold classification into what we may call the genera of philosophic schools, Marcus Varro by careful and minute examination noted such a wide variety of opinions, in his book On Philosophy, *that by the application of certain criteria of differentiation he easily arrived at a total of 288 sects, not sects already in existence but possible schools of thought.*

AUGUSTINE OF HIPPO, THE CITY OF GOD, *XIX.1*

Chapter 1
Jesus, MBA

People have described me as a 'management bishop',
but I say to my critics: 'Jesus was a management
expert too'.
                 GEORGE CAREY, ARCHBISHOP OF CANTERBURY, 1991

Looking for leadership in the Church

In December 2007 Dr Rowan Williams, then Archbishop of Canterbury, made the following revealing remark:

> Often people demand 'moral leadership' from religious figures. Confession time: like others, I suspect, my heart sometimes sinks when I hear this, and I think, cynically, that it's just about people wanting religious leaders to tell them that they're right.[1]

He alluded to this phenomenon again in a public conversation with Ian Hislop, the editor of *Private Eye*, which took place in Canterbury Cathedral: 'The leadership thing is one of the problems here. I've

---

[1] Rowan Williams, 'The stable door is open', *The Times* (24 December 2007), 17.

sometimes said when people say, "We want you to give a lead," what they mean is, "We want you to tell *them*, not us. We don't want to be led"'.[2]

People look to those men in the Church who play a visible role in the life of the community and nation.[3] We call the visible men 'leaders' and we expect them, reasonably, to provide 'leadership', even today, in a secular and suspicious world. 'Leaders' are the go-to-guys for 'leadership'.

This is what Dr Williams's discovered. The Archbishop of Canterbury is expected to provide 'leadership', within and without the Church. In 2001 Douglas Hurd was asked by Dr Williams's predecessor, George Carey, to prepare a report how and why the Archbishop should approach his office. While the Archbishop might no longer be the 'spiritual director' of English society, Hurd reported, he does remain 'the nation's primary spiritual conscience'.[4] As a result of this 'the modern media require a personality to whom they can turn for comment. In return they scrutinize that individual's life and opinions with an intensity that must often be hard to take'. This results in a 'desire for clear and firm leadership in the Church', which is both a 'demand for missionary leadership' and, at the same time, 'assumes that the Archbishop has more control over the Church's institutions than he in fact possesses'.[5]

The Archbishop of Canterbury is therefore expected both to lead directly and to model leadership. Fair enough. If you were to ask the mythical 'person in the pew' a one-word description of the function of the Archbishop of Canterbury it would probably be something around leadership: we can see this in the amount of attention Dr William's 'leadership' received in the secular press, some of which we will examine in the next section. We will also see the way that the Archbishop of Canterbury's leadership is not

[2]Ian Hislop and Rowan Williams, in Conversation at 'The Gathering', Canterbury Cathedral, (4 September 2009).
[3]I use the word 'men' very deliberately. The question of the leadership fulfilled by women is a subsidiary one, and the reasons why it is subsidiary is all the more significant for the ideas we will explore in this book.
[4]Douglas Hurd, *To Lead and To Serve* (2001), 14. Hereafter *The 'Hurd' Report*.
[5]*The 'Hurd' Report*, 14.

thought to be unique within the life of the church: the archbishop is not, or should not be, the only leader. Everyone is a leader in the modern church. This belief (a significant and deliberate word) is signalled by writings and teachings from within and without the church. How the church (the Church of England, the Episcopal Church in the United States, the Anglican Church of Canada, for example) understands the work of its ministers is best summed up by the word 'leadership'.

This is a word which needs, and seldom receives, a critical examination. I will demonstrate in this book that there is no one such thing as 'leadership'. In fact, I will explore is the relationship between *three* different models of leadership which are at play in our society today; and these models affect you, whether you are part of the church or the secular world, a religious community or a business, whether you are a vicar or a tycoon.

The first is what I call *Managerial-Leadership*. This is the open and obvious leadership we see described in the tens of thousands of books, articles, blogs, syllabuses and programmes produced by publishers, business schools and hucksters. You may think it is clear what *ManL* involves: I will show you that *ManL* is anything but defined.

The second model is the adaptation by the Church of the first, *Missional-Leadership*. Some Christians are suspicious of the lessons proffered by the secular business world. That was the experience of the Hurd Commission: 'some of those who have helped us were evidently afraid that we would see it as our main task to create a more efficient Chief Executive'. When David Gortner evaluated secular models of leadership he 'inevitably heard [church people] attempt to separate the ecclesia from the rest of human riffraff. "The church is not a business"'.[6] Even so, *MissL* is hugely popular and influential. As Wesley Carr put it, there is a 'reasonable wish to manage the church at many levels, without... selling out to the secular themes of management techniques'.[7] We

---

[6] *The 'Hurd' Report*, 2; David T. Gortner, 'Looking at Leadership Beyond Our Own Horizon', *Anglican Theological Review* (Winter 2009): 119.

[7] Wesley Carr, 'Leading without Leadership', in *Creative Church Leadership*, Adair and Nelson (eds) (2004), 76.

shall see how popular in the remainder of this chapter, as well as looking at some warnings against its popularity.

Even so, despite the advocates of both *ManL* and *MissL*, the third, unidentified and unexamined model of leadership is the one that underlies almost all our thinking about leadership. It is what I call *Mythological-Leadership*. This identifies both its origins (in mythical thinking about human beings and their relationship), and also the medium it adopts in its transmission: *MythL* uses myths to construct our unconscious understanding of leadership, myth, which in our day and culture takes an unexpected form.

Why is this important? Is this just a pointless exercise in describing the patently obvious? Church leaders should show leadership: Meanwhile, in other news, is the Pope Catholic and do bears still live in the woods? The reason why this examination of three models of leadership is not a pointless rhetorical exercise is because, at its root, it is a moral question. *ManL* and *MissL* have unacknowledged origins in *MythL*. *Mythological-Leadership*, in turn, depends upon assumptions of violence and domination, which work out in its every cultural expression. Fundamentally, *MythL* has nothing to do with the Christian gospel.

In short, the dominant model of leadership in the Church proclaims allegiance to *Missionary-Leadership*, acknowledges the lessons to be learnt from *Managerial-Leadership*, but, ultimately, is an expression of *Mythological-Leadership*. If this seems like overstating the case to you, then may I suggest that the mythology of leadership has so completely surrounded you that you are unable to see the woods for the trees (whether or not bears are living in them)?

So, as a first step, let us look at the way *MissL* has been expressed and developed in the Church in the last 20 years. When we expect our archbishop, our bishops, our priests and people to embody 'leadership', what kinds of creatures do we expect to see?

Standing up for what you believe in

The interest the secular press shows in the life of the Church still has the capacity to surprise. For example, in February 2005 the Primates of the Anglican Communion met at Dromantine in Northern Ireland to discuss the issues facing the Communion: principally the ordination of homosexual clergy, the blessing of same-sex partnerships and the accompanying extra-diocesan interventions by bishops opposed to the first two. These discussions of ecclesial polity were minutely examined and pronounced upon in Britain's national press. Will Hutton in *The Observer* lamented the loss of the role of the Church of England in the nation's life: 'As a national church, its job is to include and tolerate us all; it is everyone's friend in need. Except now it is losing its way... suffering a crisis of confidence so severe that it has lost touch with its mission'. Part of the reason for this problem is the Archbishop of Canterbury: 'he finds himself as the prelate overseeing the gradual division of the Anglican Communion, desperately playing for time in the hope that something will come up. ...the auguries are that Williams's temporising will bring no relief'. Williams temporised rather than led; in fact his temporising was a deliberate, ineffective and disappointing part of the 'leadership' he chose to exercise: it showed 'the contemporary defensiveness of liberalism in all its guises'. Instead, Williams should have offered 'more committed leadership... Liberal leadership in almost every sphere is insecure and un-surefooted'. And for Hutton, simply and clearly, secure and surefooted leadership is based on 'conviction in the notions of progress and advance'.[8]

The 'agonising' noted by Hutton is apparent in an interview the Archbishop gave a year later to Alan Rusbridger, editor of *The Guardian,* with the painful title 'I am comic vicar to the nation'. Rusbridger begins by asking the Archbishop why he is so 'averse' to the idea that he should offer moral leadership.

---

[8]Will Hutton, 'A schism that threatens us all', *The Observer* (27 February 2005).

Leadership is, to me, a very, very murky and complicated concept... I think the question I always find myself asking of myself is, 'Will a pronouncement here or a statement there actually move things on, or is it something that makes me feel better and other people feel better, but doesn't necessarily contribute very much?'.[9]

His critics in the media are sure that the problem is one of visibility: 'Here was someone of tremendous intelligence, warmth, integrity and personal charisma and yet (that leadership issue again) for the most part he remains hidden from view'. The Archbishop refuses to comply: 'I'm just a bit cautious of this fascination in our culture with personality, making yourself an object in a particular way. ...I just feel that the centrality of highly individual drama – individual struggles, individual views – is not a comfortable place for a Christian to be, perhaps for anybody to be'. Rusbridger calls this wanting to be a 'broker', rather than a 'leader', and questions whether it is 'either possible or even desirable'. In another interview Williams described how his leadership consisted in allowing a safe forum in which the contested concepts bedevilling the Church can be addressed. Attempting to clear the space for the discussion to take place is not always appreciated: it '...leads to the characterization of being indecisive and all the other things that everybody always says'.[10] Again, like Rusbridger, the interviewer found this unconvincing. As a man with 'one of the strongest, subtlest voices in all Christianity', it is important for the Archbishop to 'moderate the discussion'. He is choosing a role not proper to a 'leader', but 'a stage manager': Williams 'should also take part in the conversation; he should somehow declare himself for the course of action he favors...'[11]

But for Williams, the clamour for 'moral leadership' from the public and media is asymmetrical. He parodies it as 'Why doesn't the archbishop condemn X, Y, Z?'. This does not persuade Rusbridger:

---

[9] Alan Rusbridger, 'I am comic vicar to the nation', *The Guardian* (21 March 2006).
[10] Paul Elie, 'The Velvet Reformation', *The Atlantic*, March 2009, 79.
[11] Elie, 'Velvet Reformation', 80.

The liberals [within and without the Church] might not quite have yearned for 'moral leadership'. But they did hope they had a church leader who would remain true to what they assumed him to believe – and many were dismayed by his apparent retreat in the face of ferocious fire from evangelicals and theological conservatives, most notably over the issue of gay priests. ...' The question you should ask him, but you can't', said one frustrated observer, 'is, why should anyone care what his beliefs are if he's never going to stand up for them?'.[12]

As Rusbridger's anonymous critic makes clear, this disappointment in the Archbishop's leadership was deeply felt within the Church as well. In February 2008, six months before the Lambeth Conference, the *Christian Science Monitor* wondered if the Archbishop of Canterbury was 'too intellectual to lead?'. Whenever Williams spoke he had a tendency to express himself in ways which are 'ponderous, studious, and given to rich, convoluted peroration'. This is almost enough to disbar him from acting as a religious leader, according to one member of the General Synod of the Church of England, Col. Edward Armitstead: 'Rowan Williams is a godly, gracious and clearly very able person in many ways, but I don't think he's got the gift of leadership that the church needs at this present time. ...[The problems faced by the Church mean] it really needs a clear Christian leadership'.[13] For Col. Armitstead, to be a Christian leader means something more than godly graciousness and great ability.

The *Christian Science Monitor* began its article with an apocryphal aphorism attributed to an unnamed Bishop of Norwich: 'If you want to lead someone in this part of the world, find out where they're going. And walk in front of them'. The leader is not expected to say too much, and certainly nothing which acknowledges subtlety or ambivalence. Rather, the secular press expects of the nation's religious leaders an uncanny ability to anticipate the direction in which his followers will drive him, rather than play catch-up.

---

[12] Rusbridger, 'Comic Vicar', 6.

[13] Mark Rice-Oxley, 'Anglican Archbishop: too intellectual to lead?', *Christian Science Monitor*, 20 February 2008.

A Church of leaders

What is sauce for the goose is also sauce for the ganders. The exercise of leadership in the Church is not limited to the Archbishop or the 'higher echelons'. In the 1990s the Church of England set out its expectations for those who are to be ordained as ministers of the Church:

> A basic ability required of leaders is to identify where the group or community stands and what it should aim to achieve. Leaders should then be able to set out the means to obtain the objectives, drawing the group or community towards the aim and motivating its members towards the goal. ...This ability [leadership] includes the capacity to offer an example of faith and discipleship, to collaborate effectively with others, as well as to guide and shape the life of the Church community in its mission to the world.[14]

All clergy within the established Church, or, at least, those appointed to posts since the early 1990s, are expected to demonstrate 'this ability'. More than ten years ago Steven Croft, in an unsystematic and informal way, quantified the expectation by examining the advertisements for incumbencies in the church press: 'I have continued to make random checks on the kind of language used since [October 1997] and find that, if anything, leadership language is becoming even more predominant across the traditions'.[15]

There are more than 600 references to 'leadership' on the Church of England website. Most of these references are to one or other of the various papers, reports, forms, notes or other official publications, produced by a bewildering variety of departments, divisions and three-letter-acronyms. We can examine two representative samples of these publications from the Church of England, and compare them with two from the Episcopal Church

---

[14] Advisory Board of Ministry, *The Report of a Working Party on Criteria for Selection for Ministry in the Church of England* (October 1993), 96,102.
[15] Steven Croft, *Ministry in Three Dimensions* (1999), notes 26, p. 203.

of the United States (TEC) and the Anglican Church of Canada (ACC). We may then have some sense of what 'leadership' in a church of leaders actually means.

In 2003 the General Synod received 'Formation for Ministry within a Learning Church: The Structure and Funding of Ordination Training' (more frequently referred to as *The Hind Report*, after its author).[16] The (modest) aim of the report was to 'to provide high-quality training for the clergy that will equip them to offer vibrant and collaborative spiritual leadership, to empower a vocationally motivated laity and, thereby, to promote and serve God's mission in the world'.[17] The result this high-quality training is clear: it will form candidates for ordained ministry so that they may fulfil the 'public role' of:

- prayer, within the Church's life of worship

- acting as a spokesperson on behalf of and to the Church

- continued theological and ministerial learning, not least to support a ministry of teaching, preaching and interpretation

- leadership of the Christian community in its calling and in its service to the wider life of the community.[18]

'Leadership' is now one of the four heads of ministerial training and formation, on a par with praying, teaching, and learning. The ordained minister will provide leadership 'of' the Christian community (not 'for' or 'within', notice), and this leadership will be 'vibrant' and 'collaborative'. Furthermore, training in 'leadership', along with 'communication', will be prioritized as a 'practical skill',[19] while at the same time, 'leadership' must be a requisite 'gift' of the ordained ministers, along with skills in 'pastoral care, worship and mission'.[20]

---

[16]Ministry Division of the Archbishops' Council, *Formation for Ministry within a Learning Church (The 'Hind Report')*, 2003.

[17]*The 'Hind Report'*, para. 9.4.

[18]*The 'Hind Report'*, para. 4.6. Notice how *Hind* describes these different functions with the singular noun 'public *role*'.

[19]*The 'Hind Report'*, para. 4.16.

[20]*The 'Hind Report'*, 57, from 'A Statement of Expectations for Ministerial Education'.

'Leadership' is central to the delivery of *Hind's* intentions, but is desperately vague. In one place it functions as a practical skill that can be transmitted by training. In another place it is a pre-existing gift of the trainee which is utilized by the Church. At one moment it is expressed within a social context ('collaborative ministry'); at another, it is placed in a separate position to its community, delineated from the community (leadership 'of' a community). What does this mean?

We are not told. Nowhere in the *Hind Report* is 'leadership' defined. We are not informed whether the authors of the report believe leadership to be a trait, a contingent relationship, an interaction of influence or transaction, a rhetorical or theological construct, all of these or none of these[21]. We are just given to understand that leadership is a given, a necessity, a social and theological good.

I believe in leadership

It might seem curious to learn, bearing in mind the huge emphasis on the place and necessity of leadership within the Church can be traced back to a short section of a report on collaborative ministry. In *A Time for Sharing*, Robert Warren[22], wrote:

> If new structures for the mission of the church are to emerge there will need to be a matching change in the church's understanding and practice of leadership within the ordained ministry.[23]

---

[21] We will see something of what these terms mean in Chapter 2.

[22] At the time Warren was the National Officer for Evangelism, and previously had been Team Rector of one of the 'largest and fastest growing churches in England'. I will mention the positions and promotions of some of the authors cited in this chapter, not because their positions validate the authors' contentions (an 'argument from authority'), but because preferment might reflect the value placed on their work by the Church as a patron.

[23] Robert Warren, 'Styles of Leadership', in *A Time for Sharing* by Board of Mission of the General Synod (1995), 25. Although 'leadership' was used before Warren (as in *ABM Policy Paper 3A*), it was only finally *defined*, as much as it is defined at all,

The problem with existing patterns of ministry (and existing models of leadership) within the Church is that they have been predicated upon the 'gifts of the incumbent', rather than the 'rich mosaic of gifts ... of the whole of the laity'. The Church (as a national and a local body) will have to move away from this, but, in order for this to happen 'the ordained minister will need to affirm, train and support such gifts...'. Do you notice the paradox at the heart of collaborative leadership? We want collaborative leadership because we don't want to rely on the gifts of one person; in order to achieve collaborative leadership we will have to rely on the gifts of one person.

Warren presents us with a series of five alternatives: a leader in this new pattern will be a 'conductor rather than a director'; 'facilitator' rather than 'provider'; 'permission-giver' rather than a 'permission-withholder'; a steersman rather than a 'rower'; and a 'person' rather than a 'parson'. This last is no more than a piece of rhetorical alliteration, because by 'person' Warren means that the leader should be comfortable in his/her humanity, and through that function as 'an icon, or representative, of Christ'. Leaders achieve this by owning and articulating 'their own sense of meaning', whilst seeking a 'discovery of wholeness' and living with an intention to 'escape from addictions'. Warren doesn't explain how this is a function of being a 'person': does he mean that seeking to be a 'parson' is somehow to capitulate to addiction and brokenness, while refusing to seek meaning?

Significantly, Warren sets out his five theses with a deliberately creedal structure. Each, with the exception of the first, begins with 'I believe...'. To say 'I believe' in a religious context means something more than acknowledging otherwise insignificant facts (like 'I believe in the Loch Ness Monster'). To say 'I believe' says something about confidence, meaning, an anchorage of assurance. To turn leadership into a creed is to say that this is the solid ground of your life. Can leadership bear that weight?

---

with Warren. All subsequent uses of 'leadership' lead back, in an almost apostolic succession, to him.

Seeking coherence

Neither is TEC immune from the search for leadership. In 2003 the Episcopal Church Foundation, a lay-led educative and capacity-building organization within TEC, published a report, *The Search for Coherence*, which attempted to quantify and qualify the attitudes towards and practice of leadership within TEC. The authors wanted to discover 'is there a uniquely Episcopal/Anglican approach to effective religious leadership?',[24] or, more simply, 'what is religious about religious leadership?'.[25] The answers were many and varied, which in itself is both answer and part of a further problem:

> 'It has something to do with reconciliation'.'Part of leadership is putting people in touch with their holy life'.'It also includes the telling of stories'.'A good leader has an authentic self; this implies the person has wrestled with transcendence'.'Theological skills are essential'.'A kind of longing and tension in seeking a coherence'.

This search for coherence has happened at a time when TEC, like all mainstream denominations in the United States, has experienced a profound and accelerating decline in denominational loyalty (indeed, it has been argued that TEC has experienced such weakening more than any other denomination). Because of this decline, Episcopalians who remain committed to the organization and those who are 'lapsed', are best described as 'spiritual seekers... engaged in their faith life as a spiritual quest'.[26] This means that a religious leader must expect to act as a 'spiritual guide who draws individual journeys together into life-giving patterns of shared discovery and social responsibility'.[27]

---

[24]L. Ann Hallisey et al., *The Search for Coherence* (Autumn 2003), 3.
[25]The title of a section heading, Hallisey et al., *Search for Coherence*, 3.
[26]Hallisey et al., *Search for Coherence*, 5.
[27]William L. Sachs and Thomas P. Holland, *Restoring the Ties that Bind* (2003), 171. Quoted in Hallisey et al., *Search for Coherence*, 5.

Tick-list leadership

In 2010 the General Synod of the Anglican Church of Canada (ACC) asked for a 'Commission on Theological Education and Formation for Presbyteral Ministry' to be set up. Like all Church bodies (dating back to the Synod of Jerusalem) its first action was to write a report, which in March 2012 it presented. The draft proposals, 'Competencies for Ordination to the Priesthood',[28] make it clear that presbyteral ministry is now to be identified almost entirely with leadership, for the hierarchy of the church, 'bishops, candidates, diocesan officers, educators, field educators, parishes, and anyone else' must seek 'to raise up leaders for the church'. How do we know that they are 'leaders'? We know when they are able to demonstrate their possession of 'necessary competencies' in five different areas: 'Personal and Spiritual Formation'; 'Anglican Heritage and Identity' (which includes 'Scripture', 'Theology', 'History', 'Contextual ministry' and 'Liturgy'); 'Cultural Context'; 'Skills for Teaching and Learning'; and, inevitably, 'Capacity for Leadership'.

What does this last competency mean? It is, partly, a sharing in the apostolic ministry of the bishop, for priests are, according to this proposal 'associates in the leadership of the diocese'. Furthermore, a priest should be able to understand and describe a theology of priesthood, as received within historic Anglicanism, relating it to their own vocation and ministry. The capacious leader-priest should be able to engage in 'pastoral leadership' (which seems to be different from demonstrating 'gifts and capacity to offer pastoral care'). They should have a 'capacity for effective collaborative leadership' which means, additionally, 'an ability to work in teams in a range of settings, including ecumenical'. They should be reflective, about the context of ministry, the call to be a justice-seeker, able to communicate effectively in preaching, and through 'worship, personal interaction, group-study, and the media'. Leadership means understanding 'basic administration',

---

[28]Commission on Theological Education and Formation for Presbyteral Ministry, *Competencies for Ordination to the Priesthood*, (March 2012).

including the allocation of resources, finances and accountability (although not necessarily demonstrating those managerial skills!). Significantly, in this nebulous list, to be a leader means to be able to 'discern the gifts of others and equip them to lead and to serve'. Whatever leadership might be, we want you to help others to get it!

A note about gender

One interesting aspect about *Search for Coherence* is that it attempts to describe the differences which gender might make to the understanding and exercise of leadership. The authors asked 'is women's approach to leadership different from their male colleagues?'.[29] They recognize two contradictory starting points for this question. Following the work of Constance H. Buchanan, where it is asserted women 'possess distinctive ways of reasoning morally, of knowing, of managing and leading, of thinking, and even of speaking'[30], it could be argued that the contribution of women will transform the general, generic, gendered understanding of leadership in the church. Alternatively, to speak of 'women's leadership', or to constantly define distinctive leadership offices in the church by a qualifying adjective (a 'woman bishop' as opposed to a 'bishop') has the danger of creating 'artificial distinctions'. While recognizing that some (male) bishops pride themselves on 'spiritual' leadership practices that are 'relational, collabo-rative and... listening',[31] the report concludes that such praxis is overwhelmingly the province of women. The report agrees with the words of one Bishop (who happens to be female) that women have been required to use their 'countervailing strengths', namely 'skills in sustaining relationships, nurturing groups, and building networks'.[32] The evidence for the report's favouring of women's

---

[29] Hallisey et al., *Search for Coherence*, 33.
[30] Constance H. Buchanan, *Choosing to Lead* (1996), 115–16. Quoted in Hallisey et al., *Search for Coherence*, 33.
[31] Hallisey et al., *Search for Coherence*, 33.
[32] Pamela W. Darling, *New Wine* (1994), 3. Quoted in Hallisey et al., *Search for Coherence*, 35.

relational leadership, from Darling and two other books,[33] appears to be based on nothing more than interviews with protagonists. This is not empirical evidence: the plural of 'anecdote' is not 'data'. Rather, it appears to be evidence of the authors of the report finding things they wanted to find.

Advocating creative church leadership

Much of the implicit yearning for this leadership has been nurtured, at least within the Church of England, by para-church organisations. In 1993 MODEM (which, at least initially, stood for 'Managerial and Organisational Disciplines for the Enhancement of Ministry')[34] was set up in order to 'promote the relevance of sound management to the churches and the mutuality of interest between churches and secular organisations'.[35] It organized conferences, published seminars, drew up directories of interested parties and membership lists: all the paraphernalia of a modern, networking, pressure group. In 1996 it published its first book, aiming to 'set the agenda for management/ministry issues in the 1990s'.[36] It included chapters on appraisal schemes, the application of ISO quality standards to ministry, human resources, and the church as a voluntary non-profit organization. The essays are brief and enthusiastic, and curiously unrealistic: a chapter on appraisal begins with the surprising admission by the author that he has never been responsible for implementing an appraisal scheme. Later MODEM publications have moderated this enthusiasm.

---

[33] Namely, Sally Helgesen, *The Female Advantage* (1995); Carol E. Becker, *Leading Women* (1996).

[34] Latterly, a suggestion has been made, presumably seriously, that the acronym stands for 'Ministerial and Ontological Disciplines for the Enhancement of Management'. In any case, much play is made of the electronic modem's function as a piece of equipment facilitating two-way communication.

[35] Editor's Note, John Nelson (ed.), *Management and Ministry: appreciating contemporary issues* (1996), iii.

[36] Editor's Note, Nelson, *Management and Ministry*, iii.

Some of the essays in *Creative Church Leadership*,[37] MODEM's third collection, recognize the limitations of a strictly managerial approach to church life: Charles Handy points out the dangers, if not the impossibility, of imposing this mode within a church community. Philip Mawer, in an essay whose title, 'Believing in Leadership' might lead one to think that he shares Robert Warren's creedal approach to leadership, concludes his analysis by saying that leadership is also about relationship, and should ultimately be grounded on something beyond the leader, 'which for Christians of course means essentially a focus on God'.[38] At the same time, Elizabeth Welch drew out the biblical grounding of a creative understanding of church leadership: 'Leadership in the church has its foundation in our understanding and interpretation of God and God's purposes for the world. The most creative church leadership is that which is deeply rooted within the life of God'.[39]

MODEM's approach was extended, and in some ways, more closely entwined with the life of the established Church, by another organisation, the Foundation for Church Leadership (FCL), whose first director was Malcolm Grundy, one of MODEM's founding fathers.[40] The FCL's aim was simple: 'to support, encourage and inspire church leaders as they tackle new challenges in leadership'.[41] It would achieve this simple aim by 'identifying emerging theologies of leadership', encouraging the development of leadership potential, 'evaluating' and 'sharing best practice'.[42] The public launch of FCL took the form of a seminar, with a series of papers and responses, held at King's College, London in January 2005. The major paper was presented by Steven Croft.[43]

---

[37] Adair and Nelson (eds), *Creative Church Leadership* (2004).
[38] Philip Mawer, 'Believing in Leadership', in *Creative Church Leadership*, 88.
[39] Elizabeth Welch, 'Leadership with vision', in *Creative Church Leadership*, 135.
[40] Grundy had been Archdeacon of Craven, in Bradford Diocese, before his appointment to the FCL.
[41] *Focus on Leadership* (2005), 61.
[42] *Focus on Leadership*, 61. This is, of course, a significantly 'managerial' model of addressing the question.
[43] Steven Croft, 'Leadership and the Emerging Church', in *Focus on Leadership*, 7–41. At the time Croft was the Archbishops' Missioner, and was subsequently appointed Bishop of Sheffield.

Croft's paper begins by acknowledging the threat posed by *ManL* to *MissL*, the challenge of the business school to the church. The business school is bright and welcoming and the church is dowdy and overlooked. But, he wonders, what would happen if the church building is discovered to be sitting atop a mine, full of the most wonderful minerals, and well-built foundations, whose air is 'sweet and inviting'[44]. The image attempts to assert the importance of the Christian tradition's insights into the question and practice of leadership. As Croft says, many secular leadership books quote Plato or Sun Tzu, but neglect the far older tradition of Moses:

> Let the Lord, the God of the spirits of all flesh, appoint someone over the congregation who shall go out before them and come in before them, who shall lead them out and bring them in, so that the congregation of the Lord may not be like sheep without a shepherd. [Num. 27:16–17]

This description in Numbers is, Croft asserts, 'possibly the earliest description of leadership...in the world'.[45] Moses is to be found at the 'head of the tradition (and the very bottom of the mineshaft)', a man whose story is an archetype for leadership, full of difficulties of administration, resourcing, opposition, and yet who is capable of expressing a 'transformative vision of a new future'[46]. The Old Testament tradition of leadership builds on the humility of Moses and his acknowledged dependence on God, and this is transfigured (a word that Croft does not use) in the person and model of Jesus Christ. In Christ we see, says Croft, 'a remarkable figure in the human story, not least for what he reveals about the nature of leadership'. According to Croft, Jesus responds to the leadership traditions of the Hebrew Scriptures in three ways. First, Jesus places humble dependency on God at the centre and heart of leadership. Second, the Church's subsequent reflection on the person and nature of Jesus disperses Jesus's self-understanding through the Church's self-understanding: doctrines of faith about

---

44 Croft, 'Leadership and the Emerging Church', 13.
45 Croft, 'Leadership and the Emerging Church', n. 1, p. 55.
46 Croft, 'Leadership and the Emerging Church', 15.

Jesus (as seen in the earliest creedal statements) become the means of transmission of ideas of Christian ministry:

> The united witness of the New Testament tradition is that the risen Christ is present with the church to build, guide and guard her life. This must affect reflection on future direction and the way the church responds to the challenges of its context.[47]

Third, and consequently, this reflection and transmission happens in the context of a community. The community reinforces its identity by approving the actions which conform to Jesus's example and condemning those which don't: Croft cites Mt. 23.13 and Luke 9.48 as examples of these two dynamics.

The three responses combine within the modern church into a four-fold pattern, what Croft calls the 'elements' and 'shape' of Christian ministry. First, leadership is 'grounded in character',[48] and (therefore?) requires a moral and ethical response, what Croft calls 'watching over yourself'. Second, leadership can only exist in action (not in potential), and must be expressed by 'building, guarding and guiding' a very particular form of community which is 'missionary'.[49] Third, it must be placed within a tradition (in the original sense of 'handing on'): others must be reached, through calling, caring and nurturing. Fourth, the leader will be concerned with placing this missionary community within the widest possible context: after all, God is God of all creation.

Croft asserts that the root of Christian leadership is, therefore, episcope, which is not limited to those who exercise an episcopal, *bishop's*, ministry: Parish priests, deacons, youth leaders and diocesan secretaries all exercise episcope. Its four distinct roles, which Croft represents in a series of increasingly elaborate figures, require seventeen 'qualities', some of which actually are qualities ('humility', 'trust', 'maturity'), some of which are behaviours ('planning', 'understanding', 'empowerment'), and some of which

---

[47] Croft, 'Leadership and the Emerging Church', 18–19.
[48] Croft, 'Leadership and the Emerging Church', 19. Significantly a 'trait-based' definition of leadership.
[49] Croft, 'Leadership and the Emerging Church', 19.

are abstract nouns with no indication of how they are to be incarnated ('alignment',[50] 'scanning'). Croft himself acknowledges that these aren't qualities *per se*, and refers to them in other places as 'skills' or 'competencies'. We see once again, an uncertainty of definition which weakened the Hind Report and the Competency Proposals of ACC.

Croft had already explored some of the ideas sketched out in his FCL lecture in *Ministry in Three Dimensions*, first published in 1999.[51] Describing how the inherited models of ministry are no longer working (the instances of stress and break-down being indicators of that[52]), Croft warns against a false solution, 'the flight into management models',[53] with the evangelical clergy of the Church being particularly susceptible to the siren dangers: 'for many younger evangelical clergy the primary focus of what it means to be ordained is focused in the very exercise of leadership skills'.[54] By the late 1990s, according to Croft, 'leader' was becoming 'the most commonly used title for a person called to full-time Christian work'[55]. 'Leader' had become the universal solvent, the shorthand expression for a General Theory of Everything. Thus, according to David Pytches,[56] everything that an ordained minister could, or should, do can be described as an expression of one form or another of leadership.[57]

---

[50] By this Croft says he means, in a Humpty-Dumptyish way, 'the skill to engage the different parts of the enterprise in a common endeavour, dealing with any conflicts of interest as they arise'. (36). He says his word is better without explaining why.

[51] Croft, *Ministry in Three Dimensions*. A second edition of Croft's book was published in 2008, but the only substantive change was a new chapter on 'pioneer ministry' and 'fresh expressions', neither of which are relevant to our task.

[52] Croft, *Ministry in Three Dimensions*, 17–21.

[53] Croft, *Ministry in Three Dimensions*, 22.

[54] Croft, *Ministry in Three Dimensions*, 22. Croft mentions 'skills' here, and 'styles' elsewhere. It is not clear from his use of the terms whether they are mere synonyms or denote some substantive distinction.

[55] Croft, *Ministry in Three Dimensions*, 25.

[56] Pytches's career is an inversion of the usual pattern for our other authors: he began as a Bishop (of the Anglican Church in Chile, Bolivia and Peru) and ended as a Vicar. However, it can be argued that the parish of St Andrew's Chorleywood is a larger and more significant pastoral charge than a diocese in the Southern Cone for the life of the Anglican Communion.

[57] David Pytches, *Leadership for New Life* (1998). So, for example, chapters 23–5 are 'Leadership and the Church Council'; 'Leadership and New Staff Members';

Some writers have noticed the disadvantages of the flight into leadership. David Brown, in a pamphlet written for the FCL in 2008 compared the exercise of leadership in the Royal Navy and the Church. Leadership should be expressed in company:

> Leadership, in seeking to draw a community into creative harmony and purpose, is intrinsically proteamworking and therefore to an extent counterindividualist, and will routinely face indifference within the Anglican setting.[58]

Often the structures of the Church itself will prevent this true form of leadership, which he calls 'unrobed friendship', from being expressed. It requires relationship, which cannot be 'stimulated', or simulated 'from an 'office' or a committee'. Unrobed friendship has to be encouraged by a person, and, in the Church, that person is the Bishop. But the Church's increasingly bureaucratic systems 'have tended increasingly to relieve bishops of significant components of their engagement with clergy'[59]. In short, *Managerial-Leadership* wins out over *Missionary-Leadership*.

Some church writers have attempted to follow a 'realist' mode of writing about leadership. A notable example is Stephen Cottrell's *Hit the Ground Kneeling* (2008), in which he intended to 'see leadership differently'.[60] He achieved this by taking eight truisms and inverting them: he calls this 'upside down wisdom'[61]. Thus the leader is advised to reinvent the wheel, shed the thick skin, let the grass grow underfoot, spoil the broth, and so on.[62] His guiding Scriptural precept is what he calls 'the parable of the trees' [Judg.

'Leadership and Maintenance' (as in 'upkeep of premises' rather than 'sustaining an existing congregation').

[58] David Brown, *Making Room for Church Leadership* (2008), 5.

[59] Brown, *Making Room for Church Leadership*, 4, 5.

[60] Stephen Cottrell, *Hit the Ground Kneeling* (2008). Cottrell was Bishop of Reading until 2009 when he was appointed diocesan Bishop of Chelmsford. Although the book contained a caveat that the opinions expressed were the author's own, and 'do not necessarily reflect the official policy of the General Synod', it was published by Church House Publishing, the official publishing arm of the Church of England.

[61] Cottrell, *Hit the Ground Kneeling*, 71.

[62] The themes of Chapters 7, 8, 3 and 5 respectively.

9:8–15] in which the olive, the fig, the vine and eventually the bramble are invited to become king of all the trees. Cottrell doesn't unpack the relevance of the parable to his model, but rather, at the end of the book, returns his reader to contemplating the meaning of the parable for the reader's own context and vocation to lead. Although Cottrell makes much of the difference between his idea of leadership and those of other secular and ecclesiastical writers, it is clear where his model can be placed. Leadership is not the gift and expression of the individual leader: whether you are responsible 'for laying on a meal for twenty unexpected family guests... [or]... a Girl Guide leader, play-group supervisor or community police office... [or]... CEO of GlaxoSmithKline', your task as leader is the same – 'to enable others to do their very best and to achieve their fullest potential'.[63] Cottrell's model has a large debt to James MacGregor Burns's 'transformational' leadership.[64]

In the end, though, Cottrell's book is less about leadership and more about the need for leaders to build-in 'down time', moments of stillness and contemplation, into the busyness of their lives: 'The wise leader will... make wise choices about how time is managed, giving first priority to that space for refreshment and discernment where decisions about the right use of the *rest* of the time can be profitably made'.[65]

Cottrell finishes his book with a characteristically contrarian stricture. The best form of leadership, especially for someone who exercises an activist model of leadership, is to sleep more: that limits the 'opportunity to do further damage'[66]. Leadership is, occasionally, a refusal to do anything: no leadership can be good leadership. Perhaps like Ronald Heifetz, this means understanding that leadership is 'disappointing people at a rate they can absorb'.[67]

---

[63] Cottrell, *Hit the Ground Kneeling*, 15.
[64] See 'Transformational theories' in Chapter 2.
[65] Cottrell, *Hit the Ground Kneeling*, 17. Emphasis in the original.
[66] Cottrell, *Hit the Ground Kneeling*, 81.
[67] Ronald A. Heifetz and Martin Linsky, *Leadership on the Line* (2002), 142.

Managerial-leadership as a religion

Why is there this fascination for leadership within the Church, even if it is so vaguely argued and understood? One answer is the glamour of the near sibling. The Church recognizes, even if unconsciously, that *ManL* is speaking the same language. It is the tribute of respect paid to a fellow religious system.

It was Stephen Pattison who, in 1997, described the parallels between managerialism and organized religion. Working as a NHS chaplain and an administrator of a Community Health Council, Pattison was intrigued by the implicit foundations he saw in managerialism.[68] This was something more than systematically allocating resources of time, energy, money and value. Those who were committed to management saw it as 'the solution to social and economic problems'; it was an 'an overarching system of authority', which had a moral right to manage.[69]

Pattison could see how this mimics religion, a system of thought and practice which, through both, supplies meaning to human activity.[70] Indeed, Pattison went further than noticing parallels with religion in general. He noted the resemblance between managerialism and a particular manifestation of religion: it can 'instructively be construed as having many of the characteristics of fundamentalist sectarianism'.[71] It is the 'faith of the manager'.

ManL religion flourished in the public sector of the late twentieth century as the result of the confluence of two new trends in management theory and practice. First there was neo-Taylorism,[72]

---

[68] Stephen Pattison, *The Faith of the Managers* (1997), 23.
[69] This definition of management is taken from Newman and Clarke, 'Going about our business? The managerialization of public services', in *Managing Social Policy*, Clarke, Cochrane and McLaughlin (eds) (1994), 16.
[70] Pattison, *Faith of the Managers*, 28.
[71] Pattison, *Faith of the Managers*, 26. Pattison gives a list of analogies between managerialism and sectarianism on 36–7.
[72] Named for Frederick Winslow Taylor, whose book on 'scientific management' was the basis of all 'classical management' writing and practices: 'The Principles of Scientific Management' (1911). See the discussion in Christopher Pollitt, *Managerialism and the Public Services* (1990), 13–17, 111–18.

in which resource efficiency was the sole (measurable) goal, overlaid with a moral purpose. A fine example is found in Michael Heseltine's bold declaration made as Secretary of State for the Environment in 1980: 'I believe we are faced, as a nation, by a task of national revival as daunting as we have ever faced. Efficient management is a key to the revival. If Britain's managers fail, we can turn out the lights'.[73] It applied to every aspect of modern society: 'public and private companies, civil service, nationalized industries, local government, the National Health Service',[74] what Christopher Pollitt has called a 'cosmic' definition of management.[75]

Entwined with the neo-Taylorian 'efficiency management', there also flourished another model, known variously as 'new wave management', 'new managerialism', or the 'Excellence School'. The high priest of Excellence was Tom Peters, with his extensive and ubiquitous series of books exploring the theme.[76] This school believed that in order to succeed, any organization, whether business or non-profit, needed to loosen bureaucratic controls in order to motivate the workers into achieving a largely self-motivated commitment to quality and innovation. It meant a different style of management: 'managers became leaders rather than controllers, providing the visions and inspirations which generate a collective or corporate commitment to "being the best"'.[77]

So we can see that neo-Taylorism and 'excellence management' both claim to be the means to achieve a moral good. They encompass a wider world-view than just selling better widgets or treating more patients. Managers have a moral purpose as agents of quality, innovation and excellence. Their *methods* were morally neutral; it was the *goals* which were elevated to an ethical good:

---

[73] Michael Heseltine, 'Ministers and Management in Whitehall', *Management Services in Government* (May 1980): 68.

[74] Heseltine, 'Ministers and Management in Whitehall', 68.

[75] Christopher Pollitt, 'Beyond the Managerial Model: the case for broadening performance assessment in Government and the Public Services', *Financial Accountability and Management* (Autumn 1986): 159.

[76] Tom Peters and Robert H. Waterman, *In Search of Excellence* (1982); Tom Peters and Nancy Austin, *A Passion for Excellence* (1986).

[77] Newman and Clarke, 'Going about our business', 15.

efficiency, public accountability, reduction of Government expenditure, workforce empowerment, and so on.

Perhaps it was this sense of mission that was the attraction for the 'religious admirers of managerialism'.[78] Perhaps it was the promise of effectiveness, actually being able to make a difference in a complex world, which seemed to be increasing in complexity. However, the religious admirers of *ManL* would have done well to hearken to the warning of Alasdair MacIntyre.

MacIntyre describes managerialism as one of the 'central moral fictions of the age' because it claims 'to possess systematic effectiveness in controlling certain aspects of social reality'.[79] Managers and writers on management claim that it is the goal of management to be effective. This effectiveness has no relationship at all with the manager's own personal morality. We don't, or shouldn't, care if the manager 'is faithful to his wife'. Rather the only important question should be 'is he able to make the trains run on time?'. And it does not matter whether the trains the manager is efficiently directing carry commuters to work or prisoners to the gas chambers – in this respect Mussolini, who got the trains to run on time, was an (effective) manager.[80] But MacIntyre warns about any glib divorce of morality from effectiveness:

> ... the whole concept of effectiveness is... inseparable from a mode of human existence in which the contrivance of means is in central part the manipulation of human beings into compliant patterns of behaviour; and it is by appeal to his own effectiveness that the manager claims authority within the manipulative mode. [81]

This 'alleged quality of effectiveness' MacIntyre calls 'expertise', but more than that it is also a 'masquerade'. It is pretence because,

---

[78] The epithet in Pattison's warning coda, *Faith of the Managers*, 157.
[79] Alasdair C. MacIntyre, *After Virtue: a study in moral theory*, 2nd edn (1985), 71.
[80] Amusingly, despite the proverbial status of this image, it is in fact, a myth: Mussolini did nothing to make the Italian railway system to work efficiently. See Denis Mack Smith, *Mussolini* (1981), 118.
[81] MacIntyre, *After Virtue*, 71.

he suggests, we are not oppressed by the misuse of power 'as some radical critics believe',[82] but by impotence. The telling image often used is 'levers of power' – 'one of managerial expertise's own key metaphors'.[83] But when political life has been taken over by technocrats, who promise to 'manage things better' than their opponents, 'levers of power' can be false instruments. Before the resignation of Tony Blair as Prime Minister and the assumption of the office by Gordon Brown, Michael Portillo (not a neutral observer) pointed out that some government actions, like raising pension rates or ages, are as simple as moving a lever, and the lever works. However, there are aspects of government such as 'organisational change' that are not susceptible to such a simple approach: 'In dealing with the Home Office, for example, the levers of power have simply broken off in his [Blair's] hand. He has no talent for managing such complex change, nor indeed has any other politician'.[84]

This is a pragmatic example of MacIntyre's criticism of the metaphor: it is no more, he says, than a rhetorical sleight of hand, desperately attempting to camouflage the fact that correlation does not mean causation:

> … all too often, when imputed organisational skill and power are deployed and the desired effect follows, all that we have witnessed is the same kind of sequence as that to be observed when a clergyman is fortunate enough to pray for rain just before the unpredicted end of a drought; that the levers of power… produce effects unsystematically and too often only coincidentally related to the effects of which their users boast.[85]

MacIntyre thus gives us four warnings: first that ManL is a cultural fiction; second, it cannot be morally neutral; third, it concerns the manipulation of people into compliancy; and fourth, it is unproven

---

[82] MacIntyre, *After Virtue*, 72.
[83] MacIntyre, *After Virtue*, 73.
[84] Michael Portillo, 'It's a dirty secret: no party has the answer to a state in chaos', *The Sunday Times* (14 May 2006).
[85] MacIntyre, *After Virtue*, 73.

as an effective social action. These warnings have gone unheeded within the Church.

Thus, before David Hope's enthronement as Archbishop of York in 1995 he was interviewed by *The Church Times*. At the end of the interview, having spent some time trying to explain to the interviewer the importance of the organizational changes in the Church's governance, he decided to quote from Charles Handy, whom he was reading. The passage describes 'the right approach to the...Archbishop's Council. It was a lesson from Silicon Valley'.[86]

Thus, before his enthronement as 103rd Archbishop of Canterbury, George Carey was interviewed for *Reader's Digest*. In the accompanying profile it was noted that he 'is a man of modern self-taught managerial methods'[87] and, in the interview itself, when asked whether it was true that he would be running the Church 'much more as a business, with vicars being assessed, attending courses and so on?', he responded 'Yes – and this is already happening'.[88]

> There are many hard-working, conscientious and gifted clergy in the Church, but I believe ministers should be assessed every five years to expose and deal with those who are incompetent, lazy, or simply inept. Bishops, too, should not hold jobs in freehold, but should be subject to evaluation. [89]

Carey aphoristically summed up his philosophy:

> People have described me as a 'management bishop', but I say to my critics: 'Jesus was a management expert too'. Christ... is looking for results. I see nothing wrong with that. [90]

---

[86] Paul Handley, 'Holder of the ring', *The Church Times* (8 December 1995), 11; Quoted in Pattison, *Faith of the Managers*, 157.

[87] David Moller, 'Bishop George comes to Canterbury', *Reader's Digest*, March 1991, 39.

[88] Russell Twisk and David Moller, 'There'll be a big party going on', *Reader's Digest*, March 1991, 42.

[89] Moller, 'Bishop George comes to Canterbury', 40.

[90] Twisk and Moller, 'George Carey interview', 42.

The model for Bishops and Priests in the established Church is not so much Jesus the Good Shepherd as 'Jesus, MBA'.

In this aspect (at least) Dr Carey's thought was original. It was not until four years after the Archbishop's interview that Jesus's career path had advanced from MBA to executive authority, with the publication of Laurie Beth Jones's 'Jesus, CEO'[91]. Her book is a whimsical collection of 85 principles, allegedly derived from Jesus's public ministry, illustrating what Jones calls the 'Omega management style'[92], and divided unequally into three different areas: 'strength of self-mastery', 'strength of action' and 'strength of relationships'. So we find the disciples described as 'staff'[93], Jesus's prayer life is presenting a report to the 'Chairman of the Board'[94], his healing ministry is self-expression[95], and the promise of the kingdom of heaven is a pension plan[96].

Laurie Beth Jones's appropriation of the Gospels for American capitalism has obviously been successful.[97] This is despite (or because of?) its deep theological flaws. 'The text is a painful combination of shallow sentiment, self-help clichés…, and triviali-zation of the Gospel accounts…'[98], in which we see a portrayal of

---

[91] Laurie Beth Jones, *Jesus, CEO* (1995).

[92] Jones, *Jesus, CEO*, xiii. Management styles for Jones are based upon the use of power, and she (unwittingly?) presents the 'Omega' style as a Hegelian synthesis between an 'Alpha' style, based the authoritative use of power, and a 'Beta' style, based on co-operative use of power. The former is 'masculine', the latter 'feminine' (although Jones presents no evidence for such a distinction). 'Omega', on the other hand, 'incorporates and enhances them both' (Jones, *Jesus, CEO*, xiii). It is also monetized, through the Jones Management Group newsletter (Jones, *Jesus, CEO*, 310), a lesson which Jones presumably learnt from, among others, Blake and Mouton (see the discussion of 'the Leadership Grid' on page 40).

[93] 'He took his staff in hand', Jones, *Jesus, CEO*, 134–7.

[94] 'He saw them as his greatest accomplishment', Jones, *Jesus, CEO*, 284–8.

[95] 'He expressed himself', Jones, *Jesus, CEO*, 39–42.

[96] 'He clearly defined their work-related benefits', Jones, *Jesus, CEO*, 200–2.

[97] She has two further books, one of which, *The Path*, is now the basis of a self-help career development programme. She has sold more than 1 million copies of her books, her name is trade-marked, and Ken Blanchard (of the Hersey-Blanchard situational theory) has called her 'One of the Great Thought Leaders of Our Time' (original capitalization): see Laurie Beth Jones's home page, www.lauriebethjones. com.

[98] Michael L. Budde, 'God is not a capitalist', in *God is Not…*, D. Brent Laytham (ed.) (2004), 83.

the cleansing of the Temple, with no account taken of the political and theological implications of Jesus's actions, but rather as an object lesson in how to be 'passionate'.[99] Furthermore, Jones's first Omega principle, 'He said "I am"' (in which she examines and approves Jesus's sense of self-identity), is taken up in her 'Affirmations for Leaders', a summary appendix of 61 bullet-points, where it exhorts the business leader to affirm 'I proudly say I AM, knowing clearly my strengths and God-given talents. I repeat my strengths to myself often, knowing my words are my wardrobe'.[100] It seems unlikely that this is an entirely appropriate use of the Divine Name as applied by Jesus to his own ministry. In what possible way can a model of (human) leadership be based upon a claim to divinity?

Others, in more modest ways ('My word goes out and accomplishes that which I sent it to do'[101]), have attempted like Jones to map the example of Jesus onto modern-day business. Hence, Peter Shaw, in a Grove Booklet, wished to look '...at Jesus as a role model in a way that is relevant both to those who fully embrace the Christian faith and those who simply regard Jesus as a significant leader', for, whatever one's faith background, 'measured by his impact on history, Jesus was an outstanding leader'.[102] By properly understanding Jesus as leader, we can deal with the dilemmas (opportunities?) facing leaders today, among which are: 'defining the clearest possible strategy against a background of continuous change... developing clarity about where the leader can add the most value; ...[and] communicating succinctly and effectively amidst a barrage of communication vehicles'.[103] Shaw's examples deal, substantially, with the higher echelons of business: he presents two lists of 'C' words which describe patterns of behaviour that should be cultivated by those

---

[99] Budde, 'God is not a capitalist', 83. Jones's treatment of the cleansing is found in 'He had a passionate commitment to the cause', *Jesus, CEO*, 50–4, where she explicitly says that a political or theological interpretation of Mt. 21:12 is 'reading too much into it'.

[100] Jones, *Jesus, CEO*, 295.

[101] 'Affirmations for Leaders', Jones, *Jesus, CEO*, 301.

[102] Peter Shaw, *Mirroring Jesus as Leader* (Grove Books E135, 2004), 3.

[103] Shaw, *Mirroring Jesus*, 4. Shaw actually gives eight dilemmas in total.

in leadership positions.[104] Many of the words/behaviour patterns address the isolation which comes from being at the top of a business.[105] Is this the idea behind the church's infatuation with leadership? That we promote people to a position of isolation, and then expect them to exercise a connected, collaborative and coherent ministry?

A brief comparison with another religious tradition

Such conflict is not limited to Christian ministry. Rabbi Natan Asmoucha was the Rabbi at Britain's oldest synagogue, Bevis Marks, in the city of London. In July 2009 he allowed an interfaith group to meet in the synagogue before marching to the headquarters of the Royal Bank of Scotland in protest against unjust interest rates. He was suspended from his post, disciplined, and eventually removed. The Board of Elders (the *mahamad*) gave a statement:

> [Rabbi Asmoucha] gave all the demonstrators access to the inside of the synagogue, in order to be addressed by him, as well as its hall and courtyard, without any security checks first taking place... He then accompanied and assisted the demonstrators with their goal of delivering a political message to the chairman of the Royal Bank of Scotland, that had not been authorised by his employer.[106]

---

[104] List 1: conviction; character; care; courage; composure; competence. List 2: consciousness; congruence; compassion; connection; communication; culture; courage; confidence; creativity; coaching style. Shaw, *Mirroring Jesus*, 14.

[105] An interesting variant on this strategy (looking to a hero of the faith for a model of leadership) may be found in Kit Dollard, Anthony Marett-Crosby, Order of St Benedict, and Timothy Wright, OSB, *Doing Business with Benedict* (2002), especially, chapter 4 and 5. It is interesting because it is more modest in its application, and the analogies between the stable, settled, ministry of Benedict and modern business are closer than with Jesus's short-term, itinerant, preaching and teaching.

[106] Alfred Magnus of the Board of Elders, quoted in Isabel de Bertodano, 'Rabbi forced out after joining bank protest', *The Tablet*, 24 October 2009, 36.

One prominent rabbinical commentator deplored this exercise of the *mahamad's* authority: 'This extreme case is representative of how rabbis are seen by the communities that hire them in the UK and in the Diaspora in general. They are expected to toe the line of their employers and not to do anything dynamic without full consultation with the board of management'.[107] Asmoucha's mistake was to think 'that he was a communal leader when in fact he is seen by the synagogue's management as little more than an employee that must follow their dictates'.[108]

Brackman diagnoses: 'With shackles like these it is impossible for rabbis to actually lead. So indeed there is a crisis of leadership within our Diaspora Jewish communities... Simply put: without real leaders there won't be any followers'.[109]

A theology of leadership?

The contrast between the two positions, isolated leadership and collaborative ministry, was recognized by *Search for Coherence*. Most Episcopalians, according to *Coherence,* say that they prefer to be part of an ecclesial community which makes decisions by 'collective discernment'. At the same time, it is thought that the church's mission should be defined with clarity, and the leaders of the church must carry out that mission effectively. The two attitudes, collectivity and clarity, are directly and fatally opposed to each other, when expressed within a wider culture of leaders and leadership. The one precludes the other; the other under cuts the one. In the absence of a 'consensus on how to lead' the report optimistically states that there is 'creative incoherence'.[110] How creative this incoherence truly is has to be judged by other criteria. But, as *Coherence* demonstrates, a vague spiritual allegiance to

---

[107] Levi Brackman, 'Traditional synagogues will die off', *Ynetnews*, 16 August 2009.
[108] Levi Brackman, 'Malice at Britain's Oldest Synagogue', 14 August 2009.
[109] Brackman, "Traditional synagogues will die off'.
[110] Hallisey et al., *Search for Coherence*, 41. This latter phrase is bolded in the original.

leadership is not enough to be effective in the world in which the church operates.

Too often it appears that the question behind much church writing on leadership (whether official or otherwise) is simply 'What do we need to do to be effective?'. That question is continually answered, in the secular world at least, by expecting and demanding leadership. The church answers its own question by playing 'me too'. The secular world is effective; the church world is ineffective. The secular world likes leadership; the church world should like leadership too. The secular world has models and examples of leadership and leaders; the church world must have models and examples of leadership and leaders too. The Church of England, TEC and the ACC have attempted to operate and foster a model of leadership predicated on a secular, business model, a model that I have called *Managerial-Leadership*.

In seeking to emulate the effectiveness of *ManL*, the religious admirers of leadership assume that they are admiring something which in itself is coherent, systematic and justifiable. The internal inconsistencies in the secular models of leadership are not acknowledged, and certainly not compensated for (and the internal consistencies are a more notable feature of leadership studies than its systematic impressiveness, as we shall see in the next chapter).

Furthermore, *ManL*'s religious admirers forget that 'effectiveness' is not a Scriptural concept, and neither is it one affirmed in traditions of Christian theological reflection. The foundational model of the Christian Church, that of Jesus and his disciples, was expressed in a radical powerlessness.[111] Two of its most pungent critics, Pattison and MacIntyre, demonstrate that *ManL* is most concerned by husbanding and extension of power. MacIntyre is clear that *ManL* is a 'masquerade' with merely an 'alleged quality of effectiveness'.[112] Pattison warns: 'Ecclesiastical hierarchy and the rights of employing churches are powerfully reinforced by the introduction of management techniques and theories'. Furthermore, there is precious little evidence of beneficial results

---

[111] I will examine the ways in which we can talk of Jesus and the disciples as models for 'leadership' in Chapter 8, below. The short version is: we can't.

[112] MacIntyre, *After Virtue*, 72. See the discussion on page 39.

for the workforce on the receiving end of such techniques and theories. Negatively, there is 'evidence of demoralization, intimidation, the need to conform and a move to unionization on the part of parish clergy'. In the end, the result is likely to be analogous to the effects of *ManL* in the public sector: 'A few people will feel more powerful and freer, while many will not'.[113]

Ironically, *Coherence*, the ACC, and the Foundation of Church Leadership have all identified the problem: 'alarmingly, there seems to be no theology of leadership among Episcopalians'.[114]

We do not know what we are talking about when we attempt to talk about leadership. When we do talk about leadership, we are, unknowingly, not being theological, in the sense of speaking coherently about the God who revealed Himself to us in the Scriptures, in the traditions of the Christian church, and, pre-eminently, in the person and ministry of Jesus Christ. There is a savage disconnect, between attempts to treat leadership in a pseudo-theological manner and the real nature of leadership, which should become apparent in the remainder of this book. We are, dangerously, attempting to yoke ourselves with unbelievers. We are pretending that heresy can be put in the service of the church.

---

[113] Pattison, *Faith of the Managers*, 162–3.
[114] Hallisey et al., *Search for Coherence*, 40.

Chapter 2

The panacea of leadership

There go my people, I must find out where they are going so I can lead them.
ALEXANDRE LEDRUROLLIN, 1807–74

In October 2009, Charles Haddon-Cave QC presented a report into the crash of an RAF Nimrod aircraft in Afghanistan in 2006. It was a carefully compiled (almost 600 pages long) and devastatingly phrased condemnation of the 'cultures' of the RAF, QinetiQ, BAE Systems, the Defence Logistics Organisation, and the Ministry of Defence, who were collectively and individually responsible for the loss of the Nimrod. They failed to uphold four key principles, chief among which was 'leadership':

> Leadership is the most common principle emphasised time-and-time again in reports into major incidents and other materials... The fundamental failure was a failure of Leadership. ...lack of Leadership manifested itself in relation to the way in which the Nimrod Safety Case was handled, in the way in which warning signs and trends were not spotted, and in relation to inexorable weakening of the Airworthiness system and pervading

Safety Culture generally. For these reasons, Leadership is a key principle for the future.[1]

Fourteen lives were lost in the crash of Nimrod XV230; according to Haddon-Cave's review those deaths would not have occurred if 'leadership' had been exercised.

The loss of aircraft XV230 is an acute example of the central role ascribed to leadership in our culture and society. Along with representative democracy and free Wifi, leadership is a necessity and a given, required in every sphere of North Atlantic society.[2] There is nothing in our society that does not require or cannot be improved by the careful, judicial and thoughtful application of leadership. It is, in the words of John Storey, 'a catch-all and a panacea'.[3] There is no area in our society in which leadership cannot be exercised. Central and local government bodies, non-governmental organizations, the health service and education bodies have all set up leadership programmes or institutions which can inculcate leadership values in their employees, or clients. And this is only what is expected and required.

So, for example, when James Purnell resigned from the cabinet in the summer of 2009 he felt the need to praise Gordon Brown's 'economic leadership'.[4] If Britain is to develop a high-speed railway system then it will require, along with financial investment, 'political leadership, some dynamism and willingness to take risks'.[5] Combating climate change will place a greater demand on international relations than anything else since the Cold War: 'Climate change is arguably a far graver threat to our long-term

---

[1] Charles Haddon-Cave, *The Nimrod Review: an independent review into the broader issues surrounding the loss of the RAF Nimrod MR2 aircraft XV230 in Afghanistan in 2006* (2009), para. 20, 16–17. Capitalisation as in the original.

[2] When I say 'North Atlantic' society, what I mean is the thing often referred to as 'western society': namely, the English-speaking world, sharing the common law tradition of the United Kingdom, with a particular emphasis on the culture and influence of the United States of America.

[3] John Storey, 'Signs of Change: 'damned rascals' and beyond', in *Leadership in Organizations: current issues and key trends*, Storey (ed.) (2004), 5.

[4] Philip Webster, 'Dear Gordon, I quit,' *The Times*, 5 June 2009.

[5] Will Hutton, 'Don't let the defeatists and cynics talk down Britain's need for speed', *The Observer*, 2 August 2009, 24.

security than terrorism and probably a greater challenge to human-kind's ingenuity and leadership than anything else ever faced'.[6] Ryan Bunning was selected 'to represent Cornwall at a South West Young Leadership Camp', in which 'football leaders' are given 'the chance to receive specialist football leadership coaching from the Football Association'.[7] Even the catering business recognizes the need for (and profitability of) leadership: the 2010 Restaurant Leadership Conference, held in Scottsdale, Arizona, in April 2010, promised to 'uncover new horizons from new vantage points, providing advantages for success'.[8]

We expect our politicians, our industrialists and entrepreneurs to exercise this leadership. Steve Jobs embodied this expectation. After his death obituaries attributed his success with Apple to his character: he was 'a single, razor-focused, deeply opinionated, micromanaging, uncompromising, charismatic, persuasive, mind-blowingly visionary leader'.[9] Other companies, such as Microsoft and Hewlett-Packard, will never be as successful as Apple, even if they ran 'its designs through the corporate copying machine', as long as they lack Jobs's leadership. To be a successful industrialist requires the quality and practice of leadership.

With the word 'leadership' in such common usage, the concept behind the word must be understood – it must surely be working within an agreed, accepted, normative definition of both word and concept.

Unfortunately, there is no such thing as a generally agreed and useful definition of leadership. In the social sciences, the usual method to achieve such a definition would be to follow its history. This chronological approach, exploring the changes and the contexts of leadership, has been the method for countless textbooks and articles on leadership: see for example, Stogdill's

---

[6] Paddy Ashdown and George Robertson, 'The Cold War is over. We must move on, fast', *The Times*, 30 June 2009.

[7] 'Bunning's a true leader', *North Devon Journal*, 4 June 2009.

[8] Restaurant Leadership Conference 2010 home page, www.restaurantleadership.com.

[9] David Pogue, 'Steve Jobs Reshaped Industries', *The New York Times*, 25 August 2011.

comprehensive survey,[10] or Western's 'timeline of the leadership discourses'.[11] But the social-science method has not managed to produce an agreed definition. If anything it has complicated the discourse on leadership. By 1995 Keith Grint could present a quantitative measurement of leadership studies:

> Between January 1990 and January 1994, 5,341 articles were published on leadership... That is getting on for four every day...: approximately every six hours, somewhere, someone publishes a paper on leadership in English.[12]

The volume has accelerated. By 2000, DuBrin could assert that there were 35,000 different definitions of leadership in academic literature.[13]

Occasionally, scholars will attempt to achieve a single, overwhelming, theory-of-everything, definition of leadership. Georgia Sorenson has called this the quest for a 'general theory of leadership'. The quest has been conspicuously unsuccessful.[14] A quest for leadership is not like, to use one of Sorenson's analogies, a 'Genome Project', as if leadership were just out there, waiting to be discovered, just as soon as the right laboratory equipment has been invented. To discover America all we needed to do was sail west for long enough: to discover the holy grail of 'Leadership', all we need to do is... what? Stogdill 40 years ago nailed the problem:

> Four decades of research on leadership have produced a bewildering mass of findings...It is difficult to know what, if anything,

---

[10] Ralph M. Stogdill, *Handbook of Leadership: a survey of theory and research* (1974), chapter 2.

[11] Simon Western, *Leadership: a critical text* (2008), Fig. 6.1.

[12] Keith Grint, *Management: a sociological introduction* (1995), 124.

[13] Andrew J. DuBrin, *Leadership: research findings, practice, and skills*, 3rd edn (2000), 3. By the time DuBrin got to the latest, and sixth, edition of his book (2010), he has given up: 'A Google search of articles and books about leadership in organizations indicates 188 million articles. In all those entries, leadership has *probably* been defined in many ways'. (p. 3; emphasis added).

[14] Quoted in J. Thomas Wren, 'A Quest for a Grand Theory of Leadership', in *The Quest for a General Theory of Leadership*, Goethals and Sorenson (eds) (2006), 2.

has been convincingly demonstrated by replicated research. The endless accumulation of empirical data has not produced an integrated understanding of leadership.[15]

If we limit ourselves to studying the results of leadership we come up with nothing more encouraging. Attempts to measure the *difference* that leadership makes to an organization have also been mired in 'ferment and confusion'.[16] The only certain conclusion that these 'fruits of leadership' studies have come up with is 'some simplistic interpretation such as more is always better'.[17]

In short, it might seem that we ought to bear heed to Chester Barnard's 1948 dictum: 'Leadership has been the subject of an extraordinary amount of dogmatically stated nonsense'.[18]

The family resemblances of leadership

We have a problem: we are overwhelmed by the volume and the incoherence of the writing on leadership. No one theory of leadership makes sense in relation to any other theory of leadership: every timeline, every chronological description, is different, and every scholar comes up with a different history of the various definitions. Perhaps we should attempt something vaguer, and less ambitious, than yet another comprehensive definition, contenting ourselves with just a 'rough scheme of classification' in Stogdill's words.[19] He came up with six categories: for the sake of sanity, let us make that an even more arbitrary division of four: namely, *behavioural* theories, *contingency* theories, *transformational* theories, and finally *trait* theories.[20]

---

[15]Stogdill, *Handbook of Leadership*, vii.
[16]Gary Yukl, 'Managerial Leadership: A Review of Theory and Research', *Journal of Management* (June 1989): 253.
[17]Yukl, 'Managerial Leadership', 259.
[18]Chester I. Barnard, *Organization and Management: Selected Papers* (1948), 80.
[19]Stogdill, *Handbook of Leadership*, 7.
[20]This follows van Maurik's summary of Jago: see John van Maurik, *Writers on*

Behavioural theories

Perhaps the simplest thing to say is that leadership is something that people do. That seems reasonable: 'Leadership is expressed in terms of overt behavior patterns rather than in terms of some intrinsic property or characteristic'.[21] 'Leadership' is something that 'people-who-are-called-leaders' do. This theory developed in the period after World War Two, and shared in two post-war factors. First, in the social sciences we began to value the empirical study of observable behaviour:[22] 'what is your evidence for that assertion?' became a reasonable question. Second, conscription and the militarization of the Western liberal democracies meant we had experience of an enormous number of men exercising some form of leadership. Needs must: leadership had to be *taught* in West Point and Sandhurst.

These two factors combined: what empirical evidence can we point to to show successful, effective leadership? One of the early studies was Tannenbaum and Schmidt's 'How to choose a leadership pattern' (1958). In this new model, leadership was a choice made in how to behave, from a range of choices:

> [the successful leader] accurately understands himself, the individuals and group he is dealing with, and the company and broader social environment in which he operates. And certainly he is able to assess the present readiness for growth of his subordinates. [Moreover, he is] ...one who is able to behave appropriately in the light of these perceptions. If direction is in order, he is able to direct; if considerable participative freedom is called for, he is able to provide such freedom.[23]

Leadership (2001), 3; Arthur G. Jago, 'Leadership: Perspectives in theory and research', *Management Science* (March 1982).

[21] Jago, 'Leadership Perspectives', 316.

[22] Thomas Mengel, 'Behavioural Theories of Leadership', in *Leadership: the key concepts*, Marturano and Gosling (eds) (2008), 11–15.

[23] Robert Tannenbaum and Warren H. Schmidt, 'How to Choose A Leadership Pattern', *Harvard Business Review* (March 1958): 101.

If leadership is a *choice*, then leaders could be taught how to choose: 'it could easily be implemented by practising managers to improve their leadership effectiveness'.[24] This also meant that, if leadership was teachable, it could be profitable. Leadership as behavioural choice 'stimulated a deluge of executive training and leadership development programs'.[25] And every one a profit centre.

For example, in the 1960s one of the most common training schemes was Blake and Mouton's 'Managerial Grid', later renamed the 'Leadership Grid' and registered as a trademark. Two dimensions of behaviour, along axes of 'concern for people' and 'concern for production', are mapped onto a 9 × 9 grid. The goal to aim for is '9,9', 'team management', as this 'style' has 'a very high consideration for both tasks and people'. Blake and Mouton's theory was based on flawed data: it came from a questionnaire in which subordinates were asked to *remember* how their leader had behaved. The leader's behaviour was never directly observed. These failings didn't stop it from being profitable, and the 'Leadership Grid' continues in business today.

Contingency theories

Contingency theories were a development of behavioural theories. If leadership is behaviour, then perhaps the really successful leaders needs to change his behaviour according to the context in which he finds himself. Whatever works best in any given situation is whatever works best. As Stogdill put it: '[a] person does not become a leader by virtue of the possession of some combination of traits' and '[t]he qualities, characteristics, and skills required in a leader are determined to a large extent by the demands of the situation in which he is to function as a leader'.[26]

---

[24] David A. Van Seters and Richard H. G. Field, 'The Evolution of Leadership Theory', *Journal of Organizational Change Management* (1990): 32.

[25] E. E. Jennings, *An Anatomy of Leadership: princes, heroes, and supermen* (1960), 3.

[26] Ralph M. Stogdill, 'Personal Factors associated with Leadership: a survey of the literature', *Journal of Psychology* (1948): 64, 63.

Contingency is combination of behaviour and environment. In 1909 Mumford argued that a leader emerges 'by virtue of abilities and skills [trait] enabling him to solve social problems [situation] in times of stress, change, and adaptation'.[27] In other words, 'cometh the hour, cometh the man'. Successful leadership is the successful negotiation between 'personality' (a novel concept of the 1930s) and the situation: the relationship between the '*affective* factors and the intellectual and action *habits* of the individual', and the situation in which he finds himself was the explanation for the successful (or unsuccessful) 'performance' of leadership.[28] By the 1960s, this approach was orthodoxy: a true leader needed to work out the 'situational variables within the task situation', to survey 'the degree of support between leader and followers, the nature of the task…, the leader's formal or informal authority' and so on.[29]

It was not a wholly convincing theory. Those who advocated other theories of leadership were scathing. Jennings, for example, said it

> …appealed to our ideal of democracy, our belief in the impact of the environment on the individual and our need to do something quickly about our shortage of leaders. … [But, the] 'right man for the right situation' is a subtle but lethal kind of fatalistic thinking that must not be cultivated if business is to maintain its necessarily dynamic and creative nature.[30]

Transformational theories

The need to be dynamic and creative was answered by *transformational* theories, which had their origin in the work of James

---

[27] E. M. Mumford, *The Origins of Leadership* (1909); this is Stogdill's summary, in *Handbook of Leadership*, 18.

[28] E. M. Westburgh, 'A point of view – studies in leadership', *The Journal of Abnormal and Social Psychology* (1931): 419. [Emphasis in the original.]

[29] Martin M. Chemers, 'Contingency Theories', Goethals, Sorenson and MacGregor Burns (eds), *Encyclopedia of Leadership* (2004), 277.

[30] Jennings, 'The Anatomy of Leadership', 2–3.

MacGregor Burns, and his immensely influential book *Leadership*, published in 1978. Burns says that there are two different styles of leadership; *transactional* (limited and not to be encouraged) and *transformational* (sophisticated and edifying).

Simply put, transactional leadership occurs when a leader exchanges something of value with his followers: 'I will give you something good, money, possession, a sense of well-being, if you promise to do something that needs to be done'. It can work both ways, from leader to follower or vice versa: 'Do this for me/us, and I/we will do that for you'. However, according to Burns, the end of the exchange marks the end of the relationship: 'The bargainers have no enduring purpose that holds them together; hence they may go their separate ways. A leadership act took place, but it was not one that binds leader and follower together in a mutual and continuing pursuit of a higher purpose'.[31] With transactional leadership both sides of the transaction are in it for what they can get out of it.

Transformational leadership, on the other hand, has a 'higher', ethical, quality: it does not 'simply describe how leaders do in fact behave but, rather, prescribes how they ought to behave'.[32] It aims to raise the moral and ethical character of both leaders and followers: 'transformational leaders engage followers not only to get them to achieve something of significance…but also to 'morally uplift' them to be leaders themselves'.[33] This is leadership for a higher purpose; it is, in Burns's phrase, 'leadership *engagé*'.[34]

But there is a problem with this model. What if the leader can't sell, or the followers won't buy, the 'bigger picture'? Will the leader then be condemned to enact the 'catch-up' leadership of Ledru-Rollin, frantically chasing after his followers? And what if the 'bigger picture' is in itself, morally suspect? Just because you have a vision doesn't mean that vision is noble, it doesn't 'make one immune to

---

[31] James MacGregor Burns, *Leadership* (1978), 19.
[32] Terry L. Price, 'Transformational Leadership', in *Leadership*, Marturano and Gosling (eds) (2008), 171.
[33] Bruce J. Avolio, 'Transformational and Transactional Leadership', Goethals, Sorenson, and MacGregor Burns (eds), *Encyclopedia of Leadership* (2004), 1558.
[34] Burns, *Leadership*, 20.

factual and moral mistakes'.[35] To be even cruder, Hitler had a 'big picture', and depth of sincerity doesn't make up for wickedness. You don't have to be Hitler for this gulf between sincerity of vision and consequences of vision to become important. As Martin Samuel said about Tony Blair:

> He did what he thought was right for his country, bless him. Big deal. So did Joe Stalin. So did Neville Chamberlain. So did John Wilkes Booth. Sincerity is no excuse. The world is full of people doing what they feel is right, which is why we judge on consequence not intent. Guess what? Every bankrupt business really believed in the product. Every referee that pointed to the penalty spot was absolutely convinced there had been a foul. And every leader that committed his country to a bloody and disastrous war was convinced of the opposite outcome.[36]

Trait theories

Behavioural, contingency and transformational theories were all developed in opposition to the earlier all-conquering explanation of leadership, the theory of the 'great man'. Sometimes this is described as 'trait theory', because, or so the argument goes, the traits, character and qualities of individual men (almost uniformly men)[37] were the essential factors in any expression of leadership. The fundamental belief of the 'great man' theory is that leaders are born not made. This didn't stop the lives and characters of the great men being analysed for common

---

[35] Douglas A. Hicks and Terry L. Price, 'An Ethical Challenge for Leaders and Scholars: What do people really need?', in *Selected Proceedings of the Leaders/Scholars Association* (1999), 56.

[36] Martin Samuel, 'Enough schmaltz about Blair. Only one thing matters', *The Times* (15 May 2007), 19.

[37] This is the academic background to my excursus on gender in the previous chapter. For an exploration of the absence of 'great women' in leadership studies, see Kruse and Wintermantel, 'Leadership Ms.-Qualified: I. The Gender Bias in Everyday and Scientific Thinking', in *Changing Conceptions of Leadership*, Graumann and Moscovici (eds) (1986), 171–98.

characteristics: age, appearance, height, intelligence, scholarship, dominance, and so on, were all thought to be important
factors which could be isolated, and factored for. Amusingly,
some studies even attempted correlations between leadership
success and weight![38] Usually, historians of leadership date the
popularity of this theory to the first half of the twentieth century,
but the true origin of the theory was from 60 years before, in the
work of the single most influential thinker on leadership studies,
Thomas Carlyle.

In May 1840 Thomas Carlyle delivered a series of lectures which
he later reconstructed and published as *On Heroes, Hero-Worship,
and the Heroic in History*. His intention was clear: 'I mean to shew
that 'Hero-worship' *never ceases*, that it is at bottom the main or
only kind of worship'.[39] In the first lecture, given the title 'The Hero
as Divinity', Carlyle began by stating his thesis:

> …Universal History, the history of what man has accomplished
> in this world, is at bottom, the history of the Great Men who
> have worked here. They were the leaders of men, these great
> ones; the modellers, patterns and in a wide sense creators,
> of whatsoever the general mass of men contrived to do or to
> attain; all things that we see standing accomplished in the world
> are properly the outer material result, the practical realisation
> and embodiment, of Thoughts that dwelt in the Great Men sent
> into the world: the soul of the whole world's history, it may be
> justly considered, were the history of these.[40]

This all he summarized, in the most famous slogan of leadership
studies, 'The History of the world is but the Biography of great
men'.[41]

---

[38] There appears to be 'a low positive relationship' of weight with leadership (i.e. it has
no effect whatsoever!); Table 1, Stogdill, *Handbook of Leadership*, 40.

[39] Letter of 2 March 1840 to John Carlyle, in Thomas Carlyle, *The Collected Letters
of Thomas and Jane Welsh Carlyle, Vol. 12 1840*, Fielding, Sanders and Ryals (eds),
(1985), 67.

[40] Thomas Carlyle, *On Heroes, Hero-Worship, and the Heroic in History
(1841)*, Goldberg, Brattin and Engel (eds), (1993), 1:3.

[41] Carlyle, *On Heroes*, 1:26.

It was Carlyle's influence which meant that more than 100 years after his lectures, Eugene Jennings could write a book on leadership subtitled 'prince, heroes, and supermen'.[42] Jennings mourns the loss of the 'towering personalities' and 'titans' of the past, and that the present world is the habitation of 'cadres of professional managers who are responsible to boards of directors, to government regulators, to organized workers and to a fickle consuming public'.[43]

There is a problem with traits as a theory about the source of leadership. We find 'leadership' too difficult to define, so we will say it is something exercised by men with these particular traits. What traits? What 'qualities' or 'competencies'? That's not an easy task. There is no agreement on the traits you need to be a great man / hero / leader.

John Adair, doyen of British leadership studies, describes the problem: by 1936, one enthusiastic study proposing traits had identified 17,000 words to describe qualities of personality;[44] by 1940, one survey of 20 experimental studies revealed that only 5 per cent of leadership qualities examined were common to four or more studies;[45] Adair attended a military conference at which 64 different traits of leadership were described; best (or worst) of all, in 2001 the Council for Excellence in Management and Leadership presented 83 attributes of leadership, condensed from a long list of more than 1,000. As Adair says:

> These long lists of 'competencies', as leadership qualities now tend to be known, are virtually useless for the purposes of development. When they are reduced to a smaller number – say less than 20 (as in the case of the NHS) – they become more general. But if they are not grounded in the generic role of

[42] E. E. Jennings, *An Anatomy of Leadership: princes, heroes, and supermen* (1960).
[43] Eugene Emerson Jennings, 'The Anatomy of Leadership', *Management of Personnel Quarterly* (1961), 2.
[44] Gordon W. Allport and Henry Odbert, *Trait-names: a psycho-lexical study: a study from the Harvard psychological laboratory*, (1936). Quoted in John Adair, *Effective Leadership Development* (2006), 9.
[45] Charles Bird, *Social Psychology* (1940), 378–9. Quoted in Adair, *Effective Leadership Development*, 9.

leader, they lack intellectual coherence and seem arbitrary, so they have little credibility or practical value.[46]

Now we have the problem of defining 'qualities / traits / competencies'. And this is as much a problem as defining 'leadership'. Simply put, there were too many traits.

Most professional scholars of leadership don't like trait theories: it isn't scientific (in the sense of being neat and predictable) and it isn't democratic (because it privileges the status and gifts of the one over the many). But leadership scholars are too quick to say that only 'vestiges of the great man theory remain'.[47] It might not be popular in academic studies, but it is still the dominant one in any number of popular works on business management, and in the wider culture.

So, for example, Luiz Felipe Scolari, sometime coach for Chelsea Football Club, eulogized the leadership qualities of his captain, John Terry:

> I think when you're born, you're born as a leader. After that maybe you read something, you study something, but if you don't have the spirit, the personality in the first place, it is difficult. A coach or businessman can read books. But what does that matter if they are weak? When you're born you know your life.[48]

Popularly, if you want to be a true leader, then you need to learn how to be a great man.

Leading who?

Almost all the bulk of the work done on leadership, scholarly or popular, has concentrated on the leader. This is a curious

---

[46] Adair, *Effective Leadership Development*, 9–10. [Emphasis in the original.]
[47] Nathan Harter, 'Great Man Theory', in *Leadership*, Marturano and Gosling (eds) (2008), 71.
[48] Chris Hatherall, 'Leadership? Watch JT, Arsene', *Sunday Mirror*, 30 November 2008, 68.

emphasis, as for every leader, even such leaders as Ledru-Rollin, there must be (at least one) follower. Walter Bennis noted this indisputable fact: 'the only person who practices leadership alone in a room is the psychotic. ...Any person can aspire to lead. But leadership exists only with the consensus of followers. ....[It] is grounded in a relationship'.[49]

Joseph Rost, who falls into the optimistic school of leadership studies (that is, it actually means something), has attempted to tease out the connection between leader and follower. He hardwires the connection into his definitive definition of leadership: 'an influence relationship among leaders and followers who intend real changes that reflect their mutual purposes'.[50] Realising that this may beg more questions, Rost breaks down his definition into four essential elements, in which each clause and word receives further clarification. Thus, the relationship is based on *influence*, which must be multi-directional and non-coercive; it is leaders *and* followers, both in the plural; real changes are intended ('real' meaning 'substantive and transforming', 'intend' meaning being purposefully desired, 'changes' meaning transformations in the present or the future; 'purposes' are not goals, and move from 'mutual' to 'common' purposes).

Everything about Rost's definition shows his concern to reject the historic, 'great-man', personal traits definitions of leadership and leader. Everything is defined on a collaborative, non-coercive, mutual basis: leadership is

> not based on authority, power, or dictatorial actions, but is based on persuasive behaviours, thus allowing anyone in the relationship to freely agree or disagree and ultimately to drop into or out of the relationship.[51]

According to Rost, leadership cannot be, therefore, a quality or the possession of the leaders themselves. It can only be expressed in

---

[49] Warren Bennis, 'The challenges of leadership in the modern world', *American Psychologist* (2007): 3.
[50] Rost, *Leadership for the Twenty-First Century*, 102.
[51] Rost, *Leadership for the Twenty-First Century*, 107.

relationship, and so 'leadership' is actually the name we give to the leader/follower relationship, a relationship of mutuality which changes both leader and follower. But aren't the terms 'leader' and 'follower' a little hierarchical? Wouldn't we be better calling 'followers' something else? Rost recognizes the need to change terms:

> The cultural imperatives of the new century have made the word *followership* less acceptable in political, business, and common-place communications....the word [is] rather demeaning and inappropriate...[52]

Therefore, according to Rost, it would be best if we ceased the use of the terms 'follower' and 'followership' and used something more appropriate for our 'flattened'[53] world. Rost's preference is for 'collaborator',[54] although that may have problems in some cultures (France?), and he recognizes, grudgingly, that some scholars have attempted to get by with the generic 'people', unqualified by any hint of hierarchy.[55] Rost's arguments haven't been successful in transforming the world of leadership studies. As he reflects, he has been on a hiding to nothing: 'I tried to transform the word followers in the book and in the presentations after the book was published. I used the word "followers" about two hundred times in the book and used the word in a very positive way. I ennobled followers by including them in the leadership dynamic'.[56] What ungrateful wretches, not recognizing how Rost's post-industrial, collaborative, paradigm of leadership is actually the actions and the possession of the 'nobility' of society! In the end, Rost's idea comes down to the insight that leadership is noble, but really we are all nobles. We shall see how this idea works out, with the leaders and followers of

---

[52] Joseph Rost, 'Followership: an outmoded concept', in *The Art of Followership: how great followers create great leaders and organizations*, Riggio, Chaleff, and Lipman-Blumen (eds) (2008), 56. [Original emphasis]

[53] Rost, 'The Art of Followership', 61.

[54] Joseph C. Rost, 'Leadership Definition', in *Leadership*, Marturano and Gosling (eds) (2008), 96.

[55] Rost, 'The Art of Followership', 56–8.

[56] Rost, 'The Art of Followership', 57.

Monty Python's *The Life of Brian* (in 'They're in a rather funny mood today', on page 156ff).

Leading in circles

So leadership studies have circled round and around, and the 'breakthrough' of each generation sooner or later becomes a problem for the following generation. 'Leadership' ends up being something that everyone, whether 'leader', 'follower', 'collaborator', or 'person', does, just so long as it is being done for good, noble, non-hierarchical, and morally upright reasons.

Some scholars have attempted to rescue leadership by being pragmatic. They treat leadership as Justice Stewart famously treated obscenity as a legal concept: all we can say is 'we know it when we see it'.[57] Some scholars seem to have unconsciously adopted this pragmatic method. So Gosling and Marturano assert 'the belief that we are all talking about more or less the same thing would seem to imply a common idea'.[58] Winston Fletcher in a review of a new journal, argued that '...because the concept of leadership is so fuzzy and carries so much baggage, *Leadership* would do better to minimise the quasi-philosophical stuff and maximise the real-life examples...'[59] We can 'believe' in leadership like Gosling and Marturano, and, paradoxically, end up with a completely pragmatic philosophy: leadership exists, and so leadership must be exercised; leadership is exercised so leadership must exist.

But there remains the problem that there is no agreed definition of what leadership is. There is no agreed system putting together all the different definitions of leadership. To use a biological metaphor, no one can agree on what sort of creature 'leadership'

---

[57] The formulation 'I know it when I see it', derived from Justice Stewart's concurrence in a pornography case, *Jacobellis v. State of Ohio*, 378 U.S. 184, 197 (American Supreme Court 1964).
[58] Marturano and Gosling, *Leadership* (2008), xxvi.
[59] Winston Fletcher, 'Lots of bark, little bite for top dogs', *The Times Higher Education Supplement*, 20 October 2006, 26.

might be (animal, vegetable, mineral?) and no one can agree on what 'animal, vegetable, mineral' might mean when applied to 'leadership'.

So it would seem that, after all the thousands of words written about leadership in the twentieth century, we come down to a choice between two assertions: is leadership predicated upon the traits / characteristics / qualities of its protagonists, or is it not? Keith Grint, with his characteristic astringency, summarises the situation thus:

- Is leadership about the Person, that is, is it *who* 'leaders' *are* that makes them leaders?

- Is it the Result, that is, *what* is effected by the efforts of 'leaders'?

- Is it the Position, that is, *where* 'leaders' work (either geographically, sociologically, or culturally)?

- Is it the Process, that is, *how* 'leaders' operate?

- Or, is it some indefinable combination of all four factors?

Grint calls this four-fold typology the 'dissensus', and, only slightly tongue in cheek, calls for the halting of all further research, so as to save us '39 years of wasted reading time'.[60]

Isn't this reasonable grounds for disposing of 'leadership' as a subject of study or investigation? After, we've given up on the search for the philosophers' stone or the elixir of life; shouldn't we confine 'leadership' to the same cupboard as the hippogriff or aether?

Management by machine gun

The reason we can't ignore 'leadership' and its immensely profitably accompanying industry is that, unlike the hippogriff or aether, 'leadership', as it is presently experienced in our society,

---

[60] Keith Grint, *Leadership: limits and possibilities* (2005), 17, 18.

has a moral component. Even more so, leadership has a moral problem, and by assenting thoughtlessly to the way in which leadership is spoken of, studied and practiced in our society, we also assent to the immorality of leadership.

We can see an example, among many, in the fad for 'business process re-engineering' (with its inevitable three-letter acronym, BPR) at the end of the 1990s. Keith Grint and Peter Case noted BPR's sudden and pervasive popularity.[61] The techniques of BPR, that is the things that it advised managers and leaders to *do* aren't really important. What intrigued Grint and Case was the *register* of BPR, that is *how* it required managers and leaders to behave. Grint and Case concede that, as all management 'requires some degree of coercion',[62] all management may tend towards violence, but BPR was peculiarly and virulently violent. So, for example, the only way 'to persuade many folks to undertake painful therapy like reengineering, followed by a permanent state of mobilization, is to persuade them that the alternative will be more painful'.[63] That pain is targeted: 'On this journey we... shoot dissenters'.[64] Although BPR's purpose is the same as all management techniques to improve the functioning of the company, BPR upped the stakes: 'dramatic improvement has to be paid for in some way, and the coinage is usually denominated in units of suffering'.[65] Those who persistently resist the 'militarization' of the company 'need the back of the hand'.[66] And if fisticuffs are not sufficient: 'It's basically taking an ax and a machine gun to

---

[61] Keith Grint and Peter Case, 'The Violent Rhetoric of Re-Engineering: management consultancy on the offensive', *Journal of Management Studies* (September 1998): 558.

[62] Grint and Case, 'Violent Rhetoric', 559.

[63] James Champy, *Reengineering Management: the mandate for new leadership* (1995), 49; cited by Grint and Case, 'Violent Rhetoric', 561. [Note the subtitle of Champy's book.]

[64] Rich Karlgaard, 'Interview: Mike Hammer', *Forbes ASAP*, September 1993, 71; cited (inaccurately) by Grint and Case, 'Violent Rhetoric', 561.

[65] Michael Hammer and Steven A. Stanton, *The Reengineering Revolution: the handbook* (1996), 174,183; cited by Grint and Case, 'Violent Rhetoric', 562.

[66] Hammer and Stanton, *The Reengineering Revolution*, 174,183; cited by Grint and Case, 'Violent Rhetoric', 562.

your existing organization'.[67] As Grint and Case laconically note 'rhetoric associated with the workplace seems to have taken a violent turn'.[68]

Grint and Case suggest five reasons why this violence-speak has percolated into business.[69] First, BPR shares with all 'new' business techniques a need to mark an absolute discontinuity with all previous methods; second, to speak violently about doing violent things effectively marks a 'Year Zero' attitude; third, to demonstrate the serious transformation that BPR will deliver its acolytes are required undergo a macho 'proving ordeal'; fourth, the transformation is not just serious but also terrifying, so much so that BPR requires leaders of the calibre of Moses, or Daniel Boone, to 'lead the faithful out of the valley of darkness into the promised land';[70] fifth, BPR assumes a 'colonizer–colonized dialectic',[71] which allows the use of 'Us' and 'Them' language to strengthen loyalty to the new way of doing things.

Why would anyone buy into this? Why would anyone think that financial planning, retail or widget manufacturing would be improved by adding warfare, red in tooth and claw? For the same reason that, for example, new computers are reviewed as the weapons of 'road warriors', even though the warrior in question is a travelling account for a widget-brokerage firm.

How does leadership exist?

The answer comes from having a proper understanding of the kind of thing that leadership is, in its essence and in its power to affect people. We cannot understand leadership if we think that it

---

[67] Joseph Maglitta, 'One on One: Michael Hammer', *Computerworld*, 24 January 1994, 85. In the same interview it is revealed that Hammer had copyrighted the word 'reengineering'. Champy and Hammer are also dealt with in Brad Jackson, *Management Gurus and Management Fashions: a dramatistic inquiry* (2001), chapter 4.

[68] Grint and Case, 'Violent Rhetoric', 559.

[69] Grint and Case, 'Violent Rhetoric', 566.

[70] Hammer and Stanton, *The Reengineering Revolution*, 132–4.

[71] Grint and Case, 'Violent Rhetoric', 566.

is just the sort of things that leaders do. Rather, I mean to ask the question that, assuming that leadership exists, *where* does it exist? How do we recognize this thing called 'leadership' *as* leadership? In other words, where do people get their ideas of leadership from? We know that there are some actions and attitudes closer to a leadership ideal than others: King Henry at Agincourt is a leader, at one extreme; Thomas Rakewell of Hogarth's series of paintings, *The Rake's Progress*, at another extreme. Why can we say Hal is leader and Tom isn't? How do we know?

Strangely, very little has been written in the leadership literature about this process. Next to no attention has been paid to the means by which leadership as an ideal is disseminated, trans-mitted, conveyed. An amusing example of the importance of vocabulary is the work of the National Health Service Delivery and Organization Research and Development Programme, when they set up a programme to address the 'transmission of leadership' within the Health Service. It wasn't well received, mostly because they had forgotten that elsewhere in the NHS 'transmission' describes the way by which 'diseases find new hosts'![72] Meanwhile Stogdill devotes a chapter to the question of 'leadership training';[73] Marturano and Gosling give an entry to 'leadership development';[74] Burns has a couple of pages on the relationship between education and leadership[75]; Goethals and Sorenson have three entries on education, but those are 'leadership *in* education' and not *vice versa.*[76]

This is a curious omission. Most leadership literature assumes that people know what leadership looks like; we are just arguing about best way to define it. Leadership is a previously existing attribute, either (unfashionably) subsisting with the character, traits

---

[72]See David Buchanan et al., 'Leadership transmission: a muddled metaphor?', *Journal of Health Organisation and Management* (2007): 247.

[73]Stogdill, *Handbook of Leadership*, chapter 16.

[74]Scott J. Allen, 'Leadership Development', in *Leadership*, Marturano and Gosling (eds) (2008), 99–103.

[75]Burns, *Leadership*, 447–50.

[76]Chandler, 'Education, Higher'; Engel, 'Education, K–12'; Finkelstein, Honig, and Malen, 'Education: Overview'; all in *Encyclopedia of Leadership*, Goethals, Sorenson, and MacGregor Burns (eds) (2004).

and qualities of individual 'leaders', or (more popularly) expressed in the relationship between those we call 'leaders' and 'followers', and agreed upon, even if vaguely, by those in such a relationship. In short, leadership either pre-exists, or it is pre-known.

This recalls, inevitably, Plato. It is the disputed problem in his dialogue *Meno*,[77] written around 387 BC Is it possible, Meno asks Socrates, for virtue to be taught? Or is it acquired by practice? Or natural aptitude? This leads to the the problem of definition: what is 'virtue'? Meno comes up with a list of virtuous behaviours (like Justice Stewart, he knows virtue when he sees it!). Ah ha! Socrates strikes. You already know what virtue is, because you are listing virtuous things. But how do you know, in the first place, why these things are virtuous? This Meno's famous paradox (although, to be more accurate, credit for it should be given to Socrates): 'a man cannot try to discover either what he knows or what he does not know. …he would not seek what he knows, for since he knows it there is no need of the inquiry, nor what he does not know, for in that case he does not even know what he is to look for'. (80d–e).

In other words, is it possible to search for knowledge of X? If you know what X is, then you have already acquired knowledge of it, and therefore cannot search for it. If you do not know what X is, you cannot search for it, because you do not know what you are searching for. Plato bumps into Donald Rumsfeld. When Secretary of Defense under the second Bush administration, Rumsfeld memorably stated the problem:

> As we know, there are known knowns; there are things we know we know. We also know there are known unknowns; that is to say we know there are some things we do not know. But there are also unknown unknowns – the ones we don't know we don't know. And if one looks throughout the history of our country and other free countries, it is the latter category that tend to be the difficult ones.[78]

---

[77] Plato, 'Meno', in *Protagoras and Meno*, trans. W. K. C. Guthrie (1956). References to Meno are to section numbers, beginning at 70a and concluding at 100b.
[78] Donald H. Rumsfeld, press briefing at the U.S. Department of Defense, Washington, DC, 12 February 2002.

Where does 'leadership' come into this spectrum? Is it a known known? Is it a known unknown? We surely can't say that it is an unknown unknown, because that would cut the legs from underneath a thousand MBA programmes in business schools around the world.

An answer comes in realising what sort of thing leadership is. It is not like knowledge, of flute-playing, medicine or navigation, all examples given by Meno. Leadership, in all its forms and definitions, does not deal with the world directly and empirically. Rather, it apprehends the world (in the sense of reading it, grasping it, understanding and describing it) through an interpretative lens, what we might call a 'mediating discourse'. Between all leadership schools, BPR included, and the world lies a layer of *mythology*, and that mythology is omnipresent, omnipotent and omni-transparent. That is, the mythology of which BPR, in particular, and 'leadership', in general, are part is all pervasive, influencing every part of our understanding of our world, and all powerful for there is no human endeavour, as we have seen, that cannot be influenced for the better by it. Furthermore, it is completely invisible, for we don't know that it is there, and even being told that 'it' (whatever 'it' might be) is there, makes us uncomfortable. In short, whereas the *definition* of 'leadership' tends towards the definition of pornography (we know it when we see it), the *functioning* of leadership tends towards a myth.

So we can begin to answer the question. Our knowledge leadership comes from believing in and living under the power of the myth of leadership. Which begs the next question: what is a myth?

Chapter 3

The myths of the mighty

...my beliefs are a strong conviction, yours a dogma, his a myth...

PERCY COHEN (1969)

Leadership is a myth. At first glance, this doesn't seem like a promising approach. If there are 35 million definitions of 'leadership', then there are almost as many of 'myth'. In fact, one recent scholar of the subject, John Lyden, has recently asserted that

> ...[the] term 'myth' is so laden with negative connotations that it is practically unserviceable for the study of religion.[1]

It is true that there are any number of bewildering attempts to describe and categorize the different definitions, descriptions, histories and categories of 'myth'. Historical surveys usually begin with Friedrich Max Müller (1823–1900) and pass through the early anthropologists Edward Tylor (1832–1917) and James Frazer (1854–1941), onto the psychological interpreters, Sigmund Freud (1856–1939) and Carl Jung (1875–1961), and their disciples, especially Joseph Campbell (1904–87), reaching the social anthropologists and sociologists Emile Durkheim (1858–1917), Bronislaw

---

[1] John C. Lyden, *Film as Religion* (2003), 56.

Malinowski (1884–1942), Claude Lévi-Strauss (1908–2009), and concluding, unavoidably, with Mircea Eliade (1907–86). Every one of these thinkers, and it is by no means an exhaustive list, could justify a study in themselves, and usually do.

Thematic surveys, like Robert A. Segal's[2] or Milton Scarborough's,[3] can be equally unwieldy (with the latter, for example, dividing myth systems into 'inside' and 'outside' categories with 'up', 'down' and 'middle' flavours).

Even simply stated definitions can be picked apart. Look at Don Cupitt's definition of myth:

> …a myth is typically a traditional sacred story of anonymous authorship and archetypal or universal significance which is recounted in a certain community and is often linked with a ritual; that it tells of the deeds of superhuman beings such as gods, demigods, heroes, spirits or ghosts; that it is set outside historical time in primal or eschatological time or in the super-natural world, or may deal with comings and goings between the supernatural world and the world of human history; that the superhuman beings are imagined in anthropomorphic ways, although their powers are more than human and the story often is not naturalistic but has the fractured, disorderly logic of dreams; that the whole body of a people's mythology is often prolix, extravagant and full of seeming inconsistencies; and finally that the work of myth is to explain, to reconcile, to guide action or to legitimate. We can add the myth-making is evidently a primal and universal function of the human mind as it seeks a more-or-less unified vision of the cosmic order, the social order and the meaning of the individual's life. Both for society at large and for the individual, this story-generating function seems irreplaceable. The individual finds meaning in his life by making of his life a story set within a larger social and cosmic story.[4]

---

[2] Robert A. Segal, 'Myth', in *The Blackwell Companion to the Study of Religion*, Segal (ed.) (2006), 337–56.
[3] Milton Scarborough, *Myth and Modernity* (1994), chapter 2.
[4] Don Cupitt, *The World To Come* (1982), 29.

To which *tour de force* Laurence Coupe adds 'up to a point, Don Cupitt', for, as Coupe admonishes '…not all myths are linked with a ritual; not all myths are about gods; and not all myths concern a time outside historical time. Exceptions to, and contradictions of, any particular paradigm are endless'.[5]

What might 'myth' mean?

Bearing this in mind, as we try to examine the mythic qualities of leadership, we proceed modestly. There is no reason to pretend that we can come up with a 'complete' or 'systematic' definition of myth. In fact, to pretend to do so might even interfere with our task – after all, we are examining 'leadership', not 'myth'. We can think of our cautious approach as a sort of conceptual carpenter's vice. The carpenter does not work upon the vice; that is the tool which holds the object worked upon. A modest approach to myth, an 'interpretative strategy', is merely a means by which we can hold on to a concept work is done to it.[6]

Lies

The most important thing to remember is that 'myth' is not neces-sarily a fancy way of saying 'lie', even if it is commonly used as a synonym for 'falsehood'. It is used, it is true, in this way in the New Testament. So, for example, 1 Tim. 1.4; 4.7 and 2 Pet. 1.16 tell us 'not to occupy themselves with myths and endless genealogies', 'have nothing to do with profane myths and old wives' tales', and 'for we did not follow cleverly devised myths when we made known to you the power and coming of our Lord Jesus Christ'

---

[5]Laurence Coupe, *Myth* (1997), 6.
[6]If you want to read more about the categorization of myth, then you would do well to look at the work of G. B. Caird, *The Language and Imagery of the Bible* (1980), chapter 13, 'The Language of Myth'. Caird's description of the different under-standings of what 'myth' might mean is modest, accessible and effective.

respectively. Other, later, writers, hostile to religion, also express this sort of hostility towards myth, for example, David Bidney:

> Myth must be taken seriously as a cultural force but it must be taken seriously precisely in order that it may be gradually superseded in the interests of the advancement of truth and the growth of human intelligence. Narrative, critical and scientific thought provides the only self-correcting means of combating the diffusion of myth, but it may do so only on condition that we retain a firm and uncompromising faith in the integrity of reason and in the transcultural validity of the scientific enterprise.[7]

For Bidney, and others like him, anyone who accepts the power of myth 'lives, at best, in cloudcuckoo land and, at worst, in a state of savage perdition', in Percy Cohen's tart phrase.[8]

Wishes

Sometimes, 'myth' is used as a synonym for 'wish-fulfilment'. Caird recognizes that there is a whole school of mythography which treats myth 'as the same expression of deep-seated and permanent human needs...'[9] This is myth as an expression of human psychology, whether Freudian, where 'the function of myth is to vent the unconscious' or Jungian, in which its function is 'to encounter the unconscious'.[10] As Otto Rank put it:

> Myths are, therefore, created by adults, by means of retrograde childhood fantasies, the hero being credited with the myth-maker's personal infantile history.[11]

---

[7]David Bidney, 'Myth, Symbolism and Truth', in *Myth: a symposium*, Sebeok (ed.) (1958), 23.
[8]Percy S. Cohen, 'Theories of Myth', *Man* (September 1969): 337.
[9]Caird, *Language and Imagery*, 223.
[10]Segal's neat distinction: Segal, 'Myth', 346.
[11]Otto Rank, *The Myth of the Birth of the Hero* (1914), 82. Quoted in Segal, 'Myth', 347.

The goal for modern, liberated, rational human beings is to remove the power of myth from their lives, and to accept that wishing won't make it so, and that fairy-tales are demeaning.

Experiences

But the triumph of rationalism is anything but. As Claude Lévi-Strauss discovered in his anthropological work, myths and mythmaking and mythologies continue in the mind of modern, 'mythless', man. In *The Raw and the Cooked*, Lévi-Strauss wrote: 'I therefore claim to show, not how men think in myths, but how *myths operate in men's minds without their being aware of the fact*'.[12] Two scholars with relatively little in common agreed with Lévi-Strauss. Louis Althusser, the Marxist philosopher, argued that ideology was an unconscious process in human beings. Ideology is a series of representations which is 'profoundly *unconscious*, even when it presents itself in a reflected form'.[13] Mircea Eliade, the historian of religions, even while admitting that the modern world 'at least apparently, …is not rich in myths',[14] recognized that

> it seems unlikely that any society could completely dispense with myths, for, of what is essential in mythical behaviour – the exemplary pattern, the repetition, the break with profane duration and integration into primordial time – the first two at least consubstantial with every human condition.[15]

---

[12] Claude Lévi-Strauss, *The Raw and the Cooked* (1970), 12. [Emphasis added.]
[13] Louis Althusser, 'Marxism and Humanism (1964)', in *For Marx* (1969), 233. [Emphasis in the original.]
[14] Mircea Eliade, *Myths, Dreams and Mysteries* (1968), 25.
[15] Eliade, *Myths, Dreams and Mysteries*, 31–2.

Meanings

This is a profound human need, it seems. We need to know that we are not experiencing 'one damn thing after another', that our experiences have some kind of meaning. Margaret Atwood, the Canadian novelist, elegantly expressed this in an interview for PBS:

> We want a beginning of the story. And we go as far ahead in the future as we can. We want an end to the story. And that's not going to be just us getting born and us dying. *We want to be able to place ourselves within a larger story*. Here's where we came from. Here's where we're going in some version or another. And when you die, this is what happens.[16]

Atwood's definition is uncannily similar to the famous definition by the Christian gnostic theologian Valentinus of *gnosis*, the secret that will make us free, namely, 'the knowledge of who we were, and what we have become; where we were or where we were placed, whither we hasten, from what we are redeemed; what birth is and what rebirth'.[17]

This is a burden, and one which weighs on our sense of who we are and what we are for. Men and women, as individuals and as a society, have always dealt with the burden of these questions through the use of what Rudolf Otto called 'metaphor and symbolic expressions'.[18] Humanity is the metaphorical animal, and, moreover, one which likes its metaphors to have a beginning, a middle and an end. Our metaphors are narratives.

---

[16] 'Bill Moyers on Faith & Reason: Margaret Atwood', (PBS, 28 July 2006). [Emphasis added.]
[17] Clement of Alexandria, *The Excerpta ex Theodoto of Clement of Alexandria* (1934), sec. 78.2.
[18] Rudolf Otto, *The Idea of the Holy* (1923), 12.

Stories, symbols, significance

We tell ourselves stories to fulfil our need for meaning. These metaphors are our 'ruling stories': they are 'framing metaphors'. Eliade thought that this applied even (especially?) in modern society. We cannot avoid them because we think that modern, empirical, scientific people only 'deal directly and scientifically with raw nature, facts, data', because we forget that such things are themselves 'already second-order abstractions'.[19] We might no longer tell tales of brave Ulysses around the camp fire, or sing sagas of the northern heroes in the gloom of the war-lord's hall, but this doesn't mean that those stories aren't told in another form. The medium is different, the meaning is the same. In an advanced capitalist society, one in which experience and culture are packaged and commodified, we value the sorts of stories that Eliade called 'public spectacles'. These

> ... take place in a 'concentrated time', time of a heightened intensity; a residuum of, or substitute for, magicoreligious time. This 'concentrated time' is also the specific dimension of the theatre and the cinema. Even if we take no account of the ritual origins and mythological structure of the drama or the film, there is still the important fact that these are two kinds of spectacle that make us live in time of a quality quite unlike that of 'secular duration', in a temporal rhythm, at once concentrated and articulated, which apart from all aesthetic implications, evokes a profound echo in the spectator.[20]

In other words, our stories, our sagas, our metaphors of meaning, help us leave the normal time experience in everyday life (the time of one damn thing after another), and enter the concentrated time, in which the damn things can be connected meaningfully. We seek out the 'profound echo' of mythic stories to make sense of our

---

[19] William G. Doty, *Mythography* (1986), 18.
[20] Eliade, *Myths, Dreams and Mysteries*, 34–5.

lives. Myths provide what Richard Slotkin has called 'a functioning memory system'.[21]

But memories work in one direction alone. Myths are bi-directional: they don't just help us make sense of the past, they work upon the present and the future as well. If a society's myths describe the society's origins, they also control the present and future forms that society will permit itself to take: 'This is who we were. Therefore this is who we should be'.

As we seek out those myths, we begin unconsciously to pattern our lives to conform to the myths we have found. According to Jerome S. Bruner:

It is not simply society that patterns itself upon the idealising myths, but unconsciously it is the individual man as well who is able to structure his internal clamour of identities in terms of prevailing myth. Life then produces myth and finally imitates it.[22]

Those who seek the *mythos* of a society, should, in the words of the intellectual historian, R. W. B. Lewis:

...look for the images and the 'story' that animate the ideas and are their imaginative and usually more compelling equivalent. ...while the vision may be formulated in the orderly language of rational thought, it also finds its form in a recurring pattern of images – ways of seeing and sensing experience – and in a certain habitual story, an assumed dramatic design for the representative life. [23]

Let us assume that all this is true. Let us assume that mythic thinking does operate within our time and culture. This mythic thinking operates at a level below our conscious thought, through the cultural artefacts we produce, and, in an advanced capitalist society, consume. Let us assume that the most powerful myths are

---

[21] Richard Slotkin, 'Our Myths of Choice', *The Chronicle of Higher Education*, 28 September 2001, B11.

[22] Jerome S. Bruner, 'Myth and Identity', in *Myth and Mythmaking* (1968), 282–283.

[23] R. W. B. Lewis, *The American Adam* (1955), 3.

the ones which operate most ubiquitously upon us, in the repeated tropes and motifs and plots of our culture, 'stories we never get tired of hearing'.[24] Let us assume that these ubiquitous myths, the 'framing metaphors' in William Doty's words,[25] gain some of their power because usually we insist that we are rational people, who are only moved by empiricism and scientific materialism. We will also assume, with Kelton Cobb, that:

> We moderns and postmoderns do have metaphysical plots with which we tell the story of forces which have made the world what it is: survival of the fittest, rational choice, secularization, globalization, the war of all against all, dialectical materialism, chaos theory, the cunning collusion of power and knowledge, the triumph of the therapeutic, the decline of civilization, the 'end of history', the 'clash of civilizations,' the Big Bang and Murphy's Law...[26]

Where can we observe these mythic ways of thinking, these metaphysical plots? Eliade has already given us the answer. Because we live in an advanced capitalist society, the public spectacles which convey our myths are the products of industry: the pinnacle of myth-making today is popular film. This is not a solitary art form, but is rather, in Robert B. Ray's elegant summary, a 'technologically dependent, capital-intensive, commercial, collaborative medium, regulated by the government and financially linked to mass audiences...'[27] It is the industrial art-form *par* excellence. In other words, films require large amounts of money, large amounts of technological expertise, and, in order to be sustainable, large amounts of cultural and social resonance. Movies make money by reflecting and making our myths. Let us examine how they achieve that.

---

[24] Kelton Cobb, *The Blackwell Guide to Theology and Popular Culture* (2005), 123.
[25] Doty, *Mythography*, 18.
[26] Cobb, *Popular Culture*, 123–4.
[27] Robert B. Ray, *A Certain Tendency of the Hollywood Cinema, 1930-1980* (1985), 6.

Are movies mythic?

If we think that 'myth' = falsehood, then the idea that movies are myths is fairly straightforward. This argument usually runs this way: cinema is dominated by escapism and fantasy; these are false-hoods, myths, 'anything opposed to reality' in the words of Paul Monaco.[28] Therefore cinema is mythic.

But there is a problem. Cinema works using photographic representations of reality. Even if the story it presents is fantasy, then it is *presented* as reality ('look at how realistic Pandora is in *Avatar* – you can count each dreadlock on the head of the Na'vi'). Because it is photo-real, it cannot be operating on a mythic level: it is an artefact of 'reality lived'[29]. As André Bazin argued, cinema has 'an integral realism, a recreation of the world in its own image, an image unburdened by the freedom of interpretation of the artist or the irreversibility of time'.[30] Therefore, according to Monaco, the debate is whether cinema is mythic or amythic, or, even more strongly, anti-mythic. Movies tell the stories we don't get tired of hearing. Therefore they are mythic. Movies tell stories by showing a realistic view of the world. Therefore, movies aren't mythic.

This might seem like an insurmountable gulf, but we can sidestep the problem (realism vs mythicism) by applying Northrop Frye's 'Theory of Modes' to the medium of cinema. Frye's theory, based on a remark by Aristotle, categorizes fictions into five different modes, according to the protagonist's competency and faculties: 'the hero's power of action'[31]. In doing so, we can see that 'myth' versus 'realism' is a both/and situation and not either/or.

Frye limits the first mode, *Myth*[32], to the actions of the hero as a divine being. For some years, since the decline in the fashion for 'Jesus-pics', this was not a common genre in popular Hollywood

---

[28] Paul Monaco, 'Film as Myth and National Folklore', in *The Power of Myth in Literature and Film* (1980), 35.

[29] Monaco, 'Film as Myth and National Folklore', 36.

[30] André Bazin, 'The Myth of Total Cinema (1946)', in *What is Cinema?* vol. 1 (2005), 21.

[31] Northrop Frye, *Anatomy of Criticism* (1957), 33.

[32] He is using the word 'Myth' here in a different way from my use.

films. However, we have seen a revival of it in recent years, with the interminable fashion for super-hero films. When *Terminator: Salvation* was released in 2009, *The Guardian* reviewer noted 'in keeping with modern incarnations of the action blockbuster, this treatment of the Terminator has been smothered in quasi-religious symbolism and primary-school philosophising'.[33] Bryan Singer's *Superman Returns* (2006) made the connection between the Man of Steel and the Son of Man explicit through its endless shots of Superman hanging, cruciform, in space, like a caped version of Dalí's *Christ of Saint John of the Cross*. Along with Arthur C. Clarke's 'Third Law' ('any sufficiently advanced technology is indistinguishable from magic')[34] perhaps we similarly need to assert that 'any sufficiently advanced super-hero is indistinguishable from divinity'. Even so, Frye's first mode need not concern us for our present purposes: the divine hero is not often a leader, even of lesser mortals.

Frye's second and third modes, *Romance* and *High Mimetic,* account for the differences between fantasy and escapist cinema. According to Frye:

> The hero of romance moves in a world in which the ordinary laws of nature are slightly suspended: prodigies of courage and endurance, unnatural to us, are natural to him, and enchanted weapons, talking animals, terrifying ogres and witches, and talismans of miraculous power violate no rule of probability once the postulates of romance have been established.[35]

Romance is expressed in the fictional genres of legends and folk tales (and the cinematic equivalents of fantasy and science fiction?).

The *High Mimetic* mode exists when the protagonist shares the same environment as other characters in the fiction, but exceeds them in degree: 'He has authority, passions, and powers of

---

[33] Andrew Pulver, 'Terminator Salvation goes forward to blank out its past', *The Guardian*, 21 May 2009.
[34] Arthur C. Clarke, 'Hazard of Prophecy: the failure of imagination', in *Profiles of the Future*, 3rd edn (1982), note on p. 36.
[35] Frye, *Anatomy of Criticism*, 33.

expression far greater than ours, but what he does is subject both to social criticism and to the order of nature'.[36] This is the mode in which cinematic tragedies and epics operate. The hero of police procedurals, especially flawed heroes, works in high mimetic.

When Monaco talks about photographic representations of reality, Frye's third and fourth modes, *Low Mimetic* and *Ironic,* come into play. In the *Low Mimetic* mode, the protagonist is 'one of us', and the problems he faces and the resources he has to deal with those problems belong to all humanity. This is the mode of realistic fiction, and most 'realistic' genres of cinema. In the *Ironic* mode, on the other hand, the protagonist is inferior to most of humanity, and we find ourselves 'looking down on a scene of bondage, frustration, or absurdity'.[37] Frye says that this is the mode of most serious fiction in the later part of the twentieth century, but, paradoxically, it is also the mode of most comic or farcical films.

But, as Monaco points out, this customary division of cinema into 'unreal fantasy' and 'reality lived' is not actually how cinema works. Just as myth is multivalent and ambiguous, so too is cinema: 'it transcends reality (quasi-magically) while maintaining a close connection to the pictorial accuracy often associated with reality'.[38] For example, my children, watching Peter Jackson's *The Return of the King,* commented that the special effects in the Battle of Pelennor Fields looked 'fake', without realising they were describing the depiction of a ghost-army attacking 30 metre high battle-elephants. Somehow the fantasy should have looked 'more real'.

Movies are quasi-magical, transcending reality, by their ability to manipulate time, concentrating and elongating it. Very early on in the history of cinema, filmmakers perfected the techniques of parallel editing so that transitions in time, as transitions, are invisible to the audiences. This meant the length of a film, measurable in real time, 90 or 150 or 180 minutes,[39] very rarely matches the time

---

[36] Frye, *Anatomy of Criticism*, 34.

[37] Frye, *Anatomy of Criticism*, 34.

[38] Monaco, 'Film as Myth and National Folklore', 37.

[39] Or 726 minutes if watching the Director's Cut Blu-Ray version of the entire *Lord of the Rings* Trilogy!

of the film's story: the 'narrative' time might be a day, a week, or millions of years – see, for example, the most famous jump-cut in cinematic history: the transition between prehistoric man throwing a thighbone into the air, and the orbiting space weapon system in *2001: A Space Odyssey*. Because of this manipulation of time (usually invisible to, or unnoticed by, the film's audience), film operates in a mythic zone, called 'concentrated time' by Mircea Eliade.[40] The way a movie interacts with time, how it 'overcomes' or 'disregards' time, shows cinema working at its most mythic, according to Monaco.[41]

Furthermore, as an individual film is a collective product (the amount of industry, capital and co-operation means that the 'auteur' theory of cinema is also a myth), it expresses collective thought: 'Movies are not 'authored' but are rather reflections of shared thoughts and structures... [and such collective thinking is] impersonal, archetypic, and prototypic'.[42]

> *Insofar* as the societies of the film age are accurately described as national ones the mythocontent and mythostructure of films function as elements of national folklore. Moreover, since the motion picture possesses elements of fantasy of a certain sort based on the suspension of time, and aspects of wish-fulfilment which are collective, these function primarily at the level of national society.[43]

I want to go a step beyond Monaco at this point. He says that national cinema reflects national societies and national folklore. But for this to be true the national cinemas and the national folklore would have to be contained, separated from other national cinemas, and national folklores. But the reality of moviemaking since about 1950 is that it is a mythic medium within an international world with

---

[40] *Myths, Dreams and Mysteries*, 34–8.

[41] Monaco, 'Film as Myth and National Folklore', 38.

[42] Monaco, 'Film as Myth and National Folklore', 39. This approach to interpreting myth is one taken by, among others, Siegfried Kracauer, and will be useful when we come to examine the 'films of affirmation' in Chapter 4, 'The Leadership Principle', below.

[43] Monaco, 'Film as Myth and National Folklore', 41. [Emphasis added.]

an international folklore. And for 'international', read 'one nation'. For the reality of moviemaking since about 1950 is that one nation has dominated the cultural and economic unconsciousness of the world.

The world's movies are American movies

There is one way of making movies and one way of consuming movies, and that is the American way. As Robert Ray says 'different ways of making movies would appear as aberrations from some "intrinsic essence of cinema" rather than simply as alternatives… because departures from the American Cinema's dominant paradigms risked not only commercial disaster but critical incomprehension, one form of cinema threatened to drive out all others'.[44]

We can see how this is true by looking at the history of the political, technological, ethical, geographic or linguistic factors which have contributed to the dominance of American cinema. There are numerous studies on this process, and one of the most readable, because it was written by a protagonist in the latter stages of the takeover, is David Puttnam's *The Undeclared War* (1997). We can give a taste of the process by looking, briefly, at two examples: economics and culture.

'Fifty dollars, a broad and a camera'

Before World War One almost anyone could become a movie mogul: 'All you needed was fifty dollars, a broad, and a camera', according to an early participant.[45] Because it didn't

---

[44]Ray, *Certain Tendency*, 26.
[45]Jesse L. Lasky, Jr, *Whatever Happened to Hollywood?* (1973), 46; Quoted in Puttnam, *The Undeclared War*, 38.

take much to become a filmmaker, most filmmakers didn't
think much of the possibilities of film. Thomas Edison, who,
if not the inventor of motion pictures, was certainly its earliest
plagiarist[46], thought of movies as little more than toys. It took
two European companies, Nordisk in Denmark and Pathé in
France, to show the Americans that movies could be serious,
profitable business.

In 1908 Nordisk, owned by the former shepherd and fairground
barker Ole Olsen, was the second largest film company in the
world. Olsen had 'built an international organization in which he
controlled all aspects of production, distribution and exhibition'.[47]
In 1908/09 Nordisk made 60 films, and distributed 36 of them in
the USA.

Olsen's Nordisk was second only to Charles Pathé, who
invented the modern movie production system. Serious profits
came when the film company was 'vertically integrated'. This
meant owning the means of production (the film company proper,
with technicians, writers, directors and actors all contracted); the
means of distribution (protecting the importance of copyright); and
the means of exhibition (the nickelodeons, theatres, and movie
houses in which the movies were actually shown). It was Pathé
who first set up such a vertically integrated system: the structure
he invented 'allowed him to minimize risk, using profits generated
by the distribution of his films to fund the production of new ones.
…[he] exercise[d] an almost seamless integrated control over the
entire operation'.[48] The results were quantifiable and profitable: by
1906 Pathé's company was making a movie a day, and its potential
worldwide reach was 300 million people per film; by 1908 it was
selling twice as many films as the entire American film industry.
His 'domination of world cinema was complete'.[49] As Pathé later
boasted: 'I didn't invent cinema, but I did industrialize it'.[50]

---

[46]See Puttnam, *The Undeclared War*, 11, 12, 22, 40.
[47]Ron Mottram, *The Danish Cinema Before Dreyer* (1988), 14. Production figures are
taken from chapter 1.
[48]Puttnam, *The Undeclared War*, 41.
[49]Puttnam, *The Undeclared War*, 43.
[50]Charles Pathé, *De Pathé Frères à Pathé Cinéma* (1970), 36; trans. by and quoted
in Puttnam, *The Undeclared War*, 43.

It did not, and could not, last. As with Nordisk, Pathé faced the unequal struggle against the American film industry's inherent advantages. It was a unified market, operating in a politically and economically unified country, with a potential audience, which, if not greater than the European market, was a reasonably large proportion of the former (325 million in Europe, 92 million in America). The motion picture industry very swiftly and effectively formed itself into a series of cartels, with the active assistance of the US Federal Government, to protect American financial interests: in August 1918, the Federal Government declared the American moviemaking businesses as an 'essential industry'.[51] The disruption caused to the European industry by World War One, and American protectionism, meant that even before the introduction of sound, the European movie companies were swiftly and comprehensively overwhelmed by the American industry.

And overwhelm it did. By 1925 Hollywood feature films, as a per centage of films exhibited, took 95 per cent of the British, 60 per cent of the German, 85 per cent of the Scandinavian, and 70 per cent of the French markets.[52] By 1923, *Photoplay*, a popular fan magazine, was able to boast: 'We're getting a throttle-hold on the old world; it's all to the jazz and celluloid right now'.[53] The 'throttle-hold' was tenacious: 'by the early 20s, the American film industry had virtually taken over world markets'.[54] Even so, the 'highest tide'[55] for American domination of all forms of media was not until the years 1947–53. In 1950, America cinema produced 622 feature films: all were available for export, and it was estimated by the United

---

[51] Puttnam, *The Undeclared War*, 203, 90–1. For the history and influence of the Creel Committee and its 'Division of Films', see Kristin Thompson, *Exporting Entertainment: America in the world film market, 1907-34* (1985), 92–9.

[52] Figures taken from 'Table 4: The Hollywood Share in Foreign Film Markets, 1925, 1928, 1937', Jeremy Tunstall, *The Media Are American* (1977), 284.

[53] Herbert Howe, 'What Europe thinks of American Stars', *Photoplay*, February 1923, 41; Quoted in Thompson, *Exporting Entertainment*, 100.

[54] Thompson, *Exporting Entertainment*, 148. Thompson's conclusion is justified by her superb quantitative analysis, presented in Appendices I & II of her book.

[55] Tunstall, *The Media Are American*, 141–3.

Nations Educational, Scientific and Cultural Organization that US-produced movies consumed three-quarters of exhibition time on the world's cinema screens.[56]

This could not last, but even if the USA lost moral high ground and sales by the early 1980s,[57] in 1985 the revenue of the American film industry had grown to $1 billion a year, and 40 per cent of its revenue came from overseas rentals. The Motion Picture Association of America (MPAA), under its president Jack Valenti, operated as a mini State Department, with 300 'diplomats' stationed in 60 countries around the world, furthering the commercial and moral interests of the major American studios.[58] By 1994 the American film industry made more money from overseas exhibitions than from domestic for the first time[59]; in 1995 the European Union's audiovisual industries were in deficit to the United States by $6.3 billion[60]; by 2000 in the European Union, the market share for American films was 73.7 per cent, an increase of 4 per cent in a single year.[61] No wonder a provocative sub-editor on *Variety* was able to summarize the situation: 'Earth to H'wood: You Win'.[62]

'America's secret weapon'

But money, protectionism and complicated cartels weren't enough to achieve this victory. The triumph of American cinema was immeasurably helped by its *cultural* dominance.

---

[56] Figures quoted in William H. Read, *America's Mass Media Merchants* (1976), 53.

[57] Tunstall's updates and gloomier thesis: *The Media Were American* (2008), 93ff.

[58] Clyde H. Farnesworth, 'Jack Valenti's State Department', *The New York Times* (18 December 1985), B12.

[59] Source: 'Worldwide rentals beat domestic take', *Variety* 358, no. 2 (13 February 1995): 28.

[60] Source: the European Audiovisual Observatory, quoted in Puttnam, *The Undeclared War*, 350.

[61] European Audiovisual Observatory, 'Cinema admissions' (23 April 2001).

[62] Leonard Klady, 'Earth to H'wood: you win', *Variety* 358, no. 2 (13 February 1995): 1; John Rockwell, 'The New Colossus: American culture as power export', *The New York Times* (30 January 1994), H1.

Neal Gabler, a historian of popular film, proposes that this cultural dominance is made up of two factors, aesthetics and ideology: in other words, *how* American movies are put together, and *what* they portray. The 'how' is to do with their aesthetic of scale, speed and action that 'made them accessible to anyone'.[63] The 'what' comes from the way that 'American films, concentrating on stars framed in close-ups, promoted the centrality and the efficacy of individual action – a world that conformed to our vicarious will'.[64] In short, American movies are successful, and will continue to be successful, because they are the universal exporters of 'the primal aesthetic of excitement and individualism'.[65]

Part of the aesthetics and ideology came out of the economic realities of moviemaking. As Ray shows, during the 'classic' period of American filmmaking (1930–45), because film studios needed to make as many films as quickly and as cheaply as possible, movie plots became 'endless variations around a few basic patterns', and, for the 'sake of a regular audience', to 'consistently deploy the basic ideologies and myths of American culture': in short, 'to repeat what had worked before', and to give the audience what they want, 'standard American stories'.[66]

Jack Valenti admitted as much. At the height of the Cold War he proclaimed the American motion picture industry as 'America's secret weapon – the supreme visual force in the world, dominating screens in theaters and in living rooms'. The reason why was simple: 'People like what we create better than what others create'.[67]

The cultural dominance of American movies can also be seen as a factor in the 2001. It wasn't enough to say that Muslim terrorists attacked the United States because they hated freedom (as George W. Bush asserted in a speech to Congress on 20 September 2001). Why should the freedom of Western liberal

---

[63] Neal Gabler, 'The world still watches America', *The New York Times* (9 January 2003), A27.
[64] Gabler, 'The world still watches America', A27.
[65] Gabler, 'The world still watches America', A27.
[66] Ray, *Certain Tendency*, 30.
[67] Farnesworth, 'Jack Valenti's State Department'.

democracies provoke such hatred? Don DeLillo attempted to answer this question in a ruminative essay published three months after the attacks. September 2001 wasn't just a political action, DeLillo thought; there must be a cultural component as well:

> ...the primary target of the men who attacked the Pentagon and the World Trade Centre was not the global economy. It was America that drew their fury. It was the high gloss of our modernity. It was the thrust of our technology. It was our perceived godlessness. It was the blunt force of our foreign policy. It was the power of American culture to penetrate every wall, home, life and mind.[68]

The same thing had already occurred to Wim Wenders. As a film student in Munich in the late 1960s he wrote article after article for the review magazine *Filmkritik* full of references to, and quotations from, American cultural artefacts. Later, after having made four films in America, he reflected on the effect of America culture and filmmaking on him, a European filmmaker:

> No other country in the world has sold itself so much
> and sent its images, its SELF-image
> with such power into every corner of the world.
> For seventy or eighty years, since the existence of cinema,
> American films – or better, this ONE American film –
> has been preaching the dream
> of the unexampled, exemplary,
> Promised Land.[69]

In short, according to David Puttnam, Hollywood cinema is a 'revolutionary cultural form' which has successfully 'synthesized the American Dream to become a universal language'.[70]

---

[68] Don DeLillo, 'In the Ruins of the Future: reflections on terror and loss in the shadow of September', *Harper's Magazine*, December 2001, 33.
[69] 'The American Dream' (March/April 1984), in Wim Wenders, *Emotion Pictures* (1989), 119–20.
[70] Puttnam, *The Undeclared War*, 334.

Technically adept, financially expansive, logistically slick, industrial-scale, vertically integrated, film making is indistinguishable from the American *mythos*.

Which means we have to ask, what is the American *mythos*? What is the meaningful story being told, over and over again, by this powerful medium?

Multiple American myths

There are almost as many American myths as there are Americans. For example, Richard Hughes, in his powerful polemic *Myths America Lives By,* identifies five national myths ('the means by which we affirm the meaning of the United States'[71]). For Hughes these are: the myth of the chosen people (originating in the colonial era); the myth of nature's nation, that is, the assumption that the political and social character of America was determined by inherent, 'natural', traits (from the time of the revolution); the myth of the Christian nation (as a result of the 'Great Awakenings' of the early nineteenth century); the myth of the millennial nation, that is, American society as a shining city on the hill, which will usher in peace and goodwill for the whole of human kind (from the early nineteenth century as well); and the myth of the innocent nation (from the twentieth century, and incorporating the reaction to the 9/11 attacks).

Usually when considering the connection between myth and movies the starting point (and frequently the end point) is Joseph Campbell's *Hero with a Thousand Faces.*[72] This work of popular, speculative anthropology and literary criticism became, in the 1970s, almost a 'screenwriting manual'. It was thought to outline 'a mythic formula'[73]: and formulas can be used to make money. George Lucas kept a copy of *Hero with a Thousand Faces* alongside

---

[71] Richard T. Hughes, *Myths America Lives By* (2004), 2.
[72] Joseph Campbell, *The Hero With A Thousand Faces* (1949).
[73] Alec Worley, *Empires of the Imagination* (2005), 265.

Tolkien's *The Lord of the Rings* while writing *Star Wars,*[74] and he later described the book as having a 'wonderful life force'[75]. By the 1990s the principles of Campbell were turned into a series of explicit 'how-to' books. Christopher Vogler, 'Director of Development at Fox 2000', says that Campbell's 'great accomplishment was to articulate clearly something that had been there all along – the life principles embedded in the structure of stories'.[76] The mythic structure of all the great popular Hollywood films 'is not an invention, but an observation'[77]. Campbell has, according to these writers, described a paradigm, 'the beauty of [which] is its simplicity and the rich interpretations and varied applications of its simple truths'.[78]

Campbell's paradigm, the so-called 'Monomyth'[79], states that every hero undertakes a three-part journey: separation from society, trials whilst separated, and reintegration to society (having been transformed by his separation and trials). This three part journey is broken down into 17 distinct units, forming a narrative process:[80]

A hero ventures forth from the world of common day into a region of supernatural wonder; fabulous forces are there encountered and a decisive victory is won; the hero comes back from this mysterious adventure with the power to bestow boons on his fellow human beings.[81]

Campbell's theory has been criticised,[82] but its usual reception, especially since the marketing and industrial phenomenon that is the *Star Wars* saga, has been praise. *Star Wars* was (among other

---

[74]Worley, *Empires of the Imagination*, 258.
[75]Mary S. Henderson, *Star Wars: the magic of myth* (1997), 7.
[76]Christopher Vogler, *The Writer's Journey*, 2nd edn (1999), xi; see also Stuart Voytilla, *Myth and the Movies* (1999).
[77]Vogler, *Writer's Journey*, ix.
[78]Voytilla, *Myth and the Movies*, 3.
[79]Campbell, *Hero*, 30. For a discussion on the origins of the term and concept, see Robert A. Segal, *Joseph Campbell: an introduction* (1990), chapter 2.
[80]Campbell, *Hero*, 36–7.
[81]Campbell, *Hero*, 30.
[82]'...Campbell may be faulted for positing a trans-historical *mythos* with little variation in the morphology...'. Frank P. Tomasulo, 'Mr. Jones Goes to Washington', *Quarterly Review of Film Studies* (1982): 332.

things) a filmed version of the Monomyth, and who can gainsay such a return on investment? Films made using the Monomyth succeed, according to Campbell's acolytes, because they answer the mythic questions we need answering (expressing the answer in Campbell's structured journey). But what are those mythic questions? Stuart Voytilla sets them out:

> First, look within *yourself*. What are *your* own needs and desires? *Your* dreams and fears? *Your* triumphs and short-comings? Second, look at the stories that attract *you*. What films are most significant in *your* life?[83]

This is curious. Campbell and his followers say that his paradigm is the 'Monomyth', the fundamental, basic, mythological structure. But Voytilla's questions show that that the 'Monomyth', when applied to American cinema, is actually no such thing. It is a second-order mythology, built upon a pre-existing (mythological) understanding of what it means to be American. Campbell's Monomyth is actually dependent upon some that reached its greatest and most enduring expression in the work of a writer, lecturer, *bien-pensant,* from 100 years before Campbell. George Lucas believed that he was filming Campbell's Monomyth: in reality the *Star Wars* cycle is dependent upon the Sage of Concord – Ralph Waldo Emerson.[84]

The indviduator of individualism

Emerson, born in New England to a family of scholarly and respectable Unitarians and following a disappointing career as

---

[83]Voytilla, *Myth and the Movies*, 293.
[84]For a brief outline of Emerson's life see Joel Myerson, 'Emerson, Ralph Waldo', *American National Biography Online* (2000). A more detailed biography is in Robert D. Richardson, *Emerson: The Mind on Fire* (1995). A superb intellectual biography, using a single essay by Emerson as the hermeneutic key, is Kenneth Sacks, *Understanding Emerson: 'The American Scholar' and his struggle for self-reliance* (2003).

a dissenting minister himself, became one of the most influential essayists, lecturers and poets of mid nineteenth-century
America. He was the leader of the Transcendentalist movement,
which gradually moved away from dissident Christianity towards
a celebration of sense and experiences, with a revulsion for
the mercantile tendencies of New England Calvinism. From the
mid-1830s onwards, Emerson was, and remains, 'a dominant
presence in American culture'[85]. This presence applies especially,
but generally unrecognized, to the cultural expression of America
we call cinema. It was Emerson who articulated, with a seductive
power, the American mythology which is prior to Campbell's
so-called 'Monomyth'. We won't understand Emerson, we won't
understand Campbell, we won't understand movies and we won't
understand the myth of 'leadership', until we understand the
importance of 'America's great philosopher-psychologist-poet of
the Self'[86] to the shape of our world today, and his synthesis in an
'Emersonian Ur-myth' of two distinct, but related American myths,
namely the myths of the Frontier and the American Adam.

The myth of Frontier

The American Frontier is not a place. It is a defining *experience*.
Although it was only named when the frontier was almost extin-
guished, it was present in the self-consciousness of America from
the very beginning.

In 1874, as part of the publication of the 1870 Federal Census,
Francis Walker wrote an essay on 'The Progress of the Nation,
1790–1870', which used, for the first time, the expression 'the
frontier line', to describe the boundary of 'continuous settlement'
of the country.[87] Walker's coinage swiftly became an immensely

---

[85] Wesley T. Mott, '"The Age of the First Person Singular": Emerson and Individualism',
in *A Historical Guide to Ralph Waldo Emerson*, Myerson (ed.) (2000), 62.
[86] Mott, 'First Person Singular', 61.
[87] Francis A. Walker, 'The Progress of the Nation, 1790–1890', in *Statistical Atlas
of the United States Based on the Results of the Ninth Census, 1870* (1874), Part
II, 1–4. It was a student of Frederick Jackson Turner, Fulmer Mood, who identified

powerful cultural description. Following the 1890 census (taken in the same year as the 'Battle' of Wounded Knee), the Superintendent of the Census declared that the frontier line was no longer traceable:

> Up to and including 1880 the country had a frontier of settlement, but at present the unsettled area has been so broken into by isolated bodies of settlement that there can hardly be said to be a frontier line. In the discussion of its extent, its westward movement, etc., it can not, therefore, really longer have a place in the census reports.[88]

The significance of the Superintendent's conclusion was to consign the 'frontier' to history. It could now be studied, and 'subjected to sociological analysis to reveal its significance'.[89] One of the first historians to recognize the importance of the Census data was Frederick Jackson Turner, a young professor of history at the University of Wisconsin. In 1893 he gave a lecture to the American Historical Association, *The Significance of the Frontier in American History*, which was later published in a collected volume of lectures and essays called *The Frontier in American History*.[90]

Turner's thesis, based on both his boyhood experience in the former frontier-town of Portage, Wisconsin and his historical training, argued that the single greatest influence on the development of the American nation was its constant movement westwards, and the continual transforming effect of the frontier upon the settlers:

Walker's as the first usage of 'frontier' in the sense which later became identified with Turner: see Fulmer Mood, 'The Concept of the Frontier, 1871-1898' *Agricultural History* (January 1945): 24–30.

[88] The significance of this judgement was camouflaged by the means of its publication: the concluding paragraph of a six-page bulletin on patterns of population density. United States Census Office, *Distribution of Population According to Density: 1890*, (20 April 1891), 4.

[89] Ray Allen Billington, *The Genesis of the Frontier Thesis* (1971), 115.

[90] Frederick Jackson Turner, 'The Significance of the Frontier in American History (1893)', in *The Frontier in American History* (1921), 1–38. For a good summary of Turner's career and intellectual formation, see Martin Ridge, 'Turner the Historian: A Long Shadow', *Journal of the Early Republic* (Summer 1993): 133–44.

The wilderness masters the colonist. It finds him a European in dress, industries, tools, modes of travel, and thought. It takes him from the railroad car and puts him in the birch canoe. It strips off the garments of civilization and arrays him in the hunting shirt and moccasin. It puts him in the log cabin of the Cherokee and Iroquois and runs an Indian palisade around him. ...at the frontier the environment is at first too strong for the man. He must accept the conditions which it furnishes, or perish, and so he fits himself into the Indian clearings and follows the Indian trails. ...here is a new product that is American.[91]

This experience had direct personal and cultural consequences:

...to the frontier the American intellect owes its striking character- istics. That coarseness and strength combined with acuteness and inquisitiveness; that practical, inventive turn of mind, quick to find expedients; that masterful grasp of material things, lacking in the artistic but powerful to effect great ends; that restless, nervous energy; that dominant individualism, working for good and for evil, and withal that buoyancy and exuberance which comes with freedom – these are traits of the frontier...[92]

The frontier originally began at Plymouth Rock, or on Manhattan Island, and the transformation of the colonists into 'Americans' began almost immediately:

At first, the frontier was the Atlantic coast. It was the frontier of Europe in a very real sense. Moving westward, the frontier became more and more American.[93]

Turner's ideas had been recognized by two earlier European visitors to the New World. John Hector St John, otherwise known as Jean de Crèvecoeur (1735–1813), wrote *Letters from an American Farmer* in 1782 in which he described American society

---

[91] Turner, 'Significance of the Frontier', 4.
[92] Turner, 'Significance of the Frontier', 37.
[93] Turner, 'Significance of the Frontier', 4.

from the point of view of a fictional, Pennsylvanian, American farmer. In Letter III, 'What is an American?', Crèvecoeur tells us that Americans begin at the coast, where 'bold and enterprising' people make a living by fishing and trade. In the northern states, close to the coast, live the chosen people: 'The simple cultivation of the earth purifies them'. They are industrious, well-informed, independently-minded, enjoy the 'cheerful cup', and tolerant (preparing to be forbearing of neighbours who would be their natural religious and political enemies back in the Old World).[94]

However the inhabitants of the frontier are very different: feral, rude, 'modern'[95] and living in semi-savagery. 'Their wives and children live in sloth and inactivity; and having no proper pursuits, you may judge what education the latter receive. Their tender minds have nothing else to contemplate but the example of their parents; like them they grow up a mongrel breed, half civilized, half savage...'[96] But this unhappy situation does not last long. For Crèvecoeur the frontier is a moral, as well as an economic and demographic region, and it moves forward: within the space of a dozen years 'the most respectable army of veterans' will follow the savages, and prosperity, virtue and the law will convert the 'forlorn hope' of pioneers into 'industrious people':[97]

> Thus are our first steps trod, thus are our first trees felled, in general, by the most vicious of our people and thus the path is opened for the arrival of a second and better class, the true American freeholders...[98]

This is the basis the 'back-story' of George Steven's *Shane*: there

---

[94] J. Hector St. John de Crèvecoeur, *Letters from an American Farmer*, Stone (ed.) (1981), 71. The passage on the pragmatic religious tolerance of the American settlers is on 73–6.
[95] For de Crèvecoeur this meant 'as opposed to adhering to the universally agreed values of civilization'.
[96] Crèvecoeur, *American Farmer*, 77.
[97] Crèvecoeur, *American Farmer*, 72–3.
[98] Crèvecoeur, *American Farmer*, 79.

the frontier progression was expressed in a 'mythical succession pattern' of 'Indians, cowboys, farmers, suburbanites'.[99]

By the late 1780s Crèvecoeur had already identified the moving frontier and the effect that it had on the colonists. Another Frenchman, two generations later, was able to come up with the definitive description of the developing American nation. Alexis de Tocqueville (1805–59) had been an assistant magistrate under the Bourbon monarchy. In 1831–2 he visited North America to research the American justice and penal system.[100] From his nine months in America, Tocqueville was able to produce the two volumes of his seminal work *Democracy in America* (1835, 1840).

Like Crèvecoeur before him Tocqueville recognised the onslaught of the frontier on the life of the nation: 'This gradual and continuous progress of the European race towards the Rocky Mountains has the solemnity of a providential event. It is like a deluge of men, rising unabatedly, and driven daily onward by the hand of God'.[101]

Always westwards

As a metaphysical place the Frontier couldn't be mapped: however, it could be pointed to. From the earliest days of the republic, the Frontier was associated with a direction – West. In James Fenimore Cooper's *The Prairie* (1827), we read how the hero Natty Bumppo, 'the trapper', has left his home in New York State, where 'the sound of axes, and the crash of falling trees'[102] had disturbed his

---

[99] Bernard Brandon Scott, *Hollywood Dreams and Biblical Stories* (1994), 56. We will see more of the mythic importance of *Shane* in chapter 7, 'The Duke of deception'.
[100] The most recent history of Tocqueville's journey, and the writing of *Democracy in America*, is Leopold Damrosch, *Tocqueville's Discovery of America* (2010).
[101] Alexis de Tocqueville, *Democracy in America (1835,1840)*, Bradley (ed.) (1994): I.xviii (p. 398 in this edition).
[102] James Fenimore Cooper, 'The Prairie: a tale', in *The Leatherstocking Tales*, Elliott (ed.), vol. 1 (1985), chapter 2 (p. 903 in this edition). The introduction to the edition of 1844 makes Bumppo's flight from civilization explicit: 'The sound of the axe has driven him from his beloved forests to seek a refuge, by a species of desperate resignation, on the denuded plains that stretch to the Rocky Mountains. Here he passes the few closing years of his life, dying as he had lived, a philosopher of the

true American sensibilities. Natty continues travelling west, even to the moment of his death:

> The trapper had remained nearly motionless for an hour. His eyes, alone, had occasionally opened and shut. When opened, his gaze seemed fastened on the clouds, which hung around the western horizon, reflecting the bright colours, and giving form and loveliness to the glorious tints of an American sunset.[103]

West is the direction of hope, even in the face of death.

The great prophet of the Wilderness and the West was Henry David Thoreau. In a lecture, published posthumously in *The Atlantic Monthly* (June 1862), Thoreau explained the connection between 'west' as a direction and 'west' as a moral attitude. Strangely and whimsically, whenever he sets out for walk, he eventually finds himself heading a little south of west: 'The future lies that way to me, and the earth seems more unexhausted and richer on that side. …Eastward I go only by force; but westward I go free'.[104] The countryside is uninterrupted in that direction, and there is no sign of human habitation ('towns nor cities…of enough consequence to disturb me'). Thoreau is not alone in his whimsy, for 'that way the nation is moving, and I may say that mankind progress from east to west. …We go eastward to realize history and study the works of art and literature, retracing the steps of the race; we go westward as into the future, with a spirit of enterprise and adventure'.[105]

For Thoreau 'west' means wilderness, and the abandonment of the compromises of European civilization. At the same time, 'westwards' is the direction of enterprise and adventure, rather than art and literature: man travels west for business; he looks east for culture, and, even then not often, as the Atlantic is a Lethean

---

wilderness, with few of the failings, none of the vices, and all the nature and truth of his position'. (Cooper, 'The Prairie (1827)', n. 885.7–11, on p. 1345.)

[103] Cooper, 'The Prairie (1827)', 34 (p. 1316 in this edition).

[104] Henry David Thoreau, 'Walking', in *Walden, Civil Disobedience, and Other Writings*, Rossi (ed.), 3rd edn (2008), 268.

[105] Thoreau, 'Walking', 268–9.

stream. Those who look east forget the west, and the future is in the west.

Shortly after Thoreau's death, his attitude to the 'west' had become a political and economic imperative. 'Go west, young man!' was Horace Greeley's advice, in various editorials and campaigning pamphlets published in New York in the 1850s and 1860s.[106] Frederick Jackson Turner, not unexpectedly, also shared in this yearning for a westward bearing, a yearning with a moral component: 'The west looks to the future, the east toward the past'.[107]

A hundred and twenty years after Thoreau, 'west' retained its connotations of progress, spiritual development and utopian anti-civilization, but, overlaid upon it, was now the sense of a cultural genre: 'west' now included 'Western'. Wenders notes this in his eulogy to the American dream:

American films spoke more clearly about America
than anything else had before.
Especially the Westerns, my favourites.
The most exciting notion: that these adventurous stories
of pioneers, of the wilderness
happened only a hundred years ago.
Somehow that was very important to me.
That was an imaginable past.
…The Wild West!
That wasn't all that long ago.
The other points of the compass meant little to me,
the frozen North, the deep South,
or even the Far East.
My direction was the West.[108]

We can see in Wenders's European yearning for the American West something of the mythical power that the Frontier and its demands

---

[106] See Thomas Fuller, '"Go West, young man!" – an Elusive Slogan', *Indiana Magazine of History* (2004): 231–42.
[107] Letter of September, 1887, quoted in Billington, *Genesis of the Frontier Thesis*, 15.
[108] Wenders, *Emotion Pictures*, 128.

still exerts on western culture. Two Presidential examples: John F. Kennedy's acceptance of the Democratic nomination in 1960 made the rhetorical contrast between the place of its delivery, Los Angeles, at the edge of the last frontier, and the 'New Frontier' stretching before his country, the 'unconquered problems of ignorance and prejudice'.[109] Bill Clinton's first inauguration speech was thoroughly Turnerian, when he described Americans as 'a restless, questing, hopeful people'.[110] And what is the prologue to every episode of the *Star Trek* television series but the Turner thesis transplanted into interstellar space?[111]

We can see how Wenders is right to assert that 'the Americans have colonized our subconscious'[112]. For Turner the frontier experience turned European colonizers into Americans: the power of the frontier myth, upon those who had never had to travel in a birch canoe or throw up an Indian palisade, was also to turn them into Americans. The colonizers were themselves, in turn, colonized.

The myth of the American Adam

Thoreau was only a theoretical frontiersman. In *Walden* he praised his isolation and independence, but the log cabin in which he lived was a gentle stroll from his mother's house, and he took his laundry home at weekends.[113] Thoreau's ideal was actually lived out by Joseph Knowles, who in 1913 spent 60 days living in the woods of north eastern Maine without any equipment, food or clothing. Knowles promised the *Boston Post* that he would live off the land 'as Adam lived'. This latter-day Adam emerged from his

---

[109] John F. Kennedy, 'Acceptance of the Democratic Party Nomination for the Presidency of the United States', Los Angeles, 15 July 1960).
[110] William Jefferson Clinton, 'The Inauguration Transcript', *The New York Times*, 21 January 1993.
[111] The immortal 'Space. The final frontier…' was actually inserted into the third draft of the 'standard opening narration' by the producer John Black. Gene Rodenberry's first two drafts omitted the Turnerian phrase (and were also lifeless and lumpen). See Solow and Justman, *Inside Star Trek: the real story* (1996), 143–9.
[112] Wim Wenders, *The Logic of Images*, trans. Hofmann (1991), 99.
[113] See Paul Theroux's introduction to *The Maine Woods*, Moldenhauer (ed.) (2004), ix.

wilderness Eden a celebrity, the most curious manifestation of what Roderick Nash has called the enthusiasm for the primitive, which in the years after 1890 (a significant date) reached the status of a 'national cult'.[114]

Knowles and his public understood something special about being an American. In order for an American to become himself, he needed the boundless West: 'The vast majority of the people of this country live by the land, and carry its quality in their manners and opinions'.[115] Unhappily, those who live in the settled east have 'imbibed [too] easily an European culture'. Fortunately, the intrusion of the 'nervous, rocky West' means that the possibility of 'an American genius' will arise: 'How much better when the whole land is a garden, and the people have grown up in the bowers of a paradise'.[116] The land will act as the 'sanative and Americanizing influence' on the populations, a sanitation which will 'disclose new virtues'.[117]

Tocqueville had already realized the effect the geography of the continent would have upon American culture: 'The valley of the Mississippi is, on the whole, the most magnificent dwelling-place prepared by God for man's abode; and yet, it may be said that as present it is but a mighty desert'.[118] This vast area, a garden in potentiality, in the midst of the American continent became a driving force in American self-understanding: 'The master symbol of the garden embraced a cluster of metaphors expressing fecundity, growth, increase, and blissful labor in the earth, all centering about the heroic figure of the idealized frontier farmer armed with that supreme agrarian weapon, the sacred plow'.[119]

The earliest travellers west of the Appalachians again and again emoted in this way. So, for example, James Smith, a Methodist

---

[114] Knowles's story is related in Roderick Nash, 'The American Cult of the Primitive', *American Quarterly* (Autumn 1966): 517–19.

[115] Ralph Waldo Emerson, 'The Young American (1844)', in *Nature, Addresses, and Lectures*, Ferguson (ed.), The Collected Works of Ralph Waldo Emerson vol. 1, (1971), 229.

[116] Emerson, 'Young American', 229.

[117] Emerson, 'Young American', 229.

[118] Tocqueville, *Democracy in America*, I. i (p. 19 in this edition).

[119] Henry Nash Smith, *Virgin Land: The American West as Symbol and Myth* (1950), 123.

minister from (eastern and settled) Virginia, in 1797 took a circuit through (western and unsettled) Ohio. Having visited, in the middle of October 1797, Deerfield (now South Lebanon), which had only been settled for 12 months, Smith exclaimed:

> O, what a country will this be at a future day! What field of delights! What a garden of spices! What a paradise of pleasures! when these forests shall be cultivated and the gospel of Christ spread through this rising republic, unshackled by the power of kings and religious oppression on the one hand and slavery, that bane of true Godliness, on the other.[120]

The great prairies of the illimitable American West were a new Eden. But Nash Smith's identification of the 'idealized frontier *farmer*' misses the central implication of this powerful myth.[121] A garden is not worked by a farmer, but by a gardener, and if the American West was an Edenic Garden, then the identity of the gardener was already known: for the nineteenth-century writers and thinkers who were immersed in the imagery of the Christian scriptures (even whilst they reacted against the doctrines and moral precepts of the Christian churches), the gardener of (the new) Eden was Adam.

So Walt Whitman within *Leaves of Grass* (1860–) wrote a cycle of poems claiming for Americans the inheritance of the 'Children of Adam'. Whitman takes upon himself the role, if not of Adam, then certainly of Adam's inheritor and vicar on earth:

> I, chanter of Adamic songs,
> Through the new garden the West, the great cities calling,
> Deliriate, thus prelude what is generated, offering these,
> offering myself...[122]

---

[120] James Smith, 'Tours into Kentucky and the Northwest Territory', Morrow (ed.), *Ohio Archaeological and Historical Quarterly* (1907): 396. Also quoted in Smith, *Virgin Land*, 132. James Smith dates his visit to Deerfield as 'Fri. 12th. [October, 1797]'. [He means Friday 13th.]

[121] The only Adam who appears in Smith's treatise is Adam Smith: *Virgin Land*, 143.

[122] 'Ages and Ages Returning at Intervals', part of the 'Children of Adam' cycle in Walt Whitman, *Leaves of Grass and Other Writings*, Moon (ed.) (2002), 92.

Whitman was following the optimism of his teacher, Emerson. On a journey to the old world, overwhelmed and oppressed by the antiquity of Naples, Emerson expressed his preference for the New World and its inhabitants:

> Here's for the plain old Adam, the simple genuine Self against the whole world.[123]

Six years later, Emerson mused on possible topics for his autumn series of lectures he intended to give in Boston:

> What shall be the substance of my shrift? Adam in the garden, I am to new name all the beasts in the field & all the gods in the Sky. I am to invite men drenched in time to recover themselves & come out of time, & taste their native immortal air. I am to fire with what skill I can the artillery of sympathy & emotion.[124]

In 1955, R. W. B. Lewis articulated this yearning for Adam and the frontier as a single structure: the myth of the American Adam. Lewis collapsed the frontiersman and the husbandsman into the single figure of the gardener who tilled 'the garden of the world', a pre-lapsarian Adam, given a second chance to live as if the Fall had never happened, and whose life and destiny would be limited only by the illimitable bounty of the American land and the sincerity of the American settler:

> ...the story implicit in American experience had to do with an Adamic person, springing from nowhere, outside time, at home only in the presence of nature and God, who is thrust by circumstances into an actual world and an actual age.[125]

---

[123] Naples, 12 March 1833 in *The Journals and Miscellaneous Notebooks of Ralph Waldo Emerson (1832-1834)*, (ed.) Ferguson, vol. 4 (1964), 141.
[124] 18 October 1839, in *The Journals and Miscellaneous Notebooks*, (ed.) Plumstead and Hayford, vol. 7 (1969), 270–1.
[125] Lewis, *The American Adam*, 89.

The European settlers had been called by Providence into a new world, one in which the mistakes of the old could be renounced.

The American Adam is the mythic background to the religions of American exceptionalism, such as the Church of Jesus Christ of Latter-Day Saints (the Mormons). However, the Mormons, under the direction of their leader and prophet, Joseph Smith, were not content to find a *new* Eden in North America. Mormon revelation went further: the old Eden was also to be found there. Having to flee the settlement in Kirtland County, Ohio, in 1838 (a combination of religious suspicion and banking fraud), Smith took his family and followers west to Zion, the 'central hub of God's millennial kingdom'[126], otherwise known as Jackson County, Missouri. Once there, visiting a bluff above the Grand River, Smith was overwhelmed:

> ...a revelation filled his soul. He announced that the apparent ruins were indeed an altar; one built by none other than Adam, the first man. In fact, the very spot on which they all stood was where Adam and his wife, Eve, had fled after being expelled from the Garden of Eden for disobeying God.[127]

The revelation was accepted by Smith's followers; after all he had already revealed that the Garden of Eden was in Jackson County:

> Father Adam was instructed to multiply and replenish the earth, to make it beautiful and glorious, to make it, in short, like unto the garden from which the seeds were brought to plant the garden of Eden. ...God the Father made Adam the Lord of this creation in the beginning, and if we are the Lords of the creation under Adam, ought we not to take a course to imitate our Father in heaven? ...By faith and works we shall subdue the earth

---

[126] Richard Abanes, *One Nation Under Gods* (2002), 103.

[127] Abanes, *One Nation Under Gods*, 147; The original revelation ('to Joseph, the Seer, given near Wight's Ferry, at a place called Spring Hill, Davis County, Missouri, May 19, 1838, wherein Spring Hill is named by the Lord') is recorded in Section 116, Joseph Smith, *The Doctrine and Covenants of the Church of Jesus Christ of Latter-Day Saints* (1908), 415.

and make it glorious. We can plant vineyards and eat the fruit thereof; we possess this power within ourselves.[128]

And yet, the American Adam remains 'an allusive figure, not definitively expressed anywhere in the literature…[but] nonetheless an intrinsic part of the American cultural tradition'.[129] This has the great advantage that American Adams can be identified at all times and in all places of the American cultural tradition. So Garry Wills could title a section of his cultural biography of John Wayne 'the American Adam',[130] and a review of Bob Dylan's autobiography, *Chronicles: Volume One*, could be headed the same way.[131]

Being Adam has social consequences: Adam may have given names to all the animals, he may have been the first gardener, but he was also alone. American Adams treasured this aloneness, so much so that, when faced with it, Tocqueville needed to coin a new word to describe a new phenomenon: 'individualism' appeared for the first time in the English translation of *Democracy in America*.[132] Tocqueville denies that individualism is selfishness, already familiar to our fathers as 'égoïsme', in which a 'passionate and exaggerated love of self', leads a man to read the whole world in terms of himself and his own needs. Individualism, on the other hand, a 'novel expression to which a novel idea has given birth', resulted in the deliberate and thoughtful withdrawal of a man from 'the mass of his fellows', forming a 'little circle of his own', and leaving 'society at large to itself'. Whereas selfishness is as old as humanity, individualism is the product of democratic societies.

---

[128] Heber C. Kimball, 'Advancement of the Saints', in *Journal of Discourses*, Watt and Long (eds), vol. 10 (1865), 235.

[129] Richard Keenan, 'American Adam', Serafin and Bendixen (eds), *The Continuum Encyclopedia of American Literature* (2005), 37.

[130] Garry Wills, *John Wayne: the politics of celebrity* (1997); the concluding chapter of which was first published as 'American Adam', *The New York Review of Books*, 6 March 1997.

[131] Bob Dylan, *Chronicles: Volume One* (2004); reviewed by David E. Anderson, 'Bob Dylan: American Adam', *Religion & Ethics NewsWeekly PBS*, 11 February 2005.

[132] For the intellectual history of the word and concept see Steven Lukes, 'The Meanings of "Individualism"', *Journal of the History of Ideas* (March 1971): 45–66; Koenraad W. Swart, '"Individualism" in the Mid-Nineteenth Century (1826-1860)', *Journal of the History of Ideas* (March 1962): 77–90.

Even so, both have the capacity to weaken social bonds, and, paradoxically, open the inhabitants of the solely private sphere to the unchecked political power of the state:

> They owe nothing to any man, they expect nothing from any man; they acquire the habit of always considering themselves as standing alone, and they are apt to imagine that their whole destiny is in their own hands.[133]

In a telling final phrase, Tocqueville concludes that democratic individualism atomizes a man from ancestors, descendants, and contemporaries, so that, finally, he is confined 'entirely within the solitude of his own heart'.[134]

For Tocqueville, therefore, individualism was 'a withdrawal from public life by Americans who felt deeply their own self-sufficiency'.[135] Turner, on the other hand, celebrated individualism. The frontier experience, and its formation of individualism, was responsible for the 'fundamental assumptions that have gone to make the American spirit and the meaning of America in world history'[136]. This is the 'ideal of democracy', which Turner defines as a 'free self-directing people', which responds to leadership, but insists that the implementation of the leadership's 'programs [and]…execution' is made through 'free choice' and not compulsion. In addition, and more importantly, the 'ideal of individualism' supplants that of democracy. It might be possible to have a democracy akin to 'a disciplined army, where all must keep step and where the collective interests destroyed individual will and work', but this is not the case with America. Rather, American democratic individualism is the result of 'a mobile mass of freely circulating atoms, each seeking its own place and finding play for its own powers and for its own

---

[133] Tocqueville, *Democracy in America*, II.ii.2 ('Of Individualism in Democratic Countries', 98-9 in this edition).

[134] Tocqueville, *Democracy in America*, II.ii.2 ('Of Individualism in Democratic Countries', 99 in this edition).

[135] Joyce Appleby, 'Individualism', Boyer (ed.), *The Oxford Companion to United States History*, (2001).

[136] Frederick Jackson Turner, 'The West and American Ideals (1914)', in *The Frontier in American History* (1921), 306.

original initiative'. It is impossible to understand America, 'the whole American movement', without comprehending this point, 'the very heart' of what it means to be America and American.[137]

The Frontier (as an experience if not a place) deepened the individualism which would eventually come to be considered the typically American trait. This was part of the story, Billington concludes, that Americans told themselves, or accepted unconsciously: for those who lived on the frontier, or who considered themselves to be formed by the frontier, 'every man was a self-dependent individual, fully capable of caring for himself without the aid of society'.[138] Those who failed ('fell by the wayside' says Billington), had failed to seize the advantages and opportunities that belonged to those who, in Emerson's words, 'begin life upon our shores, inflated by the mountain winds, shined upon by all the stars of God'.[139]

This attitude to failure had political, philosophical and economic consequences. Politically, 'the frontier was distrustful of governmental meddling with the affairs of the individual'. Philosophically, the frontier was neo-Darwinian before Darwin: the 'successful man should be let alone to achieve greater success; the unsuccessful should not be pampered for he could succeed if he tried'.[140] Economically, the 'economic elite' of the late nineteenth century was able to mouth the platitudes of 'rugged American individualism'[141] knowing that they were honouring the values of the pioneers of the nation. Thus, for example, E. H. Harriman, the director of the Union Pacific Railroad, campaigned against the

---

[137] Turner, 'West and American Ideals', 306.

[138] Ray Allen Billington, *Westward Expansion: a history of the American frontier*, 4th edn (1980), 653.

[139] Ralph Waldo Emerson, 'The American Scholar (1837)', in *Nature, Addresses, and Lectures*, ed. Ferguson, The Collected Works of Ralph Waldo Emerson, vol. 1, (1971), 69.

[140] Billington, *Westward Expansion*, 653.

[141] The expression was coined by Herbert Hoover, as a presidential candidate in the 1928 general election. The speech, on 22 October 1928 was the last he made in his presidential campaign, and was perhaps prescient: one year later Wall Street crashed, and the long economic boom of the United States was over. Herbert Hoover, 'The Philosophy of Rugged Individualism', in *Documents of American History*, Commager (ed.), 7th edn (1963), 222–5.

regulation of Interstate Commerce Commission on his railroads by persuading the 'western agrarians', against their own interests, that such regulation 'was a violation of our early pioneer ideals'.[142] This phenomenon has intensified in recent years. In the American mid-West electoral behaviour is at odds with the electorate's welfare. As the journalist Thomas Frank, puzzling about the values of his home state of Kansas, has put it:

> Strip today's Kansans of their job security, and they head out to become registered Republicans. ...Squander their life savings on manicures for the CEO, and there's a good chance they'll join the John Birch Society. But ask them about the remedies their ancestors proposed (unions, antitrust, public ownership), and you might as well be referring to the days when knighthood was in flower.[143]

What happens in twenty-first century Kansas is a result of the overwhelming might of myth. The 'functioning memory system' (Slotkin's phrase) is more powerful than the ability of people to act in their own self-interest: the tale is stronger than the teller. The tale has become more than a tale. It has become a religion.

The American religion

We have an outline of this religion, a catechism if not a systematic theology, in Emerson's essay 'Self-Reliance' (1841).[144] In this Emerson speaks of the deadening hand of society, whose weight is made up of authority, convention and precedent, pressing down upon the heads and souls of individual freemen. The deathliness

---

[142] Mody C. Boatright, 'The Myth of Frontier Individualism', in *Turner and the Sociology of the Frontier*, Hofstadter and Lipset (eds) (1968), 44.

[143] Thomas Frank, *What's The Matter With Kansas?: how conservatives won the heart of America* (2004), 68.

[144] Ralph Waldo Emerson, 'Self-Reliance (1841)', in *Essays: First Series*, Ferguson (ed.), The Collected Works of Ralph Waldo Emerson vol. 2 (1979), 27–51. Page numbers in the text refer to this edition.

of society makes the individual forget the joyous freedom of youth ('boys sure of a dinner', p. 29), under the conspiracy of conformity. This denies the humanity of humanity: 'whoso would be a man must be a nonconformist'. (p. 29). Nonconformity is needful against every sacred cow of our society: charity (p. 31); what people think of one (p. 31); consistency ('a foolish consistency is the hobgoblin of little minds' p. 33); hospitality (p. 35); and even filial duty:

> Live no longer to the expectation of these deceived and deceiving people with whom we converse. Say to them, O father, O mother, O wife, O brother, O friend, I have lived with you after appearances hitherto. Henceforward I am the truth's. (p. 41–2)

> For in the end 'nothing is at last sacred but the integrity of your mind' (p. 30).

This is not an exhortation to lawlessness, however. Emerson expects the self-reliant individual to live under the law, even if it is the law he has set for himself: it is a 'law of consciousness', which is all the more worthy in that it is hard – 'If anyone imagines that this law is lax, let him keep its commandment one day' (p. 42). To live this way it is necessary to recognize the godliness within the self-reliant individual: 'High be his heart, faithful his will, clear his sight, that he may in good earnest be doctrine, society, law to himself, that a simple purpose may be to him as strong as iron necessity is to others' (p. 43).

Thus, the life of man will be like that of the drunk, picked up from the gutter, placed in the duke's bed and treated like the duke himself; except, in the case of the self-reliant individual, the reality is the deception, and the drunken life of the gutter was 'the state of man, who is in the world a sort of sot, but now and then wakes up, exercises his reason, and finds himself a true prince' (p. 36). And the clamour that awakens is that of Emerson's new Golden Rule: 'Trust thyself: every heart vibrates to that iron string' (p. 28).

> Emerson's underlying premise, therefore, is that if we strive to be what we are, the world will be better off and all the better without the deliberate attempt to make it better. It will be better

because it will be more moral, but also more human. It will be more human because the world will be made up of individuals rather than masses, of individuals, not dependants and recipients, not instruments and followers.[145]

To understand Emersonian individualism, the Ur-myth of American culture, '...is no mere academic exercise but a matter central to our cultural identity'.[146] Robert Bellah and his colleagues in their classic work of sociology, *Habits of the Heart*, have traced the ways in which the Ur-myth of individualism continues to operate in American society. The most important means is by what they call 'expressive' individualism: this holds that 'each person has a unique core of feeling and intuition that should unfold or be expressed if individuality is to be realized'.[147] It provides 'a way of thinking about human action which can conceive of human relatedness only as the result of spontaneous feeling or calculated interest'.[148] It is a way of life that is atomized, and therefore socially and emotionally unviable[149], and its line of heritage leads directly back to Emerson:

> ...the current focus on a socially unsituated self from which all judgements are supposed to flow is a development out of aspects of American selfhood that go all the way back to the beginning. ...The American understanding of the autonomy of the self places the burden of one's own deepest self-definitions on one's own individual choice. ...Most of us imagine an autonomous self existing independently, entirely outside any tradition and community, and then perhaps choosing one.[150]

---

[145] George Kateb, *Emerson and Self-Reliance* (1995), 139.

[146] Mott, 'First Person Singular', 68.

[147] Robert N. Bellah et al., *Habits of the Heart* (1988), 334.

[148] Robert N. Bellah, 'The Quest for the Self', in *Interpreting Tocqueville's Democracy in America*, Masugi (ed.) (1991), 344.

[149] See the poignant description of modern American life in Robert D. Putnam, 'Bowling Alone: America's declining social capital', *Journal of Democracy* (1995): 65–78.

[150] Bellah et al., *Habits of the Heart*, 55, 65.

Now Americans live in a permanent 'quest for the self', which seeks autonomy (an individually determined law). We leave old social structures behind and strip off 'the obligations and constraints imposed by others, until at last we find our true self which is unique and individual'.[151] This is a fearful place to be. The atomized Adams of America are individually and collectively frightened that 'society may overwhelm the individual and destroy any chance of autonomy unless he stands against it'.[152] Into this fear steps Campbell's Monomyth: he asserts that 'the function of the society is to cultivate the individual. It is not the function of the individual to support society'.[153]

This is the 'American Religion,'[154] the American *mythos*, and Emerson is its prophet: 'the true prophet of an American kind of charisma, [who] founded the actual American religion...' as Harold Bloom puts it.[155] The American Religion ('Protestant without being Christian'[156]) is actually the cult of Self-Reliance, which 'converts solitude into a firm stance against history, including personal history'.[157] In America, there is no history, 'only biography'.[158] Although Emerson might have exercised a cold and icy morality as a result of his new religion, in today's world, when 'translated out of the inner life into the marketplace [it] is difficult to distinguish [Self Reliance] from our current religion of selfishness...'[159]

When we know what we are looking for we are able to find Emerson in the most unlikely places. In the first season of the hit American musical-drama series *Glee*, one of the main protagonists, Kurt, asserts his burgeoning identity as a gay person in a hostile school environment by singing a number from the

---

[151] Bellah, 'Quest for the Self', 334.

[152] Bellah et al., *Habits of the Heart*, 146.

[153] Joseph Campbell and Bill Moyers, *The Power of Myth* (2001), 192.

[154] Harold Bloom, 'Mr. America', *The New York Review of Books*, 22 November 1984, 20; *The American Religion* (1993).

[155] Bloom, 'Mr. America', 20.

[156] Bloom, 'Mr. America', 20.

[157] Bloom, 'Mr. America', 22.

[158] Bloom, 'Mr. America', 22. Hence Emerson's throwaway comment: 'all history resolves itself very easily into the biography of a few stout and earnest persons'. 'Self-Reliance', 36.

[159] Bloom, 'Mr. America', 23.

Broadway musical *Wicked*: 'Something has changed within me / Something is not the same / I'm through with playing by the rules / Of someone else's game / Too late for second-guessing / Too late to go back to sleep / It's time to trust my instincts / Close my eyes: and leap!'.[160]

The fact that this appears to be such an unlikely place to encounter Emerson shows us the truth of Lévi-Strauss's insight that 'myths operate in men's minds without their being aware of the fact'.[161] This is so, even if the mind belongs to a gay teenager in an American television series

Is this so bad? Is this something about which we should be concerned? Emerson's thoughts on self-reliance seem to be self-evidently humane, liberal, and nourishing:

> What I must do is all that concerns me, not what the people think. ...It is easy in the world to live after the world's opinion; it is easy in solitude to live after our own; but the great man is he who in the midst of the crowd keeps with perfect sweetness the independence of solitude.[162]

Emerson's idealisation of the individual is entirely consonant with the modern ethic of 'do no one harm, and live as you please'.[163] What can be wrong with that?

We shall see the dangers as we turn to our next section, the myths as expressed in our cultural artefacts, the movie myths of great men, their followers, and what it is necessary for great men to do to become great men.

---

[160]Stephen Schwartz, 'Defying Gravity', from *Wicked*, 2003; performed by Chris Colfer, in the role of Kurt, in the episode *Wheels* from *Glee* (2009). The assertion of self-sovereignty is intensified by the fact that the original song was intended to be sung by a female character.

[161]Lévi-Strauss, *Raw and Cooked*, 12.

[162]Emerson, 'Self-Reliance', 31.

[163]Which probably had its origins in the unexpected place of Pierre Louÿs, the nineteenth-century French sensualist poet and hedonist, and the 'Code of Tryphême' in his 1901 novel *Les Aventures Du Roi Pausole*, chapter 1.

SECTION TWO

The myths

...our myths feed us our scripts. We imitate the quests and struggles of the dominant figures in the myths and rehearse our lives informed by mythic plots. We awaken to a set of sacred stories, and then proceed to apprehend the world and to express ourselves in terms of these stories. They shape us secretly at a formative age and remain with us, informing the ongoing narrative constructions of our experience. They teach us how to perceive the world as we order our outlooks and choices in terms of their patterns and plots.

KELTON COBB (2005)

Chapter 4

The leadership principle (leadership affirmed)

... they pulled me out of the sack,
And they stuck me together with glue.
And then I knew what to do.
I made a model of you,
A man in black with a Meinkampf look...
SYLVIA PLATH, 'DADDY' (1965)

Making leadership cool

In April 2010 the West Midlands Ambulance Service gave two employees a £10,000 bursary for a leadership project in the region. Mark Iley and Paul Watkins called their project 'Making Leadership Cool; How do emerging leaders wish to be managed and supported!',[1] which took the form of a questionnaire. Seven

---

[1] Note the exclamation mark.

questions were asked with responses required on a ranked scale of 1–5, with '1 being Not Cool, 3 being Average and 5 being Cool'. 'Cool' was not defined. Question 1 gave a selection of ten 'leaders' and asked respondents whether or not they were 'cool': the list was neither alphabetical nor chronological. The ten names were, in the original order: Richard Branson; Gordon Brown; David Nicholson; Ian Cummings; Adolf Hitler; General Patton; Winston Churchill; Martin Johnson; Leroy Jethro Gibbs; Fabio Cappello.[2] National newspapers weren't impressed. *The Times* reported that 'NHS staff [were left] gasping in disbelief' at the question. The Strategic Health Authority responded by defending the project's intention, which was:

> to discuss different styles of leadership and the characteristics of leadership to help staff at all levels develop their careers. Staff were asked to look at different leadership styles, and one of those was a dictatorial style. Adolf Hitler's style galvanised a country into terrible things but it did galvanise a country. Perhaps, in hindsight, a better example could have been used.[3]

Was it appropriate to include Hitler in a project about 'coolness' and leadership? A debate was had. There was no debate about the qualifications of the other nine men to be regarded as leaders, of one kind or another. There was no debate about what defines 'leadership'. Why should there be? We all understand what leadership is, and we all accept, implicitly, unconsciously, the way in which 'leadership' functions, mythically, within our society.

We can see the cultural origins to the 'Emerging Leaders Questionnaire' as we examine the way in which movies have affirmed a very particular model of leadership, depicted in two

---

[2] Ian Cummings was the chief executive of the NHS West Midlands Strategic Health Authority; David Nicholson was the chief executive of the National Health Service; Leroy Jethro Gibbs the fictional protagonist of the NCIS television series made by CBS Television (and portrayed by Mark Harmon).

[3] Press Association, 'Ambulance Chiefs Apologise For "Cool Hitler" Questionnaire', (11 May 2010).

exemplars from the Ambulance Service questionnaire: General George S. Patton, Jr and Adolf Hitler.

'Old Blood and Guts'

The life and legacy of General George Smith Patton, Jr (1885–1945) has managed to intermingle almost completely fact and legend. As his most thorough biographer said:

> Patton's reputation has been perpetually tarnished by the facade he himself created and the public effortlessly accepted: that he was a swashbuckling, brash, profane, impetuous soldier who wore two ivory-handled revolvers and loved war so much he was nicknamed 'Old Blood and Guts' – the general who slapped two soldiers in Sicily in August 1943 and was almost sent home in disgrace, his destiny unfulfilled because of momentary, irrational acts of rage.[4]

Patton's military career was marked by intense rivalries with colleagues in Allied military command, which did not cease with Patton's death as a result of a car accident in Germany in 1945. His rivals (principally Eisenhower and Omar Bradley) continued with successful post-war careers, but it was Patton who was the subject of a blockbuster Hollywood movie. Frank McCarthy, a producer for Twentieth Century Fox and who had served as secretary to General George C. Marshall, the Army Chief of Staff, during World War Two, knew that it Patton, not Bradley or Eisenhower, was 'the guy you ought to do a movie about': Patton was 'very theatrical and very flamboyant and had several Achilles heels. All these things put together made for very fine drama'.[5] Despite initial reluctance from Patton's family and the opposition from the American Department of Defense, by the early 1960s McCarthy was in a position to

---

[4]Carlo D'Este, *Patton: A Genius for War* (1995), 4.
[5]Lawrence H. Suid, *Guts and Glory* (2002), 260–1. Suid's book contains a comprehensive account of the making of the film, 260-77.

begin the movie. He commissioned Francis Ford Coppola, newly graduated from UCLA film school, to write a script which could satisfy the interested parties, and be commercially and artistically successful. Coppola's youth (in 1964 he was 25 years old) was an advantage: 'they hired me to write the story of this American hero whom I had never heard of. I knew nothing about the Army except for a year and a half that I spent in military school'.[6] After further 'development hell', direction of the picture was given to Franklin Schaffner, who had earlier been immensely successful, artistically and commercially, in his direction of *Planet of the Apes* (1968).

Patton was released in February 1970 to (initial) slight commercial success and a great deal of ambivalence.[7] Some of the first critics seem to believe that the filmmakers had set out to pull a political confidence trick, presenting the themes of the film and character of its main protagonist as all things to all men: 'When *Patton* was released it managed to please and to enrage liberal and conservatives alike, which is probably what the producer wanted, since he sees the picture as neither a glorification nor an indictment'.[8]

Coppola also encouraged this interpretation. Because Patton was unknown to him when commissioned to write the script, he researched everything he could about the general. His immediate impression was that 'this guy was obviously nuts'.[9] He came up with what he described, modestly, as 'a brilliant solution',[10] to make Patton an anachronism, 'a 16th-century warrior trapped in the 20th century and to whom a war was a holy crusade'.[11] This gave Coppola

> ...the best of both approaches. The people who wanted to see
> him as a bad guy could say, 'He was crazy, he loved war'. The

---

[6]Stephen Farber, 'Coppola and "The Godfather"', *Sight and Sound* (Autumn 1972): 220.

[7]The film was originally subtitled in both America and the U.K.: 'Salute to a Rebel' and 'Lust for Glory' respectively. Neither subtitle was liked by the film's writers, producer or director.

[8]Gussow, 'Patton' Campaign'.

[9]Farber, 'Coppola and "The Godfather"', 220.

[10]Farber, 'Coppola and "The Godfather"', 220.

[11]Kim, *Schaffner*, 242.

people who wanted to see him as a hero could say, 'We need a man like that now'.[12]

Coppola's plan was successful: Vincent Canby noted the 'contradictory tone', ranging from 'astonishing arrogance' and 'reeking with the assumption that there is a God who is, of course, on the side of the Allies'.[13] Gerald Pratley similarly thought *Patton* to be 'an historical document of a man who glorified in war, without making a film which glorifies war'. The film was 'personal, beautifully stylised, strikingly photographed, poignant and penetrating in its dramatic and psychological truths...'[14]

Patton the legend, Patton the folk hero

Schaffner was a skilled, if not a great, director. The performance of the lead role was given by an undoubtedly great actor, George C. Scott. Scott won, and refused, the Academy Award for his performance. It is easy to see why he was so accoladed: '[Scott] dominates the film entirely, and is hardly ever off-screen, becoming alternately the foolish man and the tragic warrior'.[15] His performance is 'towering, tragic, classic',[16] full of 'odd, unexpected details that compel constant attention'[17], and is 'continuously entertaining and, occasionally, very appealing'[18]. This was Scott's intention: 'I simply refused to play George Patton as the standard

---

[12] Farber, 'Coppola and "The Godfather"', 220.
[13] Vincent Canby, 'Patton', *The New York Times*, 8 February 1970. Canby is citing the opening speech, which we examine in more detail below. Elsewhere he makes explicit the political promiscuity of the opening speech: the film opens with 'a sort of overture that liberals can view as pure Camp, and Patton fans will interpret as pure inspiration'. Vincent Canby, 'The Screen: "Patton: Salute to Rebel"', *The New York Times*, 5 February 1970.
[14] Gerald Pratley, 'Patton: Lust for Glory [review]', *Focus on Film* (August 1970): 14.
[15] Pratley, 'Patton [review]', 13.
[16] Pratley, 'Patton [review]', 13.
[17] Canby, 'Patton'.
[18] Canby, 'Movie Review: Patton'.

cliché you could get from the newspaper clips of the time. I didn't want to play him as a hero just to please the Pentagon, and I didn't want to play him as an obvious, gung ho bully either. I wanted to play every conceivable facet of the man'.[19] In the end, Scott's performance is so convincing that most viewers, critics, and historians believe that this is the way Patton *ought* to have been:

> ...he does create the man, and this, combined with his inner expression of the character brings about that magic which makes a great performance – one that convinces us that this man is indeed the character he is portraying.[20]

Coppola's script, Schaffner's direction and Scott's performance create a unity, between 'Patton', the legend and protagonist in a film, and Patton, the human being who lived and died: 'George C. Scott became Patton to those people who had never met the general'.[21] Even for those who served under the General, the film meant that 'somehow the real Patton was left behind'.[22] In reactions to the film, over and over again, we see confusion between character, performance and person. Thus, for example, Robert Johnson praises the subtlety of the Coppola-North screenplay, by saying:

> To the degree that *Patton* dramatizes the actions of a man of action, the film is a first-rate example of one traditional kind of motion picture. ...But *Patton* at its most interesting does not operate within a popular traditional framework. From the very start, its *major* emphasis is on a man's character rather than on his actions as a soldier. ...the outstanding presentation of the character of General Patton is unique and will never be superseded.[23]

---

[19] Rex Reed, 'George is on his best behavior now', *The New York Times* (New York, 29 March 1970).
[20] Pratley, 'Patton [review]', 13–14.
[21] Suid, *Guts and Glory*, 260.
[22] Gen. James Gavin, who fought with Patton in the Ardennes, interviewed in Suid, *Guts and Glory*, 260.
[23] Robert K. Johnson, *Francis Ford Coppola* (1977), 91. [Emphasis in original.]

We should read a clear distinction between the movie (italicized), the character ('Patton', properly within quotation marks) and the historical person (Patton, plain and simple). However, Johnson moves swiftly, and seemingly unconsciously, into confusion between character and person:

> At its frequent best, the presentation does make it difficult to label this character. For he will not simplify himself in order to make it easy for someone to judge him. He won't "hold still".[24]

Patton is 'shown to be a 'good guy' and a 'bad guy' simultaneously'. He was 'spurred to action by multiple motivations':

> He revered and tried to embody admirable ancient ideals, and he vaingloriously lusted after fame. He strove to utilize his intellect and create strategy that would destroy the enemy commander, and he had a raw desire to destroy. He wanted to test his courage, and he simply loved war.[25]

Who is this 'he'? George S. Patton, Jr, or the character written by Coppola and North and played by George C. Scott? Johnson does not make it clear.

D'Este realizes the impossibility of disentangling 'Patton the legend' from 'Patton the folk hero'. At the very beginning of his enormous biography of the man (978 pages), he quotes approvingly another author's judgement:

> In the shape of Scott, with his dark scowling face and rasping voice, Patton had now become the essence of America's World War II. Just like the cowboy hero of the Old West, he had stepped into American mythology… the symbol of an older, simplistic America, untouched by social change, political doubts, [and] the uncertainties of the seventies and eighties.[26]

---

[24] Johnson, *Coppola*, 92.
[25] Johnson, *Coppola*, 93.
[26] Charles Whiting, *Patton's Last Battle* (1987), 269; quoted in D'Este, *Genius for War*, 1.

'I don't want these men to love me!': Patton and leadership

There is an unquestioning assumption that George Patton is a model for leadership in the civilian world. His inclusion in the West Midlands Ambulance Service list shows this, as well as the huge number of books, published by business imprints, which demonstrate Patton's relevance for business leadership. In *Patton's One-Minute Messages* Charles Province has distilled Patton's 'message' down as far as it might go.[27] Alan Axelrod has adapted Patton's speeches into 'strategic lessons for corporate warfare',[28] and his book begins with a section on 'Patton as Management Guru', in which Axelrod unpacks the management principles contained in the opening scene from the film. The Canadian Association of Student Activity Advisors produces a regular series of DVDs containing clips to stimulate discussion on various leadership issues: *Patton* is one of the films, and the discussion questions are prefaced by a transcription of the opening speech of the film.[29] To understand 'Patton' as a leader we need to look therefore at *Patton*'s opening scene.

The 'Speech'

The opening scene of *Patton* the movie has become the Rosetta stone for understanding Patton the historical figure: D'Este has a chapter which simply refers to 'The Speech'.[30] But it is also the

---

[27] Charles M. Province, *Patton's One-Minute Messages* (1995).

[28] Alan Axelrod, *Patton on Leadership* (1999); Alan Axelrod, *Patton: a biography* (2006). The former is another in the series of corporate lessons from historical characters which we saw in Chapter 2.

[29] Dave Conlon, 'Resources: Leadership Movies', *Canadian Association of Student Activity Advisors*, March 2003.

[30] There are many places where Patton's speech is printed. See, among countless others, D'Este, *Genius for War*, chapter 38; Ian Freer, 'Classic Scene: "Patton"', *Empire*, no. 239 (May 2009): 162; Keith Yellin, *Battle Exhortation* (2008), 63–4; Charles M. Province, 'The Famous Patton Speech', *The Patton Society* website.

means by which 'Patton' has come to exemplify a particular type of mythological leadership. The image of Scott as 'Patton', standing in front of the brobdingnagian-scale American flag, is now so familiar as to function as shorthand and icon for 'American Leadership' (it is the frontispiece image for the books by Suid and Yellin). The choices the film-makers made in portraying the 'Speech' shows us the unavoidable power of mythology when attempting to get to grips with leadership.

What is referred to as 'The Speech' in movie and biographies was actually a series of speeches that General Patton made to his Third Army while stationed in England and preparing for deployment to France in the early summer of 1944.[31] Although Patton didn't use a set text on the many occasions he spoke, he tended to speak to a set pattern, and the version in the film is a fair enough summary of what was delivered: 'Scott's performance minimizes differences in historical versions, inserts a few dictums Patton used elsewhere, and provides us with a single, reasonable, memorable account'.[32] But there is a difference between the Speech as a *text*, and the Speech as a *performance*. The film's version might be a reasonable compilation of the words used historically, but what about its delivery? This diverges significantly from the historical record.

Let's examine history first, before looking at the way the performance departs from record into mythology.

Historical accounts tell us that Patton's speeches were 'gala events in themselves, with an honour guard and a band playing rousing marches'.[33] The men were assembled in a great hall. When the General arrived, with an Military Police escort, the hall would become quiet, and in his 'buff-and-dark green uniform, helmet, and highly shined cavalry boots, he would march through [the] ranks to the front of the platform and inspect the honor guard closely with

---

Finally, there is Martin Blumenson (ed.), *The Patton Papers: 1940–1945*, vol. 2 (1974), 456–8.

[31] Stanley Hirshon has identified at least four occasions from the end of May to the beginning of July, 1944 when Patton spoke to various sections of his troops: Stanley P. Hirshson, *General Patton: A Soldier's Life* (2003), 473–4.

[32] Yellin, *Battle Exhortation*, 61, 62.

[33] D'Este, *Genius for War*, 601.

his eyes, before mounting the platform with his escort'.[34] The first spoken word would be an opening prayer from a chaplain; the General would then be introduced by the Commanding Officer present, and then 'he would march stiffly to the microphone and…, as if satisfied all was well, command: "Be seated!"'[35]

Now let's observe the film version. It is the first scene of the film, running before credits or title. The scene opens with no date or location caption: it is a moment out of time and space (eventually, as we watch the film, we can locate it, if we so choose, to about half-way through the film's narrative). The scene fades in from black, and we see an enormous American flag, filling the cinemascope screen of the movie theatre. We hear 'the low-grade din of hundreds of soldiers talking among us',[36] but we don't see them, and we are never shown them. We realize that the flag is on a stage, and we are viewing it from the auditorium. The movie-theatre has become the barracks hall. Suddenly, the chattering audience (us?) is called to attention. From the bottom of the flag, up steps hidden on the other side of the stage, the General emerges. He stands to attention, salutes and a trumpet sounds a call to attention.

As the trumpet plays, we, the cinema audience, are given privileged, physically impossible, views of the General's dress and accessories (close-ups of his medals, his shining helmet, and his ivory-handled revolvers[37]). These shots, impossible for the audience in the barrack hall to see, might have threatened to break the invisible fourth wall of the camera. This doesn't happen because of the intensity of Scott's delivery of the speech, and because he, as Patton, never breaks the wall. General Patton is addressing someone, and that someone is us.

Scott/Patton's speech begins shockingly: 'Now, I want you to remember that no bastard ever won a war by dying for his country.

---

[34] D'Este, *Genius for War*, 601–2.

[35] D'Este, *Genius for War*, 602.

[36] Yellin, *Battle Exhortation*, 62.

[37] Often Patton's guns are described as 'pearl-handled' but as Patton himself said 'no real gunman would carry a pearl-handled pistol'. Private, undated, and unpublished, interview with Leland Stowe, quoted by D'Este, *Genius for War*, 689. We examine the significance of such close-ups, and their ideological parallels in Riefenstahl's *Triumph of the Will*, on page 123 below.

He won it by making the other poor dumb bastard die for his country'. This is a clear, and adept, use of a rhetorical inversion. Patton is asserting his *ethos*, a concept taken from Aristotle's *Rhetorica*. The three fundamental means of persuasion – *logos*, *pathos*, *ethos* – are all present in Patton's battle exhortation:

> Now the proofs furnished by the speech are of three kinds. The first depends upon the moral character of the speaker [*ethos*], the second upon putting the hearer into a certain frame of mind [*pathos*], the third upon the speech itself, in so far as it proves or seems to prove [*logos*].[38]

Scott/Patton's *ethos* 'explodes from the screen',[39] just as the historical General's did: 'mounting the stage, Patton, wearing riding boots and holding a riding crop, which he snapped about crisply, … with his white hair and aristocratic air'.[40] Patton, rhetorically, imposes his view of war upon his audience (the soldiers and the movie-goers).

Scott/Patton breaks the statuesque effect with his second section, begun, again, with a conversational 'Now':

> Now, an army is a team – it lives, eats, sleeps, fights as a team. This individuality stuff is a bunch of crap. The bilious bastards who wrote that stuff about individuality for the Saturday Evening Post don't know anything more about real battle than they do about fornicating.[41]

It is at this point that Scott/Patton and Patton diverge. The movie version goes on, with an interpolation from another speech Patton

---

[38] Aristotle, *The Art of Rhetoric*, I.ii.3 (1356a).

[39] Yellin, *Battle Exhortation*, 62.

[40] The recollection of Harry Kemp of the 28th Infantry Division, cited by Harry M. Kemp, *The Regiment: let the citizens bear arms!* (1990), 63–5; quoted by Hirshson, *General Patton*, 476. Interestingly, Kemp asserts that Patton had been forbidden by Bradley to wear his twin revolvers on a belt, and during the delivery of the speech wore a single revolver in a shoulder holster.

[41] The verb in the original was Anglo-Saxon, which 'brought howls of delight and clapping' from the enlisted men in the audience. D'Este, *Genius for War*, 603.

made in Sicily the year before, to assert his doctrine of continual advancing: 'I don't want to get any messages saying that "we are holding our position"'. The historic version expands on the earlier analogy between the Army and a team: 'Every single man in the Army plays a vital part. Every little job is essential to the whole scheme'. A truck-driver frightened of shelling who refuses to drive would be missed. Fortunately, this is not something Americans do. Rather, 'Every man does his job. Every man serves the whole'. This is true for every unit, from Ordnance, to Quartermaster, to the mess-hall attendants. 'Even the Chaplain is important, for if we get killed and he is not there to bury us we would all go to hell'.[42]

The historical Patton was responding to the articles in the *Saturday Evening Post*, which emphasised the role of individual heroes. For Patton, this 'gave a false impression of how battles were won. The real message of his "speech" was that training and teamwork win battles'.[43]

When Scott/Patton concludes with 'Alright, now you sons of bitches, you know how I feel. I will be proud to lead you wonderful guys into battle anytime, anywhere', we know that *we* were the 'sons of bitches', who are also 'wonderful guys', part of his great team of the Third Army.

But here we see the deep and abiding irony in the way in mythic leadership treats the historical figure of George Patton. A speech intended to repudiate society's obsession with heroic individuals has been turned, through the editing of the words spoken by the character of Patton and the visual representation of that character, into a celebration of that very thing: 'The battle exhortation of Scott's Patton is overwhelmingly about himself, the commander'.[44] The presentation of the Speech in the movie removed the historically present Commanding Officer, bugler, chaplain, for the sake of the General alone on the stage: 'the opening scene of the film is all – and exclusively – commanding general'.[45]

---

[42] Quoted in D'Este, *Genius for War*, 603.

[43] D'Este, *Genius for War*, n. 3, p. 909; quotation marks in the original.

[44] Yellin, *Battle Exhortation*, 61.

[45] Yellin, *Battle Exhortation*, 68.

This focus on the heroic commander continues all the way through the film. As Pauline Kael said in her review:

> …the landscapes are full of men; the cast must surely run into the tens of thousands. But they're all extras – even the ones that *should* be important. There's really nobody in this movie except George C. Scott.[46]

By which she means there is really nobody in this movie, except 'Patton'.

Suspicion of the masses, charisma of the one

The General Patton depicted in Schaffner's film is another expression of the myth of the American Adam, the individual who can stand against the corruption and deceit of the Old World (and even use the 'living guts' of the 'lousy Hun bastards' of the Old World to 'grease the treads of our tanks'[47]). With the myth of the American Adam, the importance of the Man (singular) is emphasised over and against the failings of mankind (plural).

There are European expressions of this suspicion of the masses, and mostly related to the work of Gustave Le Bon, who published in 1895 *La Psychologie des foules*.[48] The late nineteenth century marked, for Le Bon, the transformation of world civilization into the 'Era of Crowds' (the title of his introduction): 'To-day the claims of the masses are becoming more and more sharply defined, and amount to nothing less than a determination to utterly destroy society as it now exists…'[49] Crowds are 'little adapted to reasoning' but 'quick to act… All reasoning against it is a mere

---

[46]Pauline Kael, 'The man who loved war', *The New Yorker*, 31 January 1970. [Emphasis in original.]

[47]Again, from the prologue opening speech to *Patton*.

[48]Gustave Le Bon, *The Crowd: a study of the popular mind* (2002).

[49]Le Bon, *The Crowd*, xi.

vain war of words... [the] rule [of crowds] is always tantamount
to a barbarian phase'.[50] The mind of the crowd is fundamentally
irrational, religious, supernatural, and miraculous.[51] However, it is
possible for crowds to be swayed or directed, for the fundamental
characteristic of crowds, just like any agglomeration of creatures,
is to 'place themselves instinctively under the authority of a chief'.[52]
This authority is something magical, 'a mysterious power' which
belongs to 'the victorious leader that for the moment arouses their
enthusiasm'.[53]

Le Bon wasn't the first person to express this suspicion of
crowds and adulation of the leader. For American society, he
certainly wasn't the most influential. That person was Ralph Waldo
Emerson.

In his lecture 'The American Scholar', delivered in 1837, Emerson
gave his balanced judgement on the place of most people in civic
society: 'Men are become of no account. Men in history, men in
the world of to-day are bugs, are spawn, and are called "the mass"
and "the herd."'[54] Once or twice a century, a millennium, we see
anyone who approximates 'to the right state of every man'. The
rest, while seeing in the 'hero or the poet' the fulfilment of their
humanity, are actually 'content to be less, so that [humanity] may
attain to its full stature' in the one. The mass not only should be,
but *are*, 'content to be brushed like flies from the path of a great
person'. Thus 'justice shall be done by him', and the mass will 'sun
themselves in the great man's light'. The 'dignity of man' is surrendered from the masses onto 'the shoulders of a hero', and the
masses will therefore give themselves to 'perish to add one drop
of blood to make that great heart beat, those giant sinews combat
and conquer. He lives for us, and we live in him'.[55]

The presence of the biological libel, to become so familiar in the

---

[50] Le Bon, *The Crowd*, xi, xii, xiii.

[51] Le Bon, *The Crowd*, chapter 4.

[52] Le Bon, *The Crowd*, 72. See the whole of Book II, Chapter III, 'The Leaders of
Crowds and Their Means of Persuasion'.

[53] Le Bon, *The Crowd*, 39.

[54] Ralph Waldo Emerson, 'The American Scholar (1837)', in *Nature, Addresses, and
Lectures* (1971), 65.

[55] Emerson, 'American Scholar', 65.

twentieth century, is significant. Emerson wanted to mark the differences between America and the Old World, between American scholarship and that of Europe. Even so, we actually see at work in his writing the shared ethos of North Atlantic hero-worship in the suspicion of the spawn, the mass, the herd. The shared North Atlantic roots of *MythL*, which become so powerful with the dominance of American cultural forms and media in the twentieth century, found their initial and most influential cinematic expression in the work of the German film director Leni Riefenstahl.

The American Hero, despite Emerson's disdain for the Old World, was indelibly and cinematically conjured in *Triumph of the Will*. Patton was able to be the American Adam, because Hitler had already been the German Wotan. Emerson and Carlyle might have sketched out attitudes that tended to the 'worship of the one', but it was Leni Riefenstahl who filmed the Nazi programme. And once it was filmed, once it became mythologized into celluloid, it escaped back into North Atlantic mythology.

'Führer! Command! We will obey'

In the final days of World War Two, during the *Götterdämmerung* of April 1945, Goebbels encouraged his staff:

> Gentlemen, in a hundred years' time they will be showing another fine colour film describing the terrible days we are living through. ...I can assure you that it will be a fine and elevating picture. ...Hold out now, so that a hundred years hence the audience does not hoot and whistle when you appear on screen.[56]

The film was *Kolberg*, directed by Viet Harlan, a recreation of the siege of the Pomeranian town during the Napoleonic wars, and

---

[56] 17 April 1945: Rudolf Semmler, *Goebbels, the Man Next to Hitler* (1947), 194.

the filming of which swallowed enormous financial and material resources from the collapsing regime. But Goebbels was wrong. It is not *Kolberg* we look to in order to understand the terrible days of the 1930s and 1940s, but rather to the films of Leni Riefenstahl. Her five NSDAP[57] films – the so-called Nuremberg Trilogy of *Sieg des Glaubens* (Victory of Faith), *Triumph des Willens* (Triumph of the Will), and *Tag der Freiheit* (Day of Freedom), and the two Olympic films, *Fest der Völker* and *Fest der Schönheit* (Festival of the People and Festival of Beauty) – show, to their core, the Nazi programme, the *Ordungsprinzip* (principle of order): her Party Congress films, especially, 'provided filmmakers with an aesthetic model to guide them in observing the Party's principle of order with maximum vigour'.[58]

The Nazi *Ordungsprinzip* was, in reality, less a programme than a personalised political movement. After the Nazis achieved power in 1933 (in the so-called *Machtergreifung*), Wilhelm Frick, Minister of the Interior (and later executed following the Nuremberg trials), said, simply: 'They say we don't have a program; but the name of Hitler is program enough'.[59] For the Nazis, the personal was political, and the person was Hitler.

However, the focus on Hitler could not have achieved what it did, would not have used the traction it was afforded within Weimar Germany without the pre-existing tendency in Wilhelmine and Weimar Germany to seek salvation in 'heroic leadership'.

So, for example, in the late nineteenth century in Berlin, Karl Fischer was the leader of the *Wandervogel* movement, a nature-loving, romantic fellowship, 'sending a fresh breath of naturalism through the stuffy middle-class manners of the day…'[60] Fischer was idealised by members of the youth movement: 'When we shoot, he makes the most points; when we march, his endurance far

---

[57] *Nationalsozialistiche Deutsche Arbeiterpartei*, the National Socialist German Workers Party, the Nazi Party.

[58] Hilmar Hoffmann, *The Triumph of Propaganda* (1996), ix.

[59] Wilhelm Frick, *Frankfurer Zeitung*, 21 February 1933. Quoted in Hoffmann, *Triumph of Propaganda*, vii. See also David Welch, '"Working towards the Führer": charismatic leadership and the image of Adolf Hitler in Nazi propaganda', in *Working towards the Führer,* McElligott and Kirk (eds) (2003), 93–117.

[60] Howard Becker, *German Youth: bond or free* (1946), viii.

surpasses ours; when we laugh, his example is the most infectious; when we talk, he talks the best...' The leader was inferred to be of 'unfathomable background', possessing something that was 'irrational', and 'veiled him in mystery'. Ultimately, he was thought to have a 'standing in a higher superpersonal, and thereby super-human, complex of values'.[61]

This was not limited to uniformed youth groups. As one rightist tract from 1920 put it: 'The Leader does not conform to the masses, but acts in accordance with his mission. ...The Leader is radical; he is entirely that which he does, and he does entirely what he has to do. The Leader is responsible; that is, he carries out the will of God, which he embodies in himself'.[62]

This 'Leader' (German: *Führer*) was not yet Hitler: the idea of the Leader of the Germans existed long before 'it was fitted to Hitler', and during the parallel rise of the NSDAP and Hitler, it was not clear that Hitler was the *only* person to whom it could be applied: it was not 'obvious to the protagonists of the need for "heroic" leadership that Hitler himself was the leader for whom they had been waiting'. During the 1932 elections in Germany the role of *Führer* of the Germans was ascribed to Brüning (of the *Deutsche Zentrumspartei* and Reich Chancellor, 1930–2), Hugenberg (leader of the *Deutschnationale Volkspartei*), and the dying Hindenburg.[63]

It did not take long. During the near-permanent election campaigns of 1932 one Nazi newspaper exalted Hitler to unparal-leled levels:

Hitler is the alpha and omega of our world philosophy. Every National Socialist house must have a place in which the Führer is near at hand. Generous hands and hearts must offer him small tributes every day at such in a place in the form of flowers and plants.[64]

---

[61] Heinrich Roth, *Psychologie der Jugendgruppe* (1938), 37. Quoted in Becker, *German Youth*, 55, 56.

[62] Kurt Sontheimer, *Antidemokratisches Denken in der Weimarer Republik* (1962), 272; cited in Ian Kershaw, *The 'Hitler Myth'* (1987), 19–20.

[63] Kershaw, *Hitler Myth*, 13, 64.

[64] Cited by a socialist journal 'Das freie Wort', and quoted in Kershaw, *Hitler Myth*, 39.

For the Presidential election in the autumn of 1932, Hitler took to the air, in his *Deutschlandflug* campaign, addressing 20 rallies over six days. The effect on his listeners in Hamburg was ecstatic:

> Nobody spoke of 'Hitler', always just 'the Führer', 'the Führer says', 'the Führer wants', and what he said and wanted seemed right and good. …It was nearly 3 p.m. 'The Führer is coming!' A ripple went through the crowds. …[He had] drawn 120,000 people of all classes and ages. …How many look up to him with touching faith! as their helper, their saviour, their deliverer from unbearable distress – to him who rescues the Prussian prince, the scholar, the clergyman, the farmer, the worker, the unemployed, who rescues them from the parties back into the nation.[65]

Victor Klemperer, a more astute observer, recognized the parasitical religious mechanism of the Hitler construct. In November 1933 it was announced that the Führer would be making a live broadcast from a factory in Siemensstadt: '"In the thirteenth hour Adolf Hitler will visit the workers". This is, as everyone knows, the language of the Gospel. The Lord, the Saviour visits the poor and the prodigal. … the legend of Christ has been transported into the here and now: Adolf Hitler, the Redeemer, visits the workers in Siemensstadt'.[66]

After the Nazi takeover of power, Germany was to be identified with the NSDAP, and the NSDAP with Hitler. As the Führer said at the 1935 Party Congress: 'No, gentlemen, the Führer is the Party and the Party is the Führer'.[67] Germany had, or should have, a single will, and Hitler himself was the embodiment of that will.

Hermann Rausching, the former President of the Danzig Senate who fled Germany in 1935, described the mysterious, cloaked relationship of the Leader to the nation in his 1938 book *Die Revolution des Nihilismus*: 'Hitler is deliberately and unceasingly

---

[65] Luise Solmitz, diary entry for 23 April 1932, trans. in J. Noakes and G. Pridham (eds), *Nazism 1919-1945*, vol. 1, (1983), 74.
[66] Victor Klemperer, *The Language of the Third Reich* (2000), 39.
[67] Speech of 13 September 1935, published in *Völkischer Beobachter*, No. 257, 14 September 1935. Quoted by Kershaw, *Hitler Myth*, 104.

held up to the masses as a deity'.[68] The deity could save. The 'Messiah-figure of the leader is the indispensable centre' of NSDAP propaganda, which has deliberately calculated that the leader 'must be withdrawn more and more into seclusion and surrounded with mystery'. The Leader's appearances before the nation are carefully controlled, he 'only come[s] visibly into the presence of the nation by means of startling actions and rare speeches at critical moments'. Writing in 1938, before the *Anschluss*, Rausching was willing to predict the dynamics of the Hitler-myth: 'Only when Hitler had really become a mythical figure would the whole depth of his magical influence reveal itself'.[69]

In this way Hitler became what Joseph Stern called the 'representative individual'.[70] Hitler was representative by both being ordinary (from, and of, the people), and, simultaneously, extraordinary, able to uncover something of the nature and will of the German people which had previously been hidden. Thus, for example, during the 1936 Reichstag Election Hitler could say:

> I myself come from out of the Volk. In fifteen years I have worked my way up out of this Volk with my Movement. I was not appointed by anyone to stand above this Volk. It is from the Volk I have evolved, it is within the Volk I have remained, and it is to the Volk I shall return! I will stake my ambition on the fact that there is no statesman I know in this world who has more right than I to say he is a representative of his Volk![71]

Hitler was of the people. And yet, at the same time, he was to be distinguished from the mass of the people, even those who recognised themselves as part of the *Volk*: 'The secret of his personality resides in the fact that in it the deepest of what lies dormant in the

---

[68] Hermann Rauschning, *Germany's Revolution of Destruction* (1939), 37.
[69] Rauschning, *Revolution of Destruction*, 37–8. These are all taken from a section entitled 'The Divine Inspiration of the Leader'.
[70] J. P. Stern, *Hitler: the Führer and the People* (1984), chapter 1.
[71] 20 March 1936, Hanseatenhalle, Hamburg, in Max Domarus (ed.), *Hitler: Speeches and Proclamations, 1932-1945*, vol. 2 (1990), 794. There is a deliberate echo, noted by Domarus, of the Ash Wednesday liturgy: 'memento, homo, quia pulvis es, et in pulverem reverteris'.

soul of the German people has taken shape in full living features
... That has appeared in Adolf Hitler: the living incarnation of the
nation's yearning'.[72]

This deep connection between the person and the nation was
created, sustained and strengthened by Hitler's use of propaganda. Hitler had made the central function of propaganda explicit
as early as 1924 in *Mein Kampf*: 'The art of propaganda lies in
understanding the emotional ideas of the great masses and finding,
through a psychologically correct form, the way to attention, and
thence to the heart of the broad masses'.[73] Rudolf Hess agreed.
It was necessary

> ...that the Führer must be absolute in his propaganda speeches.
> He must not weigh up the pros and cons like an academic,
> he must never leave his listeners the freedom to think that
> something else is right... The great popular leader is similar
> to the great founder of a religion... Only then can the mass of
> followers be led where they should be led. They will then follow
> the leader if setbacks are encountered; but only then, if they
> have communicated to them the unconditional belief in the
> absolute rightness of their own people.[74]

This would not be achieved by wishful thinking. The image and
persona was consciously constructed through propaganda: 'Hitler
well understood his own function, the role which he *had* to act out
as 'Leader' of the Third Reich'; furthermore, consciously he 'transformed himself into a function, the *function of Führer*'.[75]

Hitler appointed one of his more able lieutenants, Joseph
Goebbels, to oversee the nurturing of this image through the
dissemination of propaganda in the Third Reich. Goebbels
achieved this, unsurprisingly, through the bureaucratic control of

---

[72] Georg Schott, *Das Volksbuch vom Hitler* (1924), 18. Quoted in Ian Kershaw, 'Hitler
and the Uniqueness of Nazism', *Journal of Contemporary History* (April 2004): 251.
[73] Adolf Hitler, *Mein Kampf* (1974), 165.
[74] Rudolf Hess, in a private letter of 1927: Albrecht Tyrell, *Führer befiehl* (1969), 1973;
quoted and trans. in Kershaw, *Hitler Myth*, 27.
[75] Timothy W. Mason, 'Intention and Explanation', in *Nazism, Fascism and the
Working Class*, Caplan (ed.) (1995), 225–6. [Emphasis in original.]

the media by the *Reichsfilmkammer* (RFK). As Goebbels said: 'Even entertainment sometimes has the task of arming the nation to fight for its existence, of providing it with the requisite spiritual uplift, entertainment, and relaxation as the dramatic events of the day unfold'.[76]

It was with this goal of spiritual uplift that Goebbels arranged for the filming of the Reich Party Congress, held in Nuremberg in September 1934. Leni Riefenstahl was chosen to direct the film, and *Triumph of the Will*[77] was released the following year. The Rallies held in Nuremberg were part of the series of carefully produced 'national moments' repeatedly staged by the NSDAP.[78] Hitler's appearance and speeches were the centrepiece, and these 'would be broadcast simultaneously throughout the Reich. … life would come to a standstill, demonstrating the sense of national community where the individual participant in the ritual, moved by Hitler's rhetoric and swayed by the crowd, underwent a metamorphosis…'[79]

It would be wrong to think of these occasions as mere political rallies, designed to 'get the message out' to the electorate. The task was greater, and more mystical, than that. Riefenstahl set out, unquestionably, to depict Hitler as the Messiah figure for the German people. Thus, in various sequences, his plane emerges from the clouds; he walks through the 200,000 people in the crowd, parting them as Moses parts the Red Sea; he is set

---

[76] 15 February 1941 in Gerd Albrecht, *Nationalsozialistische Filmpolitik* (1969), 465–79. Cited by Hoffmann, *Triumph of Propaganda*, viii.

[77] Hereafter referred to by its German abbreviation *TdW*. For an account of the making of *TdW* see, among many discussions, Richard Meran Barsam, *Filmguide to 'Triumph of the Will'*, (1975), and Susan Sontag, 'Fascinating Fascism', in *Under the Sign of Saturn* (1996), and other works in the bibliography. See also, with a degree of suspicion, Riefenstahl's own account in *Memoiren* (1994), 220–32; later republished as *Leni Riefenstahl: a memoir* (1995) in which the section on *TdW* is 156-66. Two posthumous biographies of Riefenstahl are necessary correctives to the director's prevaricating version: Steven Bach, *Leni* (2008), chapters 9 and 10; Jürgen Trimborn, *Leni Riefenstahl* (2008), chapter 8, 'Riefenstahl shapes the face of the Third Reich' (!).

[78] David Welch, *Propaganda and the German Cinema* (2001), 134.

[79] David Welch, *The Third Reich: Politics and Propaganda* (2002), 115. See also Peter Adam, *The Arts of the Third Reich* (1992), 88–90, for the contribution of the architect and staging of the events to the overall message.

apart, in his individuality, from the other faceless and amorphous participants.

> The visual compositions ...show Hitler as a new Siegfried and his supporters as extras in a colossal Wagner opera, an anonymous mass completely under his sway.[80]

As Vicky Stupp puts it:

> Through the rituals enacted in the film and through Riefenstahl's editing. Hitler has been deified. He is the incarnation of Odin, the All-Father, Nordic god of light and victory, of the Germanic Woden of the *Nibelungenlied*, of Christ, in his second coming to Nuremberg from the sky, bringing 'the light' with him. Photographed against the sun or sky from a camera angle which places him above the people who look up to him with adoration, Hitler enacts the role of Divine Leader.[81]

This is clearly seen in the first sequence of the film, Hitler's arrival at, and procession into, Nuremberg.[82] Riefenstahl has deliberately chosen her cinematic techniques to reinforce this message. The camera work is ostentatious, with constant movement between aerial, eye-, ground-level and overhead positions, tracking and zooming. Riefenstahl didn't invent anything new here (although putting so many different techniques in one sequence was an impressive innovation); rather she was demonstrating the aesthetics of German fascist cinema. As Siegfried Kracauer noted, German filmmakers knew how to edit long before the Nazi takeover, and their skills were swiftly utilized for the Party:

> With a pronounced feeling for editing, they exploited each

---

[80] Erwin Leiser, *Nazi Cinema* (1974), 25.

[81] Stupp, 'Myth, Meaning, Message', 47.

[82] For a superb examination of this opening sequence, see Marilyn Fabe, *The Arrival of Hitler: Notes and Analysis* (1975). I am grateful to Professor Fabe for sending me an offprint of this difficult-to-obtain study. See also a shot-by-shot aesthetic examination in Neale, 'Documentary and Spectacle', 65–76, a superb dissection on the theatricality and spectaclism of *TdW*.

medium [commentary, visuals, sound] to the full, so that the total effect frequently resulted from the blending of different meanings in different media. Such polyphonic handling is not often found in democratic war films; nor did the Nazis themselves go to great pains when they merely wished to pass on information. But as soon as totalitarian propaganda sprang into action, a sumptuous orchestration was employed to influence the masses.[83]

Riefenstahl herself acknowledged her participation and competence in this tradition: 'The editing of the film plays an important role because it helps to bring the events to life for the viewer and convey them more directly. And it's true, I have a special gift when it comes to working at the cutting table. I'm a good editor'.[84]

Riefenstahl concludes the arrival sequence with a punctuated coda of close-ups of Hitler's SS Bodyguard and their uniforms. The sequence pioneers the motif of 'statuary in film', perfected by Riefenstahl in her later film *Olympia* (1938); Kracauer calls this motif 'mass ornamentalism';[85] Hinton calls it 'the dissection of detail'.[86] The shot's aesthetic origins, also used in the filming of the 'Speech' in *Patton*, comes from the high art of the Renaissance. The low-angle point of view was 'used in the Renaissance in drawing classical statuary. Since these statues were invariably mounted on pedestals it was inevitable that they were seen and drawn from below'.[87] There is an implicit hierarchy of power, and an explicit extending of that hierarchy. Furthermore, the low-angle viewpoint allows the possibility of representing an individual human as representative of an idealised humanity. It was 'Renaissance worship of the sublime'[88] expressed in a naturalistic way, but in a way which could never, for a human being, occur in nature: we are

---

[83] Siegfried Kracauer, *From Caligari to Hitler* (1947), 278.
[84] Marcus, 'Reappraising Riefenstahl's "Triumph of the Will"', 81.
[85] Kracauer, *From Caligari to Hitler*, 302. See also Siegfried Kracauer, 'The Mass Ornament', *New German Critique*, (April 1975): 67–76.
[86] David B. Hinton, *The Films of Leni Riefenstahl* (2000), 31.
[87] Berthold Hinz, *Art in the Third Reich* (1980), 113.
[88] Hinz, *Art in the Third Reich*, 113.

not pygmies living among giants. The low-angle fetishized shots, of Riefenstahl and Schaffner, imply that we are.

> Thus a pre-fascist artistic convention, with specific connota-
> tions, is taken up by the fascists and those connotations are
> thereby extended. The result is not an automatic revulsion in
> the non-fascist viewer; on the contrary, the shared aesthetic
> effectively co-opts the viewer.[89]

The subjects of these low-angled works of art declare their independence from the viewer: they 'give the impression of not being subject to external, objective circumstances, but of determining those circumstances themselves'.[90] Those viewed in this way (the *Führer*, the General), are not like the rest of us. Because of this, Riefenstahl and Schaffner's (unconscious?) use of mass-ornamentalism has a political meaning as well. Riefenstahl's film shows the triumph of the 'Hitler Myth', the heroic, divinized, individual in opposition to and superior of the masses. Riefenstahl was a 'genius', said one of her biggest fans, by being able to 'transform… the dimensions of reality' through 'impressionistic editing, brilliant in its sustained vigour' and 'intensified' by her choice of camera angles.[91] She showed us a 'grandiose conception', in which '[p]ast and present encompass all with a mystic sense of communication, of ancient glory reborn in the deified figure of Germany's new leader… the apotheosised Führer…'[92]

This is how those who participated in the Party Congress at the time saw the role and person of Hitler:

> Here and there a brief, firm handshake, a friendly word, a glance
> of recognition. On the faces of those who were able to be there,

---

[89] Brian Winston, 'Was Hitler There?: reconsidering "Triumph of the Will"', *Sight and Sound* (March 1981): 104.
[90] Hinz, *Art in the Third Reich*, 114. Hinz is referring, in particular, to a painted triptych, reproduced on p. 125 of his book, by Hans Schmitz-Wiedenbrück, *Arbeiter, Bauern und Soldaten*, Triptych, 1941.
[91] Arnold Berson, 'The Truth about Leni', *Films and Filming* (April 1965): 17.
[92] Berson, 'Truth about Leni', 17.

there is the light of grateful confidence. With roaring cheers on all sides the Führer rides into the city. The streets tremble with the shouts of loyalty, of love, of faith! Nürnberg greets the Führer of the Germans in the proud exaltation [sic] of this festive, sun-filled day![93]

When Hitler greets individuals in the crowd directly, the writer is ecstatic:

How very much this nation belongs to the Führer, how very much this Führer belong [sic] to it! In every glance, in every shake of the hands there is expressed the confession and the vow: We belong together. In eternal loyalty together.[94]

This was the purpose of the film: it was an 'epic picture of the new German created by the victory of the movement as a triumph of the will on which it is based'.[95] *What* was shown was matched by *how* it was shown: 'it is an epic, beating the tempo of marching formations, steel-like in its conviction, fired by a passionate artistry'.[96] A review in *The Observer* agreed: 'the film is one long apotheosis of the Caesar Spirit…It is to be sincerely hoped that this film will be shown in all cinemas outside Germany if one wishes to understand the intoxicating spirit which is moving Germany these days'.[97]

Simply, in Stupp's words, 'the film is a myth told to the German people so they might embody their salvation through Hitler'.[98]

---

[93] *Illustrierter Film-Kurier*, Nr. 2302, 1935, trans. John G. Hanhardt, in 'Nazi Critical Praise for "Triumph of the Will"', *Film Culture* (Spring 1973): 168.

[94] Hanhardt, 'Nazi Critical Praise', 169.

[95] Herbert Seehofer (the chief press officer for the film) in an interview with *Licht-Bild-Bühne*, 23 October 1934. Quoted in Leiser, *Nazi Cinema*, 137.

[96] Quoted in Leiser, *Nazi Cinema*, 138.

[97] Anonymous, 'Hail, Caesar!', *The Observer* (London, 3 December 1933), 17. Quoted in Loiperdinger and Culbert, 'Leni Riefenstahl, the SA, and the Nazi Party Rally Films', *Historical Journal of Film, Radio and Television* (1988): 6. The *Observer* article is referring to Riefenstahl's earlier film.

[98] 'Myth, Meaning, Message', 47.

Triumph of the will redux

The *way* in which Riefenstahl shot the film was inseparable from the political *content* of the film: the medium was the message. Her 'Nazi aesthetic' had but a '*single* objective and a *single* method'[99] – the collapse of the individual into the collective, and the apotheosis of an individual apart from the mass:

> the moviegoer, the radio listener, the reader, and the participant in Nazi mass rallies [was given] a sense of power, of being one with the collective. In this state of intoxication, the meaning or content of idea was no longer important. Meaning was submerged in a state of total self-abnegation.[100]

One individual remained immune from the abnegation of the collective and that was the one true, real, Man, the Leader, the Führer, the General, whether Hitler or Patton.

The look of triumph

Even before the rediscovery and attempted rehabilitation of Riefenstahl in the 1960s her film exerted its influence on those impressed by auteur theory and filmmakers from within the American film schools. This was both a high-brow and a low-brow influence: after all, George Lucas has remade *TdW* in colour – six times![101]

---

[99] Hoffmann, *Triumph of Propaganda*, 31. [Emphasis in original.]

[100] Hoffmann, *Triumph of Propaganda*, 31.

[101] See, among many other studies and pieces of fan-writing, Roger Copeland, 'When Films 'Quote' Films, They Create A New Mythology', *The New York Times* (25 September 1977); Joel Frangquist, 'STAR WARS and Triumph of the Will', *The Unordinary STAR WARS Web Site*, ; HeroOfTheSovietUnion, *Triumph of a New Hope (Throne Room and End)*, 2007; Kevin J. Wetmore, Jr, *The Empire Triumphant* (2005); Winston, 'Home Movies: Playback: Triumph of the Dull'; Clive James, 'Reich Star', *The New York Times*, 25 March 2007; and Glenn Kenny, (ed.), *A Galaxy Not So Far Away* (2003), in which is to be found Tom Carson, 'Jedi Über Alles', Joe Queenan, 'Anakin, get your gun', 113–26.

Consider the parallels between the 'throne room' sequence at the end of *Star Wars* (later subtitled 'A New Hope'), and the final sequence, Hitler's speech in the Luitpoldhalle[102], from *TdW*. The final sequence of *Star Wars* is described in the fourth (and final) draft of Lucas's script thus:

> INTERIOR: MASSASSI OUTPOST – MAIN THRONE ROOM
> Luke, Han, and Chewbacca enter the huge ruins of the main temple. Hundreds of troops are lined up in neat rows. Banners are flying and at the far end stands a vision in white, the beautiful young Senator Leia. Luke and the others solemnly march up the long aisle and kneel before Senator Leia. ...[Leia] rises and places a gold medallion around Han's neck. He winks at her. She then repeats the ceremony with Luke, who is moved by the event. They turn and face the assembled troops, who all bow before them. FADE OUT.[103]

Many critics have seen the origins of this scene in the final scene of *TdW*. The parallels, the 'quotation' of Riefenstahl by Lucas, seem undeniable. So, for example, when the YouTube user 'HeroOfTheSovietUnion' interpolated both sequences in a 'mash-up', there is no cognitive or aesthetic dissonance in the resulting re-edit. Tom Carson says that Lucas 'blatantly mimics' Riefenstahl,[104] and Wim Wenders, on his first viewing of *Star Wars*, also thought the connection to be so obvious that it did not need describing; rather it was the aesthetic, commercial and political dynamics of the connection which were significant:

> A film like *Star Wars*, truly 'entertaining', makes that perfectly clear, not only because it's about war, not only because it supplies new images of war and a new mythology of war to a

---

[102] Occasionally this building is referred to as the 'Kongresshalle', which is potentially confusing, as the Congress grounds in Nuremberg had another, newer, building with that name, which remained uncompleted. The Luitpoldhalle is sometimes known as the *Alte* Kongresshalle.

[103] The revised fourth draft of the script by George Lucas, dated January 1976, reproduced in Carol Titelman (ed.), *The Art of Star Wars*, (1979), 134.

[104] Carson, 'Jedi Über Alles', 162.

whole generation of children 'world-wide', but also because in the end it reveals, in all innocence, where these images come from and where they belong: the final sequence is a faithful copy of a sequence from Hitler's greatest propaganda film *Triumph of the Will*.[105]

Lucas denies his dependency on the earlier film, or even watching *TdW* in preparation for making *Star Wars*. He asserts, unconvincingly, that the throne room parallels are 'just what happens when you put a large military group together and give out an award'.[106]

In reality, the significance of the parallels between both films is clear: 'they represent conformity underneath leadership, and the resulting power that comes from a large number of people with one focus'.[107] The imagery, and the mythic substructure conveyed by the imagery, undermine the ostensible message of *Star Wars*: that the Rebel Alliance is in rebellion *against* a totalitarian and oppressive hegemony. In reality, with the filmmaker mapping SA and SS imagery upon the Rebel Alliance, and with movie-viewers 'mistakenly rooting for the Rebel Alliance in *Star Wars*, [they] not only confuse good with evil, but also fail to see their own pellucid reflection in Darth Vader and the Empire'.[108]. *Star Wars* 'legitimizes the same conformist sentiment that made the Nazis so powerful'.[109]

The idea of triumph

Lucas quotes from Riefenstahl on logistical and aesthetic grounds. But there is no, and can be no, simple division between aesthetic and conceptual factors in an artwork's creation and reception. As Brian Winston points out any attempt to 'save *Triumph of the Will* for art by ignoring its politics'[110] is the result of wilful blindness on

---

[105] Wim Wenders, 'The American Dream (March/April 1984)', in *Emotion Pictures* (1989), 159.
[106] Quoted in J. W. Rinzler, *The Making of Star Wars* (2008), 325.
[107] Frangquist, 'STAR WARS and Triumph of the Will'.
[108] Queenan, 'Anakin, get your gun', 116.
[109] Frangquist, 'STAR WARS and Triumph of the Will'.
[110] Winston, 'Critical Eye', 25.

the part of certain cinema scholars. Art and politics are, at the very least, in dialogue with one another, and, more reasonably, are in a symbiotic relationship. In short, the conceptual legacy of *TdW* is at least as strong as its aesthetic legacy. This is summed up, in even shorter order, by the grand unifying Nazi political concept of *Führerprinzip* (the leadership principle). The *Führerprinzip* laid down that

> ...at all levels of organization, ultimate authority was concentrated in a single leader imbued with special gifts. Those special gifts were more than merely managerial. ...The leader was a mystical figure embodying and guiding the nation's destiny.[111]

The constitutional lawyer Ernst Rudolf Huber developed the theory of the *Führerprinzip*: there was no such thing as 'State power' in the *völkisch* Reich of Germany, but rather only *Führergewalt* (Führer power), for the Führer is 'the executor of the nation's common will'.[112] Everything within Reich was subject to the Führer: 'There is no position in the area of constitutional law in the Third Reich independent of this elemental will of the Führer'.[113] *Führergewalt* therefore is 'comprehensive and total' and 'embraces all spheres of national life'.[114] There are no restrictions on its exercise, there are no 'safeguards and controls... autonomous protected spheres... vested individual rights'. Rather *Führergewalt* is 'free and independent, exclusive and unlimited'.[115] This is right and proper, for the Führer is the manifestation of the nation's will. In fact, the Führer was the embodiment of the sovereign power of the Reich. He was the Reich itself.

---

[111] David Welch, *Hitler: Profile of a Dictator* (2001), 49, 42.

[112] Ernst Huber, *Verfassungsrecht des Grossdeutschen Reiches* (1939), 142; trans. in Noakes and Pridham, *Nazism 1919-1945,* vol 2, (1984), 198–9.

[113] Speech by Hans Frank, head of the Nazi Association of Lawyers and the Academy of German Law, 1938, printed in *Im Angesicht des Galgens* (1955), 466–7. Quoted in Noakes and Pridham, *Nazism 1919-1945*, 2:200.

[114] Huber, *Verfassungsrecht*, 142.

[115] Huber, *Verfassungsrecht*, 142. For more on the development of the *Führerprinzip* in Nazi Germany, see Noakes and Pridham, *Nazism 1919-1945*, 2:195–200.

The people of the Reich were swallowed by the person of the Führer. We can see this, filmed, in the sequences in *TdW* where we see the contrast between mankind (in the sense of the multitude participating in the Party Congress), and the Man (in the sense of the role of Hitler, depicted as the German Messiah, the representative human being):

> People are no longer a mass of individuals, a formless, artless mass. Now they form a unison, moved by a will and a communal feeling. They learn again to move in formations or to stand still, as if moulded by an invisible hand. A new body feeling is born, beginning simply in the feature of lifting the arm for the greeting and culminating in the mass march...[116]

People are transformed into a new form, the German People's Body, the *Volkskörper*.[117] Goebbels described the transformation in his usual menacing imagery: the 'poor little man' in the crowd was given 'the proud conviction' to go from being 'a little worm into part of a large dragon'.[118]

The 'little worm' is the people (the *Volkskörper*); the 'large dragon' is the person of Adolf Hitler, indistinguishable from his role of *Führer*.

The high priest of hero-worship

Riefenstahl was doing nothing new or original, or even, for her time, reprehensible. Rather she was reflecting the assumptions of her time and culture, assumptions so deeply embedded in European culture that they remained, and mostly remain, unexamined.

---

[116]Werner Hager, 'Bauwerke im Dritten Reich', *Das Innere Reich* (April 1937): 7; quoted in Adam, *The Arts of the Third Reich*, 88.

[117]See Boaz Neumann, 'The Phenomenology of the German People's Body', *New German Critique* (2009), 149–81, for a discussion on the importance of this concept in understanding the Nazi project.

[118]Joseph Goebbels, *Kampf um Berlin: I* (1932), 18. This dragon metaphor also occurred to Hitler himself after watching a mass demonstration in pre World War One Vienna: Hitler, *Mein Kampf*, chapter 2.

The inheritance of the nineteenth century in Europe was an enthusiasm for the achievements of the great individuals. As Coleridge put it 'All the great – the permanently great – things that have been achieved in the world have been so achieved by individuals, working from the instinct of genius or of goodness'.[119] According to Edmund Gosse, the Victorians 'carried admiration to the highest pitch. They marshalled it, they defined it, they turned it from a virtue into a religion, and called it Hero Worship'.[120]

The high prophet of the new religion, whose influence was pervasive and atmospheric even when not being directly exerted,[121] was Thomas Carlyle (1795–1881). Hero worship was, according to Carlyle 'the basis of all possible good, religious or social, for mankind'.[122] But hero worship is not an optional choice, that can be rationally made for utilitarian reasons. Hero worship is ingrained into the very nature of humanity and human society:

> Society is founded on Hero-worship. All dignities of rank, on which human association rests, are what we may call a *Hero*archy... some representation, not insupportably inaccurate, of a graduated Worship of Heroes – reverence and obedience done to men really great and wise.[123]

The Hero was to be clearly, irrevocably, distinguished from those who were incapable of such heroism. For Carlyle, the vast majority of mankind are but

> ...dull millions, who, as a dull flock, roll hither and thither, whithersoever they are led; and seem all sightless and slavish,

---

[119] 24 July 1832, Samuel Taylor Coleridge, *The Table Talk, and, Omniana*, (1903), 173. This passage is often quoted, but without its context; this is perhaps understandable when we realize that Coleridge was discussing the parliamentary reform of infant education!

[120] Edmund Gosse, 'The Agony of the Victorian Age', in *Some Diversions of a Man of Letters* (1919), 335.

[121] See George M. Young, 'Portrait of an Age', in *Early Victorian England, 1830-1865*, vol. 2 (1934), 460.

[122] Lecture 4, the Hero as Priest: in *On Heroes* (1897), 123.

[123] Lecture 1, the Hero as Divinity: Carlyle, *On Heroes*, 5:12. [Emphasis in original.]

accomplishing, attempting little save what the animal instinct in its somewhat higher kind might teach, To keep themselves and their young ones alive…[124]

However, these 'dull millions' are fortunate, in that hidden among them are those of superior nature, 'whose eye is not destitute of free vision, nor their heart of free volition' (the importance of will again). The dull millions are no more than a 'Machine… [which] is merely *fed*, or desires to be fed, and so *works*'.[125] For Carlyle there remains 'the Person [who] can *will*, and so *do*'. They live 'not by Hearsay, but by clear Vision', and thus are able to *know* and to *believe*, undistracted by 'the grand Vanity-fair of the World… the mere Shows of things', able to see 'into the Things themselves'. The Persons who can *will* and *do, know* and *believe*, are 'properly our Men' (note capitalization); they are the 'guides of the dull host', which is destined to follow the Great ones as by 'an irrevocable decree'. They are the only ones for whom we can say there is 'a *Reality* in their existence'.[126]

There is an interesting echo here of the disdain shown in the Bush White House for the 'reality based community'. As an aide told a journalist from *The New York Times*, 'We're an empire now, and when we act, we create our own reality. And while you're studying that reality – judiciously, as you will – we'll act again, creating other new realities, which you can study too, and that's how things will sort out. We're history's actors… and you, all of you, will be left to just study what we do'.[127]

---

[124] Thomas Carlyle, 'Boswell's Life of Johnson [1832]', in *Critical and Miscellaneous Essays*, vol. 3 (1899), 89.

[125] Carlyle, 'Boswell's Life of Johnson', 89. [Emphasis in original.]

[126] Carlyle, 'Boswell's Life of Johnson', 89.]Italicization in the original.]

[127] Ron Suskind, 'Without a Doubt', *The New York Times* (17 October 2004).

The Führerprinzip filmed

Carlyle cannot be held responsible, as some writers have tried to do[128], for genocide and totalitarianism. As Steinweis puts it: 'If the public image of Hitler corresponded so closely to Carlyle's hero in the eyes of Nazis and anti-Fascists alike, it was because that image was manufactured to correspond to what Carlyle was understood to have written'.[129]

But the fact remains that the model of human society advocated by Carlyle as the 'the basis of all possible good' continues with us, despite the 'fiery last days'[130] of Hitler, the self-acknowledged exemplar of Carlyle's 'Great man' and 'Person'. It continues with us in our political, social and economic discourse, and it continues by the means of depictions, conscious and unconscious, critical and uncritical, in our dominant art-form – cinema. For Riefenstahl and for Schaffner, in 'Hitler' and 'Patton', the model of a leader is an articulation of the *Führerprinzip*, an expression of *Führergewalt*. The leader is the great figure, who is able to see what must be done, and then does it; the one, and the only one, who is unafraid of the gulf that lies beneath us all; the man 'born to bring the culminating movement to its close, to calm its separate waves and stand astride the abyss, ...menaced by huge dangers and recognized by few'.[131]

We shall see, in the following chapters, how this image of the great man standing over the abyss, remains at the heart of our understanding of leadership, even within a cinema which supposedly repudiates and then reaffirms leadership as a civic virtue.

---

[128] See, for example, Manuel Sarkisyanz, *Hitler's English Inspirers* (2003).
[129] Alan Steinweis, 'Hitler and Carlyle's "historical greatness"', *History Today* (June 1995): 35.
[130] John D. Rosenberg, *Carlyle and the Burden of History* (1985), 117.
[131] Jacob Burckhardt, *Reflections on History* (1943), 189.

Chapter 5

Splitters! Leadership 'repudiated'

Americans are prisoners of their own mythology, having watched too many of their own movies. If they ever want to send Americans to the gas chambers, they won't tell us we're going to take showers, they'll herd us into cinder-block movie houses.
GUSTAV HASFORD, 'THE PHANTOM BLOOPER' (1990)

Consider yourselves already dead

In the aftermath of World War Two, with the escalation of the post-war confrontation with the Soviet Union, and before the outbreak of the Korean War, a 'new wave' of war films began to be made. Less interested in simple patriotism or depicting inspiring stories of men getting the job done, these films were 'psychological studies of men under stress'.[1] Examples include *Sands*

---

[1] Garry Wills, *John Wayne: the politics of celebrity* (1997), 154.

of *Iwo Jima*, *Battleground*, *Home of the Brave*, and *Task Force*. These films demonstrate cinema's new interest in 'the neuroses of individuals, the tensions between "men on the same side", the difficulty of maintaining the military as a social structure'.[2]

The best of the new wave was Henry King's *Twelve O'Clock High*. Acclaimed on its first release, it was, according to Bosley Crowther, incomparable with other recent films for its 'rugged realism and punch'. It was 'a top-flight drama' with 'conspicuous dramatic integrity, genuine emotional appeal... [and was] beautifully played', principally by its star, Gregory Peck, who did 'an extraordinarily able job in revealing the hardness and the softness of a general exposed to peril'.[3] Later critics concurred: it is 'a truly outstanding and timeless work', made with 'intelligence, perception and obvious affection for the human spirit...'.[4]

Peck plays Brigadier General Frank Savage of the United States Army Air Forces, stationed in England in 1942, just as the Eighth Air Force began their daylight bombing raids over Germany but before they achieved a sufficient degree of expertise and battle-hardness. Savage is posted to the 918th Bomb Group, a failing 'hard-luck' Group, as an 'iron-tail'[5] commander. Through a combination of implacable discipline and admonishment he intends to accomplish the Group's mission. The psychological cost, for both crews and general, was, from the very first, intended to be central to the story. Henry King said the film explored 'the responsibilities of officers to their men rather than merely a phase of aerial warfare'.[6] As Suid puts it:

> military officers must think of their men as numbers and impersonal units rather than as human beings, as sons, brothers, husbands, or fathers. To think of them as individuals would produce too great a psychological burden on leadership. So

---

[2]Wills, *Politics of Celebrity*, 154. For more on the transition between war films in war-time and war films post-war, see Suid, *Guts and Glory*, chapter 6 and 7, 'World War II: Pseudo-Reality' & 'First Reflections'.

[3]Bosley Crowther, 'The Screen in Review', *The New York Times*, 28 January 1950.

[4]John Griggs, *The Films of Gregory Peck* (1988), 91.

[5]Griggs, *The Films of Gregory Peck*, 92.

[6]Quoted by Griggs, *The Films of Gregory Peck*, 92.

in war, leaders must reduce their fighting men to symbols they move on maps and commit to lists – whether of numbers of battle-ready soldiers or of casualties.[7]

The first morning of his command Savage assembles the Group in the briefing hall. He begins by addressing practicalities: the 'hard luck' reputation might come from the Group's flying skills, therefore they will practise. However, the greater cause is probably the self-pity exhibited by the men in the Group. There is only one solution for that, says Savage, and it is nothing to do with morale-boosting or political indoctrination:

> Now I don't have a lot of patience with this 'What are we fighting for?' stuff. We're in a war, a shooting war. We've got to fight. And some of us have got to die. I'm not trying to tell you not to be afraid. Fear is normal. But stop worrying about it. And about yourselves. Stop making plans, forget about going home. Consider yourselves already dead.

General Savage (not an accidental name) is portrayed, in the eyes of *Twelve O'Clock High* itself, as an admirable example of Suid's removed, strategic, form of leadership,[8] but eventually he is unable to practise what he preaches. Unable to maintain sufficient distance from his men, after a series of difficult missions he breaks down into a catatonic stupor. We are not told, in the film, what happens to Savage after his breakdown. The film's script was adapted from a novel of the same name by Beirne Lay Jr and Sy Bartlett, who drew on their own wartime service experience. Most of the characters in novel and film were drawn directly from life. The '918th' was, in reality, the '306th', and 'Savage' was based on the 306th commander, Col. Frank A. Armstrong, Jr. Armstrong did not have a mental breakdown and was often puzzled, after the war,

---

[7] Suid, *Guts and Glory*, 109.
[8] Savage receives 'through camera placement and lighting and pictorial context, King's commendation, compassion and respect'. Clive Denton, 'Henry King', in *The Hollywood Professionals*, vol. 2 (1974), 41–2.

to be asked about his nervous collapse in England.[9] In the film, Savage disappears from the narrative, and, in cinema, to disappear from the narrative is to cease to exist.

Twelve O'Clock High was once, but is no longer, used by the air force to teach leadership, though it remains in use in 'leadership training seminars' to dramatize and illustrate the challenges faced in 'decision making for the commander in war, business, or education'.[10] It was not as innovative as contemporary, or some later, reviewers think: the furthest that *Twelve O'Clock High* is willing to go are the truisms that 'war is a bloody shame and leaders are dedicated but fallible'.[11]

However, contained within its effective and affective portrayal of a variety of characters and responses to war (Dean Jagger's wryly compassionate outsider, Paul Stewart's thoughtful doctor, Peck's understanding martinet), are the seeds of what I call a 'cinema of suspicion', a suspicion and repudiation of leaders and leadership. Savage is portrayed from a distance: he is physically and emotionally separated from the men he leads. Major Cobb refuses to accept a drink from him, and (so?) Savage closes the mess-bar; when Stovall brews a cup of coffee for him, Savage is able neither to ask Stovall for help directly in delaying transfer requests, nor to thank him for the proposed, administrative, solution: 'you red-tape adjutants are all alike'. His concern is to save his Group by destroying, if necessary, his men, just as, in a later American war, it became necessary to destroy a town in order to save it.

Paradoxically, and yet necessarily, cinema continued to nurture these seeds of repudiation within the genre of war films. It was a fruitful medium. As Denton puts it, 'Films feed on films and wars, unhappily, seem to feed on wars'.[12] We can go further: films feed on wars and wars feed on films. The consummation of this

---

[9] Beirne Lay and Sy Bartlett, *Twelve O'clock High!* (New York: Harper, 1948). For the connections between reality and the fictional depictions in novel and film, see John T. Correll, 'The Real Twelve O'Clock High', *Airforce Magazine*, January 2011.

[10] Suid, *Guts and Glory*, 109.

[11] Denton, 'Henry King', 41.

[12] Denton, 'Henry King', 41.

symbiosis, a full-blown cinema of suspicion, can be seen in the works of Stanley Kubrick.

Full Metal legions

Shortly after the cinematic release of *Paths of Glory* in 1957, Stanley Kubrick gave an interview to the critic Colin Young: his next film was going to be another war movie, *The German Lieutenant*, based on a novel by Richard Adams.[13] Two war films in a row intrigued Young. He asked Kubrick why he wanted to make another genre film: 'was there nothing about the contemporary scene which interested him?'. Young described Kubrick's reply as 'crucial'.[14] For Kubrick the war film 'provides an almost unique opportunity to contrast an individual of our contemporary society with a solid framework of accepted value'. This framework can be revealed to the audience – they become 'fully aware' of it – and the framework then acts as 'a counterpoint to a human, individual, emotional situation'. Furthermore, the experience of individuals within a war is a dramatic situation: war 'acts as a kind of hothouse for forced, quick breeding of attitudes and feelings'. Attitudes can reasonably, and convincingly, be depicted, not in moral black and white, but as a form of 'spectacle': they 'crystallize and come out into the open'. The spectacle derives from conflict, which, in war, is 'natural', and which, not in war (or 'a less critical situation'), would have to be introduced 'almost as a contrivance', and thus appear 'forced', or, worse, 'false'. War allows contrasts, and 'within these contrasts you can begin to apply some of the possibilities of film...'[15]

Although some critics celebrated Kubrick as a 'genre-blind' director (making psychological, morality, science fiction, dystopian,

---

[13] The film was never made, although versions of the script, with unstated provenances, are available on the internet: see the example in the bibliography under Kubrick and Adams.

[14] Colin Young, 'The Hollywood War of Independence', *Film Quarterly* (Spring 1959): 10.

[15] All quotations in this paragraph are from Young, 'War of Independence', 10.

and costume dramas[16]), he did favour the war film for its 'contrasts' and for the latitude it gave him to examine one of his favourite themes.[17] We can see an exploration of that theme in Kubrick's first major studio film, *Spartacus*.

Large Spartacus vs small Spartacus

The place of *Spartacus* in the oeuvre of Stanley Kubrick is an embarrassment for some critics.[18] The famous perfectionist and auteur, who was so dissatisfied with the corporate Hollywood system of film production that he left the U.S. for the delights of independent filmmaking in Hertfordshire, once made a big-budget, mainstream, robes-and-sandals epic. Some critics deal with *Spartacus* by bracketing it out of consideration of Kubrick's work. But *Spartacus* is an important piece of evidence of the way in which cinema can function mythologically, even in the work of a director so often celebrated as an auteur. The function of myth is almost, by definition, independent of the conscious creativity and directivity that the auteur theory requires. The world-view we detect is the *unconscious* world-view. And Kubrick himself has given us permission to approach his work in this way:

> I have always enjoyed dealing with a slightly surrealistic situation and presenting it in a realistic manner. I've always liked fairy tales and myths, magical stories. I think they are somehow closer to the sense of reality one feels today than the equally stylized

---

[16]Mario Falsetto, *Kubrick: a narrative and stylistic analysis* (2001), 8. 'Kubrick virtually reinvented each genre in which he worked, whether it was horror or science fiction…', from Phillips and Hill, *The Encyclopedia of Stanley Kubrick* (2002), xxiv.

[17]Kubrick completed 16 films: at least five may be, broadly, defined as war films. Furthermore, there were a number of unmade films which are part of this genre: for example, *The German Lieutenant*, and *Napoleon*.

[18]And, seemingly, for Kubrick himself: 'The only film he disclaims is *Spartacus*. He says he worked on it as just a hired hand'. Joseph Gelmis, 'Stanley Kubrick', in *The Film Director as Superstar* (1970), 294.

'realistic' story in which a great deal of selectivity and omission has to occur in order to preserve its 'realist' style.[19]

In other words, Kubrick was a mythic filmmaker, and his mythic films are susceptible to a mythic interpretation. When critics do engage with *Spartacus* however, its mythic qualities are neglected for its alleged allegory: it is often read as allegorical of the political situation in late 1950s America. The scriptwriter, Dalton Trumbo, was one of the ten Hollywood workers black-listed as a result of the House Committee on Un-American Activities (HUAC) investigations into the Communist infiltration of American society: he hadn't written a film script, under his own name, for ten years. Thus, it does not take a great imaginative leap to read the contemporary overtones in the threat made by the victorious, but oppressive, Marcus Licinius Crassus (Laurence Olivier) to the populist Senator Gracchus (Charles Laughton):

The enemies of the state are known. Arrests are in progress. The prisons begin to fill. In every city and province, lists of the disloyal have been compiled. Tomorrow they will learn the cost of their terrible folly...their treason.

Alternatively, Kirk Douglas, star and executive producer, was an enthusiastic Zionist: 'Looking at [Roman] ruins... I wince. I see thousands and thousands of slaves carrying rocks, beaten, starved, crushed, dying. I identify with them. As it says in the Torah: "Slaves were we unto Egypt". I come from a race of slaves. That would have been *my* family, *me*'.[20] In making the film he wished to reflect the heroism of the nascent state of Israel: 'Douglas... saw *Spartacus* as an opportunity to make a large-scale Zionist statement... and reinterpreted the slave-rebel's story as a Roman variation on the let-my-people-go theme'.[21] In this way Spartacus becomes a Moses-figure; slavery in Italy stands for slavery in Egypt

---

[19] Penelope Houston, 'Kubrick Country (1971)', in *Stanley Kubrick: Interviews*, (2001), 114.

[20] Kirk Douglas, *The Ragman's Son (*1988), 304. [Emphasis in original.]

[21] Derek Elley, *The Epic Film: Myth and History* (1984), 110.

and Crassus for Pharaoh; the (unspecified) Promised Land is reachable, not across the Red, but the Ionian Sea, and not by foot through the miraculous intervention of God, but by ship with the commercial assistance of pirates. The history of slavery in America is also part of the allegorical interpretation of *Spartacus*. The hero meets Draba (Woody Strode), an African slave who refuses to tell him his name, for gladiators 'don't make friends. If we're ever matched in the arena together, I'll have to kill you'. And yet, when Draba and Spartacus are matched in the arena, for the pleasure of the villainous Marcus Crassus (Laurence Olivier), Draba ultimately refuses to kill Spartacus, and instead attempts to kill the Roman. In this we see, supposedly, 'an individual and group demand for freedom'.[22] *Spartacus* was released at the beginning of the civil rights movement, and Girgus draws parallels between the gladiator ('an amazing black figure') and Martin Luther King, both embodying 'the readiness of African Americans to lead their fight for equality'. Draba, in the person of Strode, 'assumes a special status in the film, exercising his right to speak for freedom'; he transfers the 'contemporary realities of discrimination and racism onto the back of the black gladiator who fights Spartacus'. Ultimately Strode's performance 'renegotiates the relationship of history and fiction'.[23]

Thus *Spartacus* can variously be an allegory for McCarthyite witch-hunts in the United States, Zionism or African-American civil rights. It is simpler to say that its major theme is more universal: inspired by the story of the rebel slave leader told in Howard Fast's self-published book, but indifferent to the specific political concerns of the author, Douglas 'wanted to make an epic film that articulated the eternal human fight for freedom against oppression'.[24] The publicity material for the film certainly emphasised this universal aspiration: 'Man's Eternal Struggle For Freedom Theme Of New

---

[22] Sam B. Girgus, *America on Film* (2002), 94.

[23] Girgus, *America on Film*, 94–95. This last is quite a hermeneutical weight for a five-minute sequence, and one which remains to other, reliable, critics, puzzlingly opaque in its motivations: see, for example, Phillips and Hill, *Kubrick Encyclopedia*, s.v. 'Strode, Woody (Woodrow)', 363.

[24] Monica Silveira Cyrino, *Big Screen Rome* (2005), 103. See Douglas, *The Ragman's Son*, 304.

Film'.[25] Douglas, in a letter to an opponent of Trumbo, said emphatically of the completed film, 'it is a courageous and positive statement about mankind's most cherished goal – freedom'.[26]

In reality these are all subsidiary themes in *Spartacus* as a whole. The film reflects, despite the disavowal of the director and its dismissal by the critics, a thematic continuity with the rest of Kubrick's work. Stanley Kubrick, as a director, was interested in exploring, and repudiating, the idea of leadership. What else can we say about a man whose great, uncompleted, film was a life of Napoleon? Such a project was, in 1969, Kubrick's 'next' film: Napoleon's life was, for Kubrick, 'a fantastic subject for a film biography'. As a character and historical protagonist Bonaparte fascinated Kubrick, as his life was (rightly) 'described as an epic poem of action'. He was 'one of those rare men who move history and mold the destiny of their own times and of generations to come – in a very concrete sense, our own world is the result of Napoleon...' Any film, any good film (and there has never been 'a good or accurate movie about him'), would be able to explore 'oddly contemporary' issues: 'the responsibilities and abuses of power, the dynamics of social revolution, the relationship of the individual to the state, war, militarism, etc'. To make a film about Napoleon is to make a film 'about the basic questions of our own times'.[27]

Kubrick was unable, despite years of expensive and exhaustive research, to secure funding for the film. Following his death Alison Castle was invited by his estate to collate and curate the director's Napoleon Archives. In a sumptuous series of volumes, with accompanying scholarly essays, we learn that 'the story of Napoleon moved Kubrick to look at the glory and frailty of mankind through the character of a charismatic leader with unparalleled gifts, a man who was worshipped and who genuinely loved himself, but who, constrained by his arrogance, brought about his own downfall'.[28]

---

[25] See the illustration reproduced in Jeffrey P. Smith, "A Good Business Proposition", *The Velvet Light Trap*, (Spring 1989): 93.

[26] Letter from Kirk Douglas to J. David Johnson, 6 May 1960: cited in Smith, 'Good Business', 92.

[27] Gelmis, 'Kubrick (Superstar)', 297.

[28] Jan Harlan, 'Stanley Kubrick's "Napoleon"', in *Stanley Kubrick's 'Napoleon'*, Castle (ed.) (2011), 25 / 15.

Thus, to return to *Spartacus*, we can see that the main theme of the film, its ostensible rhetoric, is a depiction, and repudiation, of a particular ideology of leadership. It was the deliberate intention of the scriptwriter (Trumbo) and star-cum-producer (Douglas) to depict the protagonist and hero as an unequivocal hero and leader, in distinction to the opportunist and totalitarian corruption of the Roman state with its economic and moral slavery. This intention was stated explicitly in an 80-page memorandum written by Trumbo after he had repeatedly viewed a rough cut of the film.[29] In it Trumbo made a distinction between two different interpretations and depictions of Spartacus which he named 'Large' and 'Small' Spartacus. If the film ended up with a depiction of 'Large Spartacus' then the audience would see: a man who led a major revolt which (inadvertently) led to the destruction of republican Rome and the creation of a totalitarian Empire; whose generalship was so successful that it required three Roman armies to suppress him; who, despite his slave background developed a political and intellectual capacity equal to that of the greatest patrician of his day, and possibly equivalent to that of the greatest in history; and whose commitment to his followers extended beyond narrow self-interest to an absolute commitment to noble objectives. With a 'Large Spartacus' we would see how:

> ...in the moment of his supreme test, ...[Spartacus] never doubts the rightness of his cause, or the need for all of them to have engaged in it, even unto death.[30]

A 'Small Spartacus' would show us, instead: a man who repeatedly doubts his strategy and his tactics; who suffers in comparison with the rhetorical and political leadership of Crassus; who is obsessed with the physical safety of himself, his wife and his unborn child; who acts for the sake of fame and glory. A 'Small Spartacus' would

---

[29]Part of the memo is printed in Dalton Trumbo, 'Report on Spartacus', *Cineaste* (June 1991). It is extensively discussed by Duncan L. Cooper's two chapters in *Spartacus: Film and History*, (ed.) Winkler (2007).

[30]Trumbo, 'Report on Spartacus'.

'probably [have] had leadership thrust on him, that he exercised it reluctantly, that he never be seen discussing destinations or planning strategy'. He would not, like his rival 'feel and think', but 'feel' only: he would not be the 'equal of Crassus'.

Trumbo's preference, and the preference of the star, was for the former, the Large Spartacus. Trumbo sought to secure a rhetorical depiction of an individual as symbol and inspiration:

> ...That the essence of manhood is to rise above the petty ambitions of one's own self, and identify oneself with something larger, with mankind as a whole, with the good of mankind. That the spirit and intellect of Spartacus in his moment of defeat and moral agony rose so far above himself that it symbolized the spirit and intellect of the whole murdered slave community.

Trumbo's aspirations and rhetoric, although surviving in part in the completed film, are doubly subverted, first, by the inadequacies of the script and Kirk Douglas's acting ability. We hear too often exactly how heroic Spartacus is, exactly how much more of a man he is than his opponents (see, for example, Varinia's last conversation with Crassus): any script which is 'too insistent about the honesty and intuitive vision of the film's proletarian hero'[31] will inevitably elicit the opposite opinion from a half-way conscious audience. When Douglas is required to act 'head-to-head' with Olivier, the British actor's understatement and variation of tone, pace and expression, is more than a match for Douglas's simple glowering.

Secondly, and paradoxically for those who dismiss *Spartacus* as the work of an auteur, the heroic status of Spartacus as a moral being and dramatic protagonist is undermined by Kubrick's directorial decisions. We can examine two examples.

---

[31] Thomas Allen Nelson, *Kubrick: inside a film artist's maze* (2000), 58.

The political exhortations on the mount

In the first, it has become apparent that the Roman state, person-ified by Crassus, will not allow the slave army to flee the Italian mainland. Crassus has manoeuvred them into fighting one last battle (although, interestingly, it is the first and only battle which Kubrick chose to depict). Just as Spartacus realises this, Crassus in Rome assumes, unhistorically, full dictatorial powers ('election as first consul, command of all the legions of Italy, and the abolition of senatorial authority over the courts'.). This is 'order'.

Kubrick shows the two situations, the slave resolution to face Crassus' legions and the totalitarian *Machtergreifung* through a montage sequence: Spartacus and Crassus, in moral and hierar-chical equivalences, addressing their 'troops', both from elevated positions, Spartacus on a hill above Brundusium, Crassus on the podium before the Roman Senate. For Spartacus his hearers are the mixed audience of the slave army: men, women, children, the elderly and the young, all dressed in homely robes of brown and greys. Crassus addresses the regular soldiers of the Roman legions, ranked in military discipline, and equipped with the impressive *lorica segmentata* and *heroic cuirass*.

Spartacus tells his people that they have no choice 'but to march against Rome herself and end this war the only way it could have ended: by freeing every slave in Italy'. At this point Kubrick changes the point of view. Spartacus is given his first close-up, from a side angle: it is, says Winkler, as if 'he were standing between *two* crowds, his own people and those in the theatre',[32] a division between what is technically called the intra- and extradiegetic audiences. More significantly, Spartacus is filmed from the 'Renaissance' angle. We (and here the theatre audience and the slave army audience are identified) view him from a slightly inferior position. The evening sky glows behind him: 'In this way

---

[32]Martin M. Winkler, 'The Holy Cause of Freedom' in *Spartacus: Film and History* (2007), 180.

Spartacus is elevated above all others and becomes almost godlike'.[33]

The point of view is shared with that of Crassus. We see him from slightly below the podium level of the Senate House, although behind Crassus we see the architectural glory of republican Rome. Crassus is the personification of military and economic might.

The distinctions between the two, Crassus and Spartacus, seem clear, in the way in which the interlocutors are depicted and the way they speak. Thus: 'Crassus addresses a faceless mass which submits willingly to him as savior'.[34] Whereas Spartacus' army, 'young and old, men and women are shown literally looking up to him', they do so as 'to someone who can federate disparate victims ready to take their own destiny in hand, if only to lose at this particular moment of history'.[35] In other words, the surrender of autonomy has been made willingly and knowingly, and we know this because Kubrick shows us their faces. And yet, as we have seen in the previous chapter, close-ups of individuals in a crowds, contrasted with images of the *Führer* or *imperator*, are not necessarily anti-totalitarian. In fact, rhythmic editing between *imperator* and crowd, even if the crowd is a slave army, may be the means of expressing and reinforcing the power of the *Führer*. Humphries undermines his own thesis, in a footnote to the same passage, when he reminds us that the crowd cry 'Heil [sic] Crassus!' ('which is obviously intended to remind us of "Sieg Heil!"'[36]): Humphries is either unable, or unwilling for ideological reasons, to mark the difference between the German 'Heil' and the English 'Hail' (for the Latin 'Ave'). A vowel can mark a totalitarian difference. We see close-ups of the Senators, including Gracchus and Caesar as Crassus is acclaimed. Furthermore, Winkler notes the way in which the sequence concludes. Crassus moves for the first time, his head turning to follow the movement of his soldiers. This parallels the exclamatory movement of Spartacus during his speech, and

---

[33]Winkler, 'Holy Cause of Freedom', 180.
[34]Reynold Humphries, 'The Specter of Politics', in *Kubrick: essays on his films and legacy*, Rhodes (ed.) (2008), 91.
[35]Humphries, 'Specter of Politics', 91.
[36]Humphries, 'Specter of Politics', 91, n. 23.

yet Winkler asserts that the 'visual similarity with the movements of Spartacus' head points to a strong underlying contrast between them'.[37] Surely the similarity of movement is intended to compare rather than contrast the two speakers?

Some critics attempt to make a distinction between the delivery of the two speeches: Crassus delivers his lines 'in a clipped, haughty tone', whereas Spartacus is 'calm and affectionate'.[38] Crassus promises 'a new Italy and a new empire. And I promise you the body of Spartacus'. Spartacus promises something less hopeful: 'We've fought many battles and won great victories. Now, instead of taking ship for our homes across the sea, we must fight again'. There is no goal, or end result, here. The slave army is not given a way of knowing when their war will be concluded, other than an abstracted principle: 'I do know that we're brothers, and I know that we're free'. How free? As Spartacus speaks we are given close-ups of his audience (without armour or weaponry, as Winkler notes[39]) including a shot of a young girl with her mother. We see that girl again, on the night before the decisive battle, when Spartacus wanders through the sleeping encampment. The girl is awake, and pleads with her mother: 'Mummy? Mummy? When do we go home?'. There is no answer. The young girl does not go home – she is not free to go home, or to choose not to die. She is killed in the battle the next day, and we see her body in the aftermath. Here Kubrick is setting up an equivalent moral dilemma to the famous theodicy of *The Brothers Karamazov*. Does the majesty of God justify the death of an innocent child? Is Spartacus' freedom of brotherhood confirmed or denied by the death of a toddler?

Victory is resistance is death

The question is answered in the second example, when we see the consequences of Spartacus' leadership. Spartacus and Antoninus

---

[37] Winkler, 'Holy Cause of Freedom', 181.
[38] Phillips and Hill, *Kubrick Encyclopedia*, s.v. 'Olivier, Laurence', 278.
[39] Winkler, 'Holy Cause of Freedom', 180.

(Tony Curtis) are chained to a cart outside the walls of Rome, the last two slaves remaining to be crucified. Antoninus asks if the slave army could ever have won? Could've won? replies Spartacus. We did win, and our victory was in our resistance:

> When just one man says, 'No, I won't', Rome begins to fear. And we were tens of thousands who said no. That was the wonder of it. To have seen slaves lift their heads from the dust, to see them rise from their knees, stand tall, with a song on their lips, to hear them storm through the mountains shouting, to hear them sing along the plains.

But Spartacus' inspiring rhetoric in the face of an actual, empirical, imperial defeat is brutally undercut by Antoninus, with a quick glance down the Appian Way: 'And now they're dead'. As Winkler unwittingly affirms, the slave army was made up of 'fathers with young children, old people, young girls, women and children. ... They are Everyman and Everywoman, and viewers can readily identify themselves with them: There, but for the grace of God, go I!'.[40] Kubrick concurs, but not in a heroic or affirming way. Rather the director repudiates the leadership of Spartacus. Follow Spartacus, Kubrick says, follow any leader, and death will be your fate, even if it is not crucifixion along the Appian Way. Spartacus was as responsible as Crassus for the crucifixion of his followers.

Is that you, John Wayne? Is this me?

Kubrick made *Full Metal Jacket* at the tail-end of the 1980s cycle of Vietnam war-films, which had begun, while the war was still being fought, with John Wayne's *The Green Berets.* Critics were excited to see what the director of *Spartacus*, and, more pertinently, *Paths of Glory*, would make of the miring of American imperialism in

---

[40]Winkler, 'Holy Cause of Freedom', 181.

the 'living-room war'. In other words, most critics expected *Full Metal Jacket* to examine war and anti-war, and that is what they found. Private Joker, Mathew Modine's character, we are told, is 'a humanist in the process of being permanently bent by the war', illustrated by a photograph captioned 'War Is Hell'[41]; it tells 'a story hinged on the trauma of the Tet offensive in the Vietnam War'[42]; the film 'exemplifies the Vietnam War film in its mature stage', in which the 'crucible of combat is rendered with state-of-the-art technology and showcased for maximum effect';[43] it is 'an anti-war film', which depicts 'the dark desolation of war', and yet 'that offers no ready answers to the painful political and moral issues it raises'.[44] Kubrick himself acknowledges the ambivalent way in which violence and human culpability was depicted: he was attracted to the original novel, Hasford's *The Short-Timers,*[45] because the 'book offered no easy moral or political answers; it was neither pro-war nor anti-war. It seemed only concerned with the way things are'. Kubrick attempted to continue this descriptive discourse in the making of the film: 'There may be a fallacy in the belief that showing people that war is bad will make them less willing to fight a war. But *Full Metal Jacket*, I think, suggests that there is more to say about war than that it is bad'.[46]

Kubrick's admirers believe that he replicated this neutral naturalism in his film. As Philips says, the final sequence of the film, the third stanza, in which the marine platoon are engaged in extended and traumatic urban warfare, was shot 'with the raw immediacy of a wartime documentary'.[47] Kubrick himself boasted

---

[41] Vincent Canby, 'Kubrick's "Full Metal Jacket"', *The New York Times* (26 June 1987).

[42] Francis X. Clines, 'Stanley Kubrick's Vietnam', *The New York Times* (21 June 1987).

[43] Thomas Doherty, 'Full Metal Genre', *Film Quarterly* (Winter 1988): 24,29.

[44] Phillips and Hill, *Kubrick Encyclopedia*, s.v. 'Full Metal Jacket', 127,128.

[45] Gustav Hasford, *The Short-Timers* (New York: Harper & Row, 1979). Hasford later concluded the story of Joker in *The Phantom Blooper* (New York: Bantam Books, 1990). Kubrick also used as a source Michael Herr, *Dispatches* (London: Picador, 1978). Herr was employed as a consultant and scriptwriter for the film.

[46] In an interview with Michael Ciment printed in *Kubrick: the definitive edition*, by Ciment (2001), 243.

[47] Introduction, Phillips and Hill, *Kubrick Encyclopedia*, xxiii.

of the authenticity of the *mise-en-scène* of his film: 'We also flew in two hundred large palm trees from Spain and shipped a hundred thousand artificial tropical plants from Hong Kong. Set into marsh-lands covered with chest-high yellow grass, amidst helicopters and pink smoke – everything looked absolutely authentic'.[48]

And yet, simultaneously, there is something fairy-tale like about the film. It is episodic, rather than narrative-driven. The characters remain no more than ciphers, made up of nicknames and the customizations of their uniforms: Jim Davis is baptised 'Joker' by the drill sergeant in the first scene of the film and his given names are never mentioned again; he wears a CND 'Peace badge' on his jacket and the slogan 'Born to Kill' on his helmet. Even more noticeably Kubrick eschewed the temptations and dangers of filming in south east Asia and North America: the Parris Island training depot scenes were filmed at RAF Bassingbourn in Cambridgeshire; the Vietnamese rice paddies were played by the salt marshes of Cliffe-at-Hoo in Kent, the ruins of Hué city were filmed in the semi-demolished gas works in Beckton, E6, eight miles east of Charing Cross. How seriously is the audience supposed to take the 'documentary authenticity' of the film when an American marine base is filled with English street furniture?[49] Kubrick is, intentionally or not, putting quotation marks around both his film and its subject: this is not Vietnam, it is 'Vietnam'. The film and the war are 'constructs', operating within a 'symbolic space'.[50]

So we can see, taking into account the deconstructed narrative structure, the disinclination to provide full depictions of well-rounded characters, and the signifying of the fairy-tale making and depiction of the film and war, Kubrick is signalling to us that *Full Metal Jacket* is not 'about' Vietnam. If so, then what is it 'about'?

Running just under the surface of Kubrick's adaptation of Hasford and Herr's books is a meditation on the American myth

---

[48] Under a section entitled 'Beckton' in 'Kubrick on 'Full Metal Jacket'', 243.
[49] Note the 'Give Way' signs, double-yellow lines and dotted lane markings around 'Parris Island' in the double-timing marches.
[50] Robert Castle and Stephen Donatelli, 'Kubrick's Ulterior War', *Film Comment* (October 1998): 25.

of individual heroism, and the temptations of leadership. Let us examine three sequences in the film.

The film opens with medium close-ups of unprepossessing young men having their heads shaved. Extradiegetic music (a soundtrack) plays over: Johnnie Wright's sentimentally patriotic and bloodthirsty 'Hello Vietnam'. We do not know who these men are, but we watch them losing one of the great signifiers of individuality to young men in the late 1960s, their hair. These young recruits have lost their 'freak flag'. Immediately the scene cuts to the interior of a barracks. In a bare and empty room, with a shining blood-red floor, the recruits stand by their bunks in shapeless olive green fatigues. The middle of the room and screen is occupied by Master Gunnery Sergeant Hartman (the only person in the room who is allowed to be self-identified). Hartman is played by Lee Ermey, a career marine (a 'lifer' in Marine slang) who was employed by Kubrick as a military advisor, and impressed the director with his ability to improvise scatologically.[51] It is a bravura performance (and Ermey was nominated for a Golden Globe), aided by bravura filming. Kubrick must have consciously realized the parallels with Schaffner's opening scene in *Patton*: a 'lifer' instructs reluctant soldiers on the realities of war. Whereas Schaffner is content to keep the scene static with all attention on General Patton and his military accoutrements, Kubrick almost immediately begins to move the camera. Hartman strides in a wide ellipse around the echoing barracks, and the camera leads the way in a characteristically Kubrickian reverse dolly-tracking shot. We are distracted from the fluency of the filmmaking by the fluency of Hartman's cursing:

> Because I am hard, you will not like me. But the more you hate me, the more you will learn. I am hard, but I am fair! There is no racial bigotry here! I do not look down on niggers, kikes, wops or greasers. Here you are all equally worthless![52]

---

[51] At least, this is the story told by Kubrick to Alexander Walker, and by Ermey himself. In reality, much of Hartman's dialogue is taken directly from Hasford's novel: Walker, Taylor, and Ruchti, *Stanley Kubrick, Director* (1999), 318–23; Aljean Harmetz, "Jacket' Actor Invents His Dialogue', *The New York Times* (30 June 1987).

[52] Kubrick, Herr, and Hasford, *Full Metal Jacket: the screenplay* (1987), 3–4 (Sc. 2).

Hartman asserts his authority through rhetoric, through action and through violence: when Private Joker mocks Hartman's bravado,[53] Hartman pounces on him.

> What have we got here, a fucking comedian? Private Joker? I admire your honesty. Hell, I like you. You can come over to my house and fuck my sister. *Sergeant* HARTMAN *punches* JOKER *in the stomach.* JOKER *sags to his knees.*

As Hasford tells us in the source novel:

> Beatings, we learn, are a routine element of life on Parris Island. And not that I'm-only-rough-on-'um-because-I-love-'um crap civilians have seen in Jack Webb's Hollywood movie *The D.I.* and in Mr. John Wayne's *The Sands of Iwo Jima.*[54]

The drill instructors (in the book the Gunnery Sergeant is called Gerheim) 'administer brutal beatings to faces, chests, stomachs, and backs. With fists'. As Hasford writes, and Kubrick shows, leadership in the Marines is not just for the (sentimental) conditioning of the recruits into a body of men worthy of 'the Corps'. It is also an exercise in naked, Nietzschean, violence. Gunnery Sergeant Gerheim / Hartman attacks 'any part of our bodies upon which a black and purple bruise won't show'.[55] He beats the men, not because he loves them, but because he can.

Once out of training the leadership displayed is no more inspiring. In Vietnam, Joker (promoted to Sergeant himself) is a Marine Correspondent reporting on a suspected mass grave. He is admonished by a 'poge'[56] Colonel to 'get with the program... jump on the team... for the big win':

Quotations from the movie are from *FMJ Screenplay* corrected against the film's soundtrack.

[53] We shall examine the significance of the *way* Joker does this below, on p. 156.

[54] Hasford, *The Short-Timers*, 7.

[55] Hasford, *The Short-Timers*, 7.

[56] A rear-echelon soldier. General Savage is a good example, in the beginning of *Twelve O'Clock High* at least, of a poge airman.

Son, all I've ever asked of my marines is that they obey my
orders as they would the word of God. ...It's a hardball world,
son. We've gotta keep our heads until this peace craze blows
over.

But it is not just the 'poges' and the 'lifers' who fail in leadership:
even 'salty' and 'righteous' Marines fail.

Joker's training buddy Cowboy is assigned to combat infantry,
and Joker meets up with him in the battle for the Citadel in Hué
city. Cowboy has become, by death and default, the leader of the
'Lusthog Squad'. He leads the squad through the ruined city, until
realising they are lost, he calls a halt. One marine, Eightball, is sent
out from cover to recon. He is hit by a sniper's bullet and collapses,
mortally wounded, in an exposed position. Cowboy is unable to
persuade the squad either to cease fire or to stay put:

> I think we're being set up for an ambush. I think there may
> be strong enemy forces in those buildings over there. I've
> requested tank support. We're gonna sit tight until it comes...

Cowboy is not obeyed. First one, then another, then five more
Marines, including Cowboy, move to try and rescue Eightball. Two
are killed, including Cowboy. His last words are 'I... I can hack
it'. Cowboy's leadership ends in failure, from the point of view of
Kubrick and his civilian viewers. From the point of view of Gunnery
Sergeant Hartman and the Marine Corps, Cowboy's death is all
that can be expected of a Marine: as Hartman said to the recruits
at graduation 'always remember this: marines die, that's what
we're here for! But the Marine Corps lives forever. And that means
you live forever!'.

Finally, Joker achieves his ambition to be the first kid on his
block with a 'confirmed kill' when he shoots the mortally wounded
sniper who had killed Cowboy: she was 'a beautiful Vietnamese girl
of about fifteen'. The Marines withdraw, through a night lit by the
burning ruins of the Citadel. We have a final voiceover from Joker,
celebrating his continued existence: 'We have nailed our names in
the pages of history enough for today... I am so happy that I am
alive, in one piece and short. I'm in a world of shit... yes. But I am

alive. And I am not afraid'. As Joker's voice-over ends, we hear clearly the song that the Marines are singing together, the theme from Disney's 'Mickey Mouse Club', with 'the transcendental, ideologically prompted and universally memorized Mickey Mouse question'[57]: 'Who's the leader of the club that's made for you and me?'. As the oral historian Mark Baker says, the Vietnam War, as experienced by the Americans, turned out to have been 'a warped version of *Peter Pan*. Vietnam was a brutal Neverneverland, outside time and space, where little boys didn't have to grow up'. It was 'billed on the marquee as a John Wayne shoot-'em-up'.[58]

Here we see the person whom Hasford, Herr and Kubrick identify as Mickey Mouse's alter ego: 'Mr John Wayne'. John Wayne was the reason the soldiers of Vietnam accepted their role: 'I was seduced by World War II and John Wayne movies'.[59] Michael Herr in his own work concurs. He recalls how the 'grunts' were affected by the presence of TV cameras in the battlefield:

> You don't know what a media freak is until you've seen the way a few of those grunts would run around during a fight when they knew there was a television crew nearby; they were actually making war movies in their heads, doing little guts-and-glory Leatherneck tap dances under fire, getting their pimples shot off for the networks.[60]

They were killed, not by the VC bullets, but by 'seventeen years of war movies before coming to Vietnam to get wiped out for good'[61]. They were seduced into dying by Hollywood and John Wayne.

Hasford and Kubrick vehemently repudiate this seduction.[62] Hasford recalls how he saw Wayne's *The Green Berets* in a forward

---

[57] Janet C. Moore, 'For Fighting and for Fun', *The Velvet Light Trap* (Spring 1993): 43–4.

[58] Mark Baker, *Nam* (1982), 24. A significant metaphor.

[59] Baker, *Nam*, 12.

[60] Herr, *Dispatches*, 169. Kubrick dramatizes this phenomenon with a series of straight-to-camera interviews by the members of the Lusthog Squad.

[61] Herr, *Dispatches*, 169.

[62] For an evaluation and enumeration of Hasford's demolition of John Wayne, see Matthew Ross, 'The Life and Work of Gustav Hasford' (2010).

area: it was 'a Hollywood soap opera about the love of guns. ...
The audience of Marines roars with laughter. This is the funniest
movie we have seen in a long time'.[63] But if a Marine 'does a John
Wayne' it means he has gone berserk, and in such a way that he
is likely to get himself killed.[64]

In the first scene, as a minor rebellion against Hartman's
hectoring, Joker asks out loud 'Is that you, John Wayne? Is this
me?'[65] The distinction is unclear at the beginning of the movie; it is
impossible to make at the end: 'Life-as-movie, war-as-(war)-movie,
war-as-life; a complete process if you got to complete it'.[66]

Kubrick has enacted a solid and terrifying demolition of the
myth of John Wayne, and the adolescent heroism of the American
Adam. In the Brueghel-like atmosphere of the final scene, the
Marines, socialised into being 'killers... indestructible men, men
without fear',[67] psychologically process their experiences in the
urban fighting of Hué by regressing to childhood. They are in a
'world of shit', according to Joker's voice over, but they are also
members of a gang, whose leader is a mouse with white gloves.
According to Kubrick, all leaders are 'M-I-C-K-E-Y-M-O-U-S-E',
and they will lead you to the grave, singing Mouseketeer songs as
you go.

'They're in a rather funny mood today'

According to Sartre, to be truly in hell we require other people:
there is a quorum for damnation. If we require other people for hell,

---

[63] Hasford, *The Short-Timers*, 38.

[64] Joker speaks to himself: 'Legs, don't do any John Waynes. My body is serviceable.
I intend to maintain my body in the excellent condition in which it was issued'.
Hasford, *The Short-Timers*, 98. See also 107.

[65] Hasford, *The Short-Timers*, 4. In the novel, it is Cowboy who asks the question,
and Joker who responds with the significant assessment 'I think I'm going to hate
this movie'.

[66] Herr, *Dispatches*, 58.

[67] Joker's VO description at the end of the Parris Island training.

do we require other people for such relational states as 'leadership' or 'followership'? If an order is given to no followers, can it be enacted?

As we discovered in Chapter 2, Bennis, for one, denies the possibility of leadership without followers:[68] leadership and followership are states of human interaction which require, at a fundamental level, a social context. In other words, leadership and followership must happen in (some form of) community, whatever social or religious organisation that community takes. As a corollary, there is no such thing as leadership or followership which happens in social isolation, at least, there is no such thing as socially isolated leadership which is not depicted for satirical or humorous purposes.

Which brings us to *Monty Python's Life of Brian,* 'this squalid little film...morally without merit and undeniably reprehensible'.[69] When *Life of Brian* was released in 1979 it was, almost reflexively, seen as an anti-religious film. For this reason, it was censored and/or banned in numerous local authority areas in England, Wales and Scotland.[70] It was also, like Gunnery Sergeant Hartman, an equal opportunity offender, disgusting Christians and Jews alike: Robert E. A. Lee of the Lutheran Council of North America said 'if blasphemy is still an operative word in our society we must apply it... [to this] outrageous' satire, and Rabbi Abraham Hecht of the Rabbinical Alliance of America declared it to be 'foul, disgusting, blasphemous'.[71]

Ironically, this was the intention of at least one of the members of the Python team. For Eric Idle religion *was* the target of the film:

---

[68] See the discussion on p. 48 above.

[69] Malcolm Muggeridge's ill-informed judgement, on a television chat show hosted by Tim Rice: 'Friday Night, Saturday Morning' on BBC 2, 9 November 1979). Gavin Millar says that although Muggeridge's critique was 'incoherent', he should be forgiven. The Bishop of Southwark on the same programme, however, is unforgivable for the way he 'alternated boastful facetiousness with insulting condescension'. Gavin Millar, 'Blessed Brian', *The Listener* (15 November 1979): 673.

[70] Robert Hewison, *Monty Python: The Case Against* (1981), chapters 5 and 6.

[71] 'Lutheran Broadcast Slam at "Life of Brian"', and 'Rabbinical Alliance Pours on Condemnation of "Life of Brian"', *Variety* (29 August 1979). See also Robert Sellers, *Always Look on the Bright Side of Life* (2003), 15.

Here were some of the basic thoughts and impulses of Western society, which had been inculcated into everyone and yet no one was allowed to refer to them or deal with them unless they were part of a religious body or organization which was dedicated to the promulgation of the very things we wanted to examine. We were drawn to the fact that this area was indeed taboo for all kinds of comedy.[72]

Subsequently, Terry Jones, the film's director, has repeatedly made a distinction between 'blasphemy' (which he defines as touching on 'belief'), and the film's true, heretical, nature (which he defines as touching on 'dogma', that is to say 'the priesthood, the interpretation of belief, rather than belief itself'[73]). The distinction is a subtle one, and does not necessarily protect Jones's position. For example, Thomas Aquinas also notes a distinction between blasphemy and heresy. Blasphemy is 'to cast insult or abuse at the dignity of our creator'.[74] There are three kinds of blasphemy: attributing something to God which is not his, denying something of God which *is* his, and lastly, attributing something to a creature which properly belongs to God.[75] Heresy, on the other hand, 'is a species of infidelity, attaching to those who profess faith in Christ yet corrupt his dogmas'.[76] Heresy, therefore, is not just to do with ideas, but rather practice, and practice within a social context: it is a 'socially embodied notion', which raises a 'social and political' threat by the heterodox, subsisting within a larger orthodox community. It is 'an enemy of faith that sows the seeds of faith's destruction'.[77]

---

[72] An unpublished essay, quoted by Hewison, *Case Against*, 59.

[73] From an interview given in Jones, Parker, and Timlett, 'Monty Python: Almost The Truth – The BBC Lawyer's Cut' (BBC 2, 3 October 2009). See also Graham Chapman et al., *The Pythons' Autobiography* (2003), 281, where Jones makes a distinction between blasphemy, which repudiates belief in 'the Bible story as gospel' (sic), and heresy, which repudiates the Church's 'interpretation' of the Bible.

[74] St Thomas Aquinas, *Summa Theologiae: Consequences of Faith (2a2ae. 8–16)*, trans. Thomas Gilby, O.P., vol. 32 (London: Blackfriars; Eyre & Spottiswoode, 1975), q.13 a.1.1, 'Blasphemy in General.'

[75] Aquinas, *Summa (2a2ae. 8–16)*, 32:q.13 a.1.3.

[76] Aquinas, *Summa (2a2ae. 8–16)*, 32:q.11 a.1, 'Heresy'.

[77] Alister E. McGrath, *Heresy* (2009), 34. See the whole of Chapter 2 for a discussion on the character of heresy.

Such distinctions, between heretical and blasphemous intentions, are of no concern to Eric Idle, always the most outspoken of the Pythons in delineating of the film's targets. It was Idle who quipped at the New York premiere of *Monty Python and the Holy Grail* that the team's next project would be *Jesus Christ: Lust for Glory*.[78] The Pythons, after reviewing the pomposity of most 'reverent, choir-laden, star-studded gospel dramatizations'[79], realized the lack of humour to be found in the person and teaching of Jesus, 'since what he says is very fine (and Buddhist)'.[80] But there were satirical possibilities to be had in lampooning those around or associated with Jesus: according to Idle the film began life, and is intended to be seen, as 'an attack on Churches and pontificators and self-righteous assholes who claim to speak for God, of whom there are too many still on the planet'.[81]

There was, and is, no consensus within the Pythons on the nature of *Life of Brian*'s target. John Cleese gives a moral and political component: 'What is absurd is not the teachings of the founders of religion, it's what followers subsequently make of it. And I was always astonished that people didn't get that'.[82] Michael Palin insists, in disagreement with Jones and Idle, the film is not 'attacking Jesus' or 'anyone's faith or religion'. Rather, it attacks 'a kind of authoritarianism', one which 'tells you what to believe and what to do'. In carrying out this political and ethical critique, it uses a 'religious metaphor' to explore how, 'nowadays', people want 'to have their own independent voice heard', and people are 'critical of those in authority telling them what to say'. He concludes, simply, 'that's really what it's about'.[83] Gavin Millar's perceptive contemporary review concurs: 'Insofar' as the film has a 'moral

---

[78] David Morgan, *Monty Python speaks!* (1999), 224. The throwaway remark betrays a significant connection with the attitudes and belief-system of *Patton,* which we explored in the previous chapter.

[79] Clyde Jeavons, 'Review' *The Monthly Film Bulletin* (November 1979): 229.

[80] According to Idle; Morgan, *Monty Python speaks!*, 226.

[81] Morgan, *Monty Python speaks!*, 226. For a discussion on the blasphemous nature of the film see David S. Nash, *Blasphemy in the Christian World* (2007), 211–9.

[82] Chapman et al., *The Pythons' Autobiography*, 280.

[83] All Palin's quotations in this paragraph are taken from a broadcast interview with Simon Mayo, BBC Radio 5 Live, 14 September 2009.

charge', it is predicated upon 'pragmatism, common sense and tolerance'. English morality is implicitly and explicitly anti-political: the only 'stand' Brian will take is his sexual affair with the 'spitfire revolutionary', Judith. Brian is the *'homme moyen sensuel'*.[84]

However, Palin wishes to retain a political dimension to the film. In order to depict or understand Jesus, he says, we have to rely 'on interpretation, and interpretation is a *political* thing',[85] which, therefore, is susceptible to a political depiction and a political critique.

David Jasper concurs. For him the success of *Life of Brian* lies in the way it subverts the pious Jesus-films. It is a 'far more serious comedy' as it 'leaves theology out of it and endlessly exposes what we do with theology and institutional religion as a means of self-justification'. Jasper's argument doesn't make clear what the 'it' is, from which the theology has been left: is it 'hope', 'religious experience', or just the film itself? Even so, his political and ethical approval stands.[86]

The politics of Brian

What is there in in *Life of Brian* to justify this political interpretation? First, we see the way in which Brian, a sincere but inept Jew (who identifies himself as such, despite his half-Roman ancestry[87]), attempts to associate himself with an anti-Roman resistance group. Brian does not care which resistance group he joins, as long as they are opposed to the Romans. He asks 'Are you the… Judean People's Front?'. The leader of the group (whom we have already learnt has the archetypical 1970s trade-unionist's name of

---

[84] Millar, 'Blessed Brian', 673.

[85] Morgan, *Monty Python speaks!*, 227. [Emphasis in original.]

[86] David Jasper, 'Systematizing the Unsystematic', in *Explorations in Theology and Film,* Marsh and Ortiz (eds) (1997), 243.

[87] 'I'm not a Roman, Mum and I never will be! I'm a Kike! A Yid! A Hebe! A Hook-nose! I'm Kosher, Mum. I'm a Red Sea Pedestrian and proud of it!' in the screenplay, Graham Chapman et al., *Monty Python's The Life of Brian (*1979), 15. Quotations from the film will be taken from the published screenplay, (hereafter *Brian Screenplay)* corrected against the soundtrack on a DVD release of the film.

'Reg') responds angrily: 'Fuck off!... Judean People's Front!???
We're the People's Front of Judea. Judean People's Front! Cor!'.
We learn that the PFJ hate the Romans, but they hate the JPF
more: the latter are 'Wankers! 'Splitters! Bastards!'. There is
momentary confusion within the PFJ: they are not the *Popular*
Front of Judea, but the *People's* Front. The Popular Front exists,
but 'He's over there'. The sole representative of the Popular Front
is, inevitably, a 'splitter!': we have the absurdity of a *Popular* Front,
which consists of only one member, emphasised by the comic
technique of bathetic incongruity. Along with this depiction of the
lonely leader, note also the depiction, later in the film, of the solitary
follower (played by Spike Milligan), the only person in the crowds
pursuing Brian who calls upon the mass to 'stop to consider the
great significance of what Brian's coming may mean'.[88]

Brian's second mission for the PFJ is an assault on Pilate's
Palace, through the drains, as a result of which they intend to
kidnap Pilate's wife and hold her to ransom. Reg, the 'glorious
leader and founder of the PFJ' does not participate in the assault,
but rather co-ordinates from the sewer entrance, 'as he has a bad
back'.

So we see how, in an organization which 'exhibits a pretentious
and sanctimonious display of corporate equality',[89] the ideals of
co-ordinated action are both unrealistic ('two days to dismantle the
entire apparatus of the Roman imperialist state'), and undermined
by the 'utterly self-interested ambitions and desires of individual
members',[90] most clearly in the hypocritical actions of Reg, the
group's 'glorious leader'.

Inside the palace the PFJ encounter the Campaign for Free
Galilee (whose leader, 'Deadly Dirk', is played by John Cleese,
with a high-pitched North Welsh accent). The two revolutionary
groups begin to fight until Brian reminds them 'Brothers! We
mustn't fight with each other. Surely we should be united against
the common enemy'. The revolutionaries pause, 'in horrified
unison': 'The Judean People's Front?????'. The PFJ, the CFG,

---

[88]Stern, Jefford, and DeBona, *Savior on the Silver Screen* ((1999), 244.
[89]Cyrino, *Big Screen Rome*, 189–90.
[90]Cyrino, *Big Screen Rome*, 189–90.

the 'Judean Popular People's Front', and, presumably, the JPF, are all 'paralyzed to inactivity', by the 'gender-pronoun precision and the inflated rhetoric of oppression' in which they are required to 'to draw up resolutions and exercise the democratic process'.[91] Leaders, like Reg, are not to be trusted. Popular movements, which pay lip-service to democratic processes, are sclerotically ineffective.

On the other hand, Brian's naïve idealism does lead to accomplishments: he is able to paint 'Romanes Eunt Domus' ('People called Romanes, they go the house?!') a hundred times, in letters ten feet high! across the Forum. He is also able to escape Roman arrest (with the assistance of an alien spacecraft), and, despite having led the Fifth Legion to the headquarters of the PFJ, is able to escape again by pretending to be a prophet. A small crowd is initially impressed by his entrance (falling from a great height), but they are hostile and sceptical when he begins to teach ('Don't pass judgment on other people, or else you might get judged, too'). His pastiche of the Sermon on the Mount is greeted by literalistic questions: which birds need to be considered, why should the lilies of the field get jobs, what were the names of 'two servants'? In panic, as Romans come closer to arrest him, Brian's pastiche breaks down into nonsense ('Blessed are they... who convert their neighbour's ox, for they shall inhibit their girth,... and to them only shall be given – to them only... shall... be...given...').

Unconvincing to a modern, extradiegetic, audience, this is the moment that Brian's intradiegetic audience begins to get intrigued by his message – which is the whole point of Python's critique of both the leader (the messiah) and the followers (the crowd / disciples): the message is unconvincing, nonsensical, and lacking in coherence, and *because* of those very characteristics will be believed as the gateway to 'the secret of Eternal Life'. It is by refusing to tell the 'secret', because he knows there is no secret, that Brian is first called 'Master' (by 'Arthur', played by Cleese). The crowd, portrayed as those who seek answers, are 'depicted in a markedly negative way, first hostile and demanding, then fawning

---

[91] Cyrino, *Big Screen Rome*, 189–90.

and fanatic'.[92] This is the nature of followers, according to the anthropology of Python.

The crowds of Brian

In this respect, Philip Davies is wrong when he contrasts the treatment of the crowd in *Life of Brian* and the crowds in the New Testament. In the New Testament, according to Davies, the crowd is merely a 'foil for dominical exploits', passively 'hearing, receiving, or just gathering'.[93] Instead, he says, they are the 'hero' in *Life of Brian*, 'stealing the initiative in listening to sermons, in stoning, in heckling the teller of parables, in creating a messiah, in ridiculing the Roman governor…'[94] But these are still *reactive* actions. The crowd never takes the initiative. Rather, they are so blinded by their need to be a *crowd*, to find someone, anyone, to follow, that they do not see the absurdity of their actions. As Palin put it, he was always more interested in 'people who get in the way of heroes *being* heroes'.[95] Thus, Brian, who is, if not the hero, then at least the protagonist, is pursued into the wilderness by the crowd, as they divide on the nature of the sign that the new Messiah has given them – is it a shoe or is it a gourd?[96] Everything is over-interpreted by the crowd: following Brian to the desert is a sign, a juniper bush is a miracle, being told to leave is 'a blessing!'. Even when Brian tells the crowd to 'Fuck off!', it can be incorporated into their followership: 'How shall we fuck off, O Lord?' asks Arthur, who has promoted himself into a Peter-role of chief interpreter, guardian and confessor of Brian's messianic status. It is Arthur who leads the crowd in a salutation of Brian's true, revealed nature:

---

[92] Cyrino, *Big Screen Rome*, 189.

[93] Philip R. Davies, '"Life of Brian" Research', in *Whose Bible Is It Anyway?* (2004), 153. Davies enumerates 14 occasions in Matthew, 24 in Mark, 15 in Luke, and 9 in John for this passive role.

[94] Davies, "Life of Brian' Research', 153.

[95] Morgan, *Monty Python speaks!*, 227. Emphasis in original.

[96] As Davies perceptively points out, also the sign of Jonah [Jonah 4:6-10, AV]: "Life of Brian' Research", 147.

ARTHUR: Hail Messiah!

BRIAN: I'm not the Messiah!

ARTHUR: I say you are Lord, and I should know. I've followed a few.

When violence breaks out Brian escapes again. He spends the night with the object of his lust, Judith Iscariot, but, in a moment of post-coital bliss, he opens the shutters of his house onto a view of the assembled mob, one even greater than the day before. He attempts once more to preach ('Please, please, please listen. I've got one or two things to say'); it is the Gospel of individualism and personal individuation:

BRIAN: Look. You've got it all wrong. You don't need to follow *me*. You don't *need* to follow anybody! You've got to think for yourselves. You're *all* individuals!

FOLLOWERS: Yes, we're all individuals!

BRIAN: You're all different!

FOLLOWERS: Yes, we are all different!

DENNIS: I'm not.

'Dennis', played by Terence Bayler, is the drunk who originally tried to buy Brian's gourd. The only person who recognizes a distinction between individual and crowd is a drunk, who denies the existence of that distinction. In a self-consciously English pantomime idiom, we can see clearly what Michael Palin later called the 'message' of the film, a message identical to the essence of the Pythons' humour: 'It was the freedom of the individual, a very Sixties thing, the independence which was part of the way Python had been formed...'[97] In a curious way, the Pythons reflected an anthropology which seems innate to the British Isles, indeed, has been called the 'British heresy'.[98] It follows the work of Pelagius,[99] who

---

[97] Palin in Chapman et al., *The Pythons' Autobiography*, 306.

[98] Named as such by Leo Sherley-Price's introduction to Bede, *History of the English Church and People* (1968), note to Bk. 1.10 on 339, without a source, as if it were a proverbial identification.

[99] The usual caveats apply: Pelagius was most likely not a 'Pelagian' – just as Karl

taught 'the need of the individual to define himself, and to feel free to create his own values in the midst of the conventional, second-rate life of society'.[100]

John Godfrey relates an instance of the working out of (semi) Pelagianism in British society. A British bishop named Fastidius (a Pythonesque name?) taught 'A Christian is he who shows pity to all, who is not in any way troubled by injury, who does not allow a poor man to be oppressed if he be present'.[101] Godfrey's description of Fastidius' work could, almost, be applied to the self-expressed ideology of Python: 'The book is free of fanaticism or rancour, and with its humane, pious, and cultured tone, represents a type of Christianity which may well have been common in Britain at this time, and which has much to commend it'.[102]

Certainly, Davies believes that the portrayal of Brian adheres to this form of exemplary humanism. Brian is Everyman, the 'human nature of the dichotomized Messiah'. He represents a 'meek and mild' humanity, victimised and 'rarely, if ever, the instigator', a 'true "man for others"'. He is betrayed by everyone in whom he places his trust; mother, fellow revolutionaries, girlfriend, disciples:

> He is never the real leader, but rather that parodic leader, the stooge. He is the disciple of others, even when having messi-ahship foisted on him and when being betrayed by his own band of revolutionaries.[103]

It is unclear why Davies qualifies 'parodic leader' with 'stooge'. The Oxford English Dictionary says that 'stooge', possibly deriving from 'stage assistant', means: 'A person whose function is merely to carry out another's directions; an unquestioningly loyal or obsequious subordinate, a lackey; a person used as an instrument by someone behind the scenes, a cat's paw' (OED). Surely,

---

Marx was never a Marxist.

[100] Peter Brown, *Augustine of Hippo* (2000), 346–7.

[101] Fastidius, *De Vita Christiana* XIV, cited by John Godfrey, *The Church in Anglo-Saxon England* (1962), 28. Fastidius probably wrote between AD 420 and 430.

[102] Godfrey, *The Church in Anglo-Saxon England*, 28.

[103] Davies, "Life of Brian' Research', 151.

therefore 'stooge' is the better definition of the way in which *followers* are regarded in the film?

Brian's passivity, for Davies, is admirable: 'His inability to accept any initiative and his willingness to be led into even the most dubious of causes displays a benevolence towards fellow humans that induces sympathy in the audience'. The audience can self-identify with Brian, in the richness of his humanity: an '*imitatio Briani* is almost inevitable'.[104]

The nihilism of Brian

This is a far too optimistic and benevolent interpretation of the way in which Brian is depicted, and the real 'message' of the film. If there is a hero in *Life of Brian*, and the political outlook of the Pythons probably precludes such a creature, then the only feasible candidate is neither Brian, nor Davies's corporate candidate of the crowd, but rather 'Mr Cheeky', a character played by Eric Idle.

Cheeky is the man who begins the fight at the Sermon on the Mount, and the crucifixion victim who, at first claims to have been freed ('They said I hadn't done anything, so I could go free and live on an island somewhere'), then refuses to be intimidated by the soldiers crucifying him ('You mean I might have to give up being crucified in the afternoons?'), and finally has the presence of mind to claim to be Brian of Nazareth when a pardon arrives ('No, I'm only joking. I'm not really Brian... It was a joke'.). Contrast Mr Cheeky's existential insouciance with the parodic 'I am Spartacus' reaction of the rest of those being crucified, all of whom claim to be Brian: 'I'm Brian. And so's my wife'. Kubrick's celebration of collective solidarity is now parodied as 'the clamorous urge for self-preservation among those being crucified, with no thought whatsoever to Brian's survival'.[105]

The anthropology of Monty Python is deeply pessimistic. In the face of the fact of existential annihilation, the best that can be said

---

[104] Davies, "Life of Brian' Research', 151.
[105] Cyrino, *Big Screen Rome*, 192.

is to 'look on the bright side of life'.[106] This, paradoxically, undercuts the Pythons' Pelagianism: there is an unconscious contrast between what is expressed and what is depicted. Whereas for Pelagius, and the Pythons' espoused anthropology, the target is 'the heavy artifice of society', in order to uncover the 'raw bones of heroic individuality',[107] the actual performance of the Python world-view shows that there are no heroes, and there can be no moral value expressed through being either a leader or a follower. Both roles are merely opportunities to exhibit the venal and corrupt nature of humanity. If one did not know the Pythons' approach to organized religion, one might say that they exhibit an almost Augustinian anthropology. For, as Augustine expressed it in one of his anti-Pelagian writings, 'many sins are committed through pride; but yet not all things which are wrongly done are done proudly – at any rate, not by the ignorant, not by the infirm, and not, generally speaking, by the weeping and sorrowful'.[108] Which sounds like motivation notes for the protagonists of *Life of Brian*.

Suspicion and leadership redux

We have seen how in Kubrick's genre-films, and in the humour of *Life of Brian*, there is 'a kind of hothouse for forced, quick breeding of attitudes and feelings'.[109] The hothouse has displayed the deep, focused, and passionately held antipathy towards the forms of leadership which constitute military and religious societies (and thus, by extension, all society). In *Life of Brian* the antipathy is directed against everyone who seeks to act as a leader, and also everyone who seeks to be a follower. In Kubrick's *Full Metal Jacket* the antipathy is personified, on a vicarious level, by Mickey Mouse,

---

[106] It is not insignificant that the closing song is sung by Idle, if not as Eric Idle the Monty Python member, then certainly as an protagonist from outside the world of the film: Mr Cheeky's creator is the man who chews on life's gristle.

[107] Brown, *Augustine of Hippo*, 350.

[108] Augustine of Hippo, 'On Nature and Grace', in vol. 5, *Nicene and Post-Nicene Fathers of the Christian Church*, chapter XXIX (33).

[109] Young, 'War of Independence', 10.

who stands as an avatar for John Wayne, who stands, in turn, as the avatar of Leadership. 'John Wayne' never went away, and in the next chapter we shall explore how he re-emerged in the cinema of 'leadership redux'.

Chapter 6

Citizen soldiers:

Leadership redux

The West is the best,
The West is the best.
Get here and we'll do the rest...
The killer awoke before dawn
He put his boots on
He took a face from the ancient gallery
And he walked on down the hall...

'THE END', THE DOORS, 1967

We saw in Chapter 3 how the American *mythos* came to dominate cinema from all countries and cultures. We further saw how this *mythos* developed from the American experience of the Frontier. We saw the importance for American self-understanding of the cardinal bearing, Westwards, which functions as the locus of the American *mythos*. We saw how Emerson, through his synthesis of the myths of the American Frontier and the American Adam, formed the true 'American Religion', a quest for the self and the individual. We saw in the last chapter how American cinema attempted, following World War Two, to repudiate traditionally understood and enacted values of heroism and leadership, and how one man, John

Wayne, became the focus for this rejected concept of leadership. In this chapter, we shall examine why and how Wayne became the personified avatar of *MythL,* and how, despite *and because of* the repudiation, the avatar remains intact today.

The free man, living greatly

The triumph of *MythL* in our culture is the triumph of the American Adam, who finds expression, most powerfully, in the symbiosis of the West and Wayne. Wayne himself recognized, at the end of his career, the importance of the 'West' as the touchstone of American culture and myth:

> The fellows I worked with over the last 30 years authenticated what the West was like. Now people making movies are running out of ideas. They're making up all kinds of things. It used to be that the western was folklore and legend. Now it's all psychological, innuendos and petty fights.[1]

Wayne responded romantically to the idea and the possibilities of the West. In this he was characteristic of wider American culture. According to one of the earliest, and most astute, commentators on the American West, Bernard De Voto, to both understand and be realistic about the Westward *mythos*, is to respond to its romanticism:

> Sure you're romantic about American history. ...[I]t is the most romantic of all histories. It began in myth and has developed through centuries of fairy stories. Whatever the time is in America it is always, at every moment, the mad and wayward hour when the prince is finding the little foot that alone fits into the slipper of glass. ...Ours is a story mad with the impossible, it is by chaos out of dream, it began as dream and it has continued as dream down to the last headlines you read in a newspaper.[2]

---

[1] P. F. Kluge, 'First and Last, a Cowboy', *Life*, 28 January 1972.
[2] In a letter to his collaborator Catherine Drinker Bowen, quoted by her in *Adventures*

It was only by being romantic that the myth of the American West could exist, and in doing so, be psychologically useful. In an article for *Harper's*[3], published 40 years before Wayne's complaint, De Voto showed how the actor's complaint was inaccurate: folklore and psychology were doing the same thing. De Voto described the political, economic and psychological factors involved in the formation of the Western folklore. He noted, first, that westerners originally did not have a good reputation in American society: in the 'metropolitan press' the westerner is depicted as 'the national wildman, the thunder-bringer, disciple of madness, begetter of economic heresy, immortal nincompoop deluded by maniac visions'. He is endlessly complaining, being a drain on the public purse, 'forever scuttling the ship of state'.

But immediately you place the clamouring ninny in cowboy clothes ('Put a big hat on his head, cover the ragged overalls with hair pants and let high heels show beneath them, knot a bandanna round his neck'), he becomes 'one of the few romantic symbols in American life'. He is no longer a profligate fool but 'a free man living greatly, a rider into the sunset, enrapturer of women in dim theaters, solace of routine-weary men who seek relief in wood pulp, a figure of glamour in the reverie of adolescents, the only American who has an art and a literature devoted wholly to his celebration'. As De Voto say, dryly, '[o]ne perceives a certain incompatibility between these avatars'.

De Voto identified two different and incompatible public protagonists in American society: the Westerner (a nincompoop) and the Cowboy (an atavistic hero). The latter is the former with 'a mere change of clothes'.[4] We have here, intended or otherwise, an impersonation, and, as with all impersonations, a question of authenticity. Who, and what, is real?

---

of a Biographer (Boston; Toronto: Little Brown, 1959), 106.
[3]Originally in an article for *Harper's Magazine* in 1934; later reprinted as 'The West: a plundered province', in *The Western Paradox* (2000).
[4]All from De Voto, 'Plundered Province', 4.

Faking authenticity

That isn't a valid or a necessary question. Reality, when it comes
to mythology, isn't an important factor. We can see how this is so
with an example from the life and career of a man so important
to *MythL*: John Wayne. When *Sands of Iwo Jima* was released it
was singled out for praise by General Douglas MacArthur, no less,
at a Convention for the American Legion Convention. He said of
John Wayne, in his portrayal of Sergeant Stryker, 'You represent
the American serviceman better than the American serviceman
himself'.[5] Wayne was 34 when America entered the war, seven
years younger than Clark Gable, six years younger than Tyrone
Power, and the same age as Gene Autry, all of whom served with
distinction. Wayne began the war classified for the purposes of the
draft as 3-A (family deferment), and ended it as 2-A (deferment in
'support of national health, safety, or interest') following the intervention of Republic Pictures. He did not serve in the military during
World War Two.[6]

John Wayne did not serve, and yet he came to personify
and embody American military service. MacArthur's statement
'suggests that Wayne's mythic figure is not merely a representation
but a valid substitute for and even improvement on the real thing'.[7]
Or, as Eco neatly summarised in another context:

> ...the American imagination demands the real thing and, to
> attain it, must fabricate the absolute fake.[8]

John Wayne is both absolute fake, and absolutely authentic when it
comes to the *MythL* based upon the myth of the American Adam.

---

[5] At least, as reported by Wayne himself to Richard Warren Lewis in an interview
for *Playboy Magazine*, May 1971; reprinted in Judith M. Riggin, *John Wayne: a
bio-bibliography* (1992), 31–67.
[6] See Garry Wills, *John Wayne* (1997), 107–10; Roberts and Olson, *John Wayne,
American* (1997), 211–213.
[7] Richard Slotkin, *Gunfighter Nation* (1992), 514.
[8] Umberto Eco, *Travels in Hyperreality* (1975), 8.

Half myth, half movie star[9]

This transformation of John Wayne, from the sidelines (of war) to the heroic heart, we can see most clearly in his participation in the three films made by John Ford beginning in 1948, *Fort Apache*, *She Wore a Yellow Ribbon* and *Rio Grande*:[10] the so-called 'Cavalry Trilogy'.

Wayne had worked with Ford before the war, in which Ford himself had served with distinction as a military photographer and filmmaker.[11] When Ford returned to civilian filmmaking in the post-war period his films were influenced by his wartime experiences, and the uncertainties of the developing Cold War. The Cavalry Trilogy films are explorations of the 'ideological concerns of the World War and its aftermath',[12] concerns which are all the more powerful by moving the setting from combat in the Pacific theatre (which Ford had shown in his documentary *The Battle of Midway* and his feature film *They Were Expendable*), into the 'mythic landscape of the Western'.[13] By doing so, Ford 'proposed a mythic response'[14] to, and critique of, both the Western victory in Europe and the Pacific and the West's response to super-power Soviet Communism. He used the American past 'to seek historical or mythical answers to the problems that troubled him in the present'.[15] It was inevitable that Ford chose the genre of the Western as it was 'a vital medium for reflecting and articulating crucial issues of modern American society'.[16] The Western, because it takes place in the mythological heart of American self-understanding, and because it is so 'implicitly bound up with

---

[9]A subheading description of Wayne in Kluge, 'First and Last, a Cowboy'.

[10]The best biography of John Ford is Joseph McBride, *Searching for John Ford* (2003). To this may be added two works of 'Fordolatry', Peter Bogdanovich, *John Ford* (1968); Lindsay Anderson, *About John Ford* (1981). An excellent examination of Ford's films is William Darby, *John Ford's Westerns* (1996).

[11]See McBride, *Searching*, chapter 10. Ford was injured during the Battle of Midway.

[12]Slotkin, *Gunfighter Nation*, 334.

[13]Slotkin, *Gunfighter Nation*, 334.

[14]Slotkin, *Gunfighter Nation*, 334.

[15]McBride, *Searching*, 418.

[16]Michael Coyne, *The Crowded Prairie* (1997), 33.

pride in the American experience',[17] Ford was able to affirm 'the importance of the patriotic solidarity that made victory possible'[18]; victory in the Indian Wars of the 1870s and 1880s, and victory in the war against fascism in the 1940s. More pertinently for our requirements, 'all three films of the loosely connected Cavalry trilogy revolve around a crisis of leadership'.[19]

John Ford did not think that he was doing anything particularly sophisticated: he had a modest description of his career: 'My name's John Ford. I make Westerns'.[20] He denied that he was making art:

> You say someone's called me the greatest poet of the Western saga. I am not a poet, and I don't know what a Western saga is. I would say that is horseshit. I am just a hardnosed, hard-working, run-of-the-mill director.[21]

Lindsay Anderson did not think much of *Fort Apache*: it was not 'a very satisfactory film'. He thought the 'casting was weak', with some minor parts 'poorly played' and Henry Fonda was 'unhappily miscast'.[22] His opinion is in the minority. Bosley Crowther said Ford's work was that of a 'genuine artist', in which '[e]very episode, every detail of drama and personality is crisply and tautly realized'.[23] James Agee was prepared to forgive John Ford the poor acting ('Shirley Temple and her husband, John Agar, handle the love interest as if they were sharing a soda-fountain special...') for the verve of the direction and 'a good deal of the camera work which sneaks by as incidental are somewhere near enduring the rest for'.[24] Later critics were able to recognize the film's narrative and aesthetic pleasures:

---

[17] Coyne, *Crowded Prairie*, 33.

[18] Slotkin, *Gunfighter Nation*, 334.

[19] McBride and Wilmington, *John Ford* (1974), 97.

[20] This is the pithier version of what Ford might actually have said: see the discussion in McBride, *Searching*, 759.

[21] Walter Wagner, *You Must Remember This* (1975), 65.

[22] Anderson, *About John Ford*, 79.

[23] Bosley Crowther, review in *The New York Times* (25 June 1948).

[24] James Agee, review in *The Nation*, 24 July 1948.

More impressive even than the credit sequence's sweeps across Monument Valley are the vast, epic compositions of Thursday leading his columns, backed by thunderous skies, with Archie Stout's camera scarcely a foot off the ground.[25]

And *Fort Apache*'s cinematographic achievement is more than matched by its 'remarkable' ideological achievement that 'enables us to see… that an insane system may be perpetuated by noble men, and, indeed, that it needs noble and dedicated men to perpetuate itself'.[26] It is 'a seminal work of mythography'.[27]

Because Ford set all three 'Cavalry' films in the middle of the experiences of the American Cavalry during the Indian Wars he had a 'convenient structure'[28] to explore his themes: the dangers posed by the outside world, by the land and 'a fanatical race-enemy',[29] and the tensions within the regiment, ('static, unchanging… almost entirely severed from the outside world…'[30]). The regiment symbolizes American values, and yet the greatest threat to it is 'Easterners'.

Fort Apache begins with the stage coach bringing Colonel Owen Thursday[31] through the barren lands of Monument Valley. Thursday is frustrated that he has not yet arrived at his destination:

THURSDAY: What a country! Forty miles from mud hole to mud hole. *[He consults his notebook]* Mule Creek. Dead Man's Squaw. Schmidt Wells. Hangman's Flats. Hassayampa. At the end of the rainbow, Fort Apache. Fort Apache. Blast an ungrateful war department that sends a man to a post out here.[32]

---

[25] Tag Gallagher, *John Ford* (1986), 317.
[26] McBride and Wilmington, *John Ford*, 109.
[27] Slotkin, *Gunfighter Nation*, 343.
[28] Coursodon and Sauvage, *American Directors* (1983), 131.
[29] Slotkin, *Gunfighter Nation*, 335.
[30] Coursodon and Sauvage, *American Directors*, 131.
[31] The exact historical sources of Ford's film are much less important than the mythology celebrated.
[32] The screenplay was by Frank S. Nugent, 'suggested by' the short-story by James Warner Bellah, 'Massacre', *Saturday Evening Post*, (1947).

With him is his daughter, Philadelphia (played by Shirley Temple, in her first film with John Ford since *Wee Willie Winkie*). Their conversation tells us that Thursday has recently been stationed in Europe, where Thursday wishes he were still.

When Colonel Thursday arrives in Fort Apache, complete with daughter, history and grievances, his new command react with suspicion towards him. Those suspicions are justified by his origins in the East, and his desire to return there as swiftly as possible:

> The kind of man they [the Westerners] most admire is one who has evolved rules for the conduct of life out of his own brain by the help of his own observation; and they entertain a strong distrust of men who have learned what they know by a fixed course of study, mainly because persons who have passed the early part of their lives in learning out of books or from teachers are generally found less fitted to grapple with the kind of difficulties which usually present themselves in Western life, than those who were compelled to learn to conquer them by actual contact with them.[33]

Thursday immediately and unpatriotically antagonizes his men with his interruption of the dance held in honour of General Washington's birthday. The next morning Thursday calls his senior officers to him, and reads his orders to them. York is relieved of command, Captain Collingwood (George O'Brien) is relieved as adjutant, and both are returned to their troops. Thursday makes it clear that he did not wish to be in command at Fort Apache, but as he has to be there, 'I intend to make this regiment the finest on the frontier'. He will achieve this by eliminating the carelessness that has grown up around 'dress and deportment... The uniform, gentlemen, is not a subject for individual, whimsical expression'.[34] York and his fellow officers are implicitly criticised by the camera

---

[33] Edwin L. Godkin, 'Aristocratic Opinions of Democracy', *North American Review* (1865): 218.

[34] Gradually, though, we see Thursday adapting to his environment and deviating from regulation uniform. On his first patrol against Diablo's band he adopts non-regulation head-gear.

through the use of close-ups for their slouch hats and bandanas. In a tropic use of 'Hollywood irony', Thursday tells the officers 'Understand me, gentlemen, I am not a martinet'. The inference we take is that he is exactly that. Later, Thursday realizes that the Apache revolt is being fomented by a 'well-known' warband leader, Cochise. Over six campaigns Cochise has 'out-generaled us, out-fought us, out-run us', Collingwood recalls. Thursday muses on the possibility of being 'the man who brought Cochise back', and Collingwood stares at him in shock, realizing that from then on 'the commander will be working for his own posterior glory at the expense of his men's lives'.[35]

Thursday is portrayed, made into, the anti-archetype of the right, proper, and noble hero. He cannot possibly be a Cavalry man. Opposed to the values and actions of Thursday is York. At the beginning of the film the contrasts between them are so clear that they can be tabulated:[36]

Thursday	York
East	West
Europe	Frontier
West Point	Fort Apache
book knowledge	wilderness knowledge
individual	family and community
glory	duty

This is the beginning of the film. By the end, after Thursday's futile death, York has been transformed. His anti-regulation dress and manner have changed into an imitation of his dead commander. He wears Thursday's havelock cap, instead of a slouch hat. As McBride and Wilmington put it: 'It is impossible to put too much stress on this gesture; it implies nothing less than York's tragic

---

[35] McBride and Wilmington, *John Ford*, 106.
[36] Jim Kitses, *Horizons West* (2004), 64.

submission to Thursday's vainglory, and, through this 'obedient rebel', the submission of the Cavalry itself'.[37] York is the memorial of Thursday, both through his imitation and also in what he says to the press about the dead colonel:

> YORK: No man died more gallantly. Nor won more honour for his regiment.
> REPORTER: Of course, you're familiar with the famous painting of 'Thursday's Charge', sir?
> YORK: Yes, I saw it when last in Washington.
> SECOND REPORTER: That was a magnificent work. There were these massed columns of Apaches in their warpaint and feathered bonnets. And here was Thursday, leading his men in that heroic charge.
> YORK: Correct in every detail.

The second reporter consciously or unconsciously uses the word 'legend' to describe Thursday's new status: 'the newspapers – with the help of those Army men who witnessed the spectacle – are writing the birth of a legend, creating a noble leader who died with his men…'[38]

It would seem on a first viewing (and repeated viewings) of *Fort Apache*, that York is portrayed as the archetypical Western hero, and that Thursday is (clearly) the Easterner villain, shallow, self-seeking, socially isolated, and destined to come to a bad end. But the final scene tells us and shows us that Thursday, through mythological action and then in reality, secured by his actions the future of the regiment and the victory of Ameica, represented by the American Cavalry and its flags: Mrs Collingwood, watching her husband and his men riding out to battle from the rooftops of Fort Apache, declares 'I can't see him – all I can see is the flags'.[39] Her husband has been visually, and completely, subsumed into the symbols of the Cavalry and the state. Thursday thus has truly

---

[37] McBride and Wilmington, *John Ford*, 108.
[38] Bogdanovich, *John Ford*, 34.
[39] For the mythological and ideological importance of this scene, see McBride, *Searching*, 30; Leland Poague, 'All I Can See Is the Flags' *Cinema Journal* (1988).

become, in the eyes of the film, a leader worthy of imitation, even if it is a leadership of symbolism. But in order for him to be that, he had to fail as a man, a father and a friend. Thursday is a leader *by being* socially isolated.

York glorified the memory of Thursday for the sake of the regiment and its morale in the Indian wars. It was an attitude and a sacrifice that Wayne himself imbued: 'I don't believe in giving authority and positions of leadership and judgment to irresponsible people'.[40] York was not an irresponsible person: he realized that the war would continue and so the regiment, and its *mythos*, needed to continue as well:

> Ford is saying that the Cavalry, in fact the country, lives on despite the errors of any one leader; and if printing a falsehood will help the morales [sic] of the Cavalry or the nation – then print the legend.[41]

But Ford has actually depicted something more than the mere printing of the legend: he has shown how events have become legendary, and in doing so, begin to exercise their influence over men, even men as sympathetically portrayed as Captain York. 'Truth' and 'reality' have nothing to do with the power of the legend: as Slotkin puts it: 'We are to continue to believe in our myths despite our knowledge that they are untrue'.[42]

Michael Coyne gives an interesting suggestion as to why this might be so, to explain why York ends up doing what he does. He suggests that York's surrender to the ethos of the regiment shows that he is actually 'the consummate organization man, a true corporate liberal'.[43] He cites William Whyte's sociology of business, *The Organization Man*, in which white-collar (if not yellow bandana) workers are the ones

---

[40] Warren Lewis, 'Playboy Interview'. Wayne was controversially, but unsurprisingly, talking about 'giving' leadership responsibilities to black Americans.
[41] Bogdanovich, *John Ford*, 34.
[42] Slotkin, *Gunfighter Nation*, 342.
[43] Coyne, *Crowded Prairie*, 59.

of our middle class who have left home, spiritually as well as physically, to take the vows of organization life, and it is they who are the mind and soul of our great self-perpetuating institutions. Only a few are top managers or ever will be. ...But they are the dominant members of our society nonetheless. ...it is from their ranks that are coming most of the first and second echelons of our leadership, and it is their values which will set the American temper.[44]

This explains why York 'capitulates' at the end of *Fort Apache*, taking on the myth and the uniform of Thursday: 'between themselves and organization they believe they see an ultimate harmony and, more than most elders recognize, they are building an ideology that will vouchsafe this trust'.[45] York's final speech in the film, over the ghostly image of the dead troopers, shows the surrender of individual to the collective, the triumph of the organization. The dead soldiers (like 'Collingworth') haven't been forgotten, because

...they haven't died. They're living, right out there. Collingwood and the rest. They'll keep on living as long as the regiment lives. ...The faces may change, the names, but they're there, they're the regiment. The regular army, now and fifty years from now. They're better men than they used to be. Thursday did that. He made it a command to be proud of.[46]

In *Rio Grande* John Wayne plays Lt Col. Kirby Yorke (the same character, in all but rank and a variation in spelling his surname, as he played in *Fort Apache*), an American cavalry officer estranged from his (Confederate) wife and son since he burnt down her family plantation during the Civil War 15 years before. When Yorke learns that his son (Claude Jarman Jr.) has been expelled from West Point, enlisted as a trooper and been posted to his father's command, he addresses the recruits:

---

[44] William H. Whyte, *The Organization Man* (1956), 3.

[45] Whyte, *Organization Man*, 4.

[46] Note the echoes of Sergeant Hartman's 'regimental immortality' from *Full Metal Jacket* discussed on p. 154.

YORKE: I don't want you men to be fooled about what's coming up for you. Torture? At least that. The war department promised me at least one hundred eighty men. They sent me eighteen all told. You are the eighteen. [CLOSE] So, each one of you will have to do the work of ten men. If you fail I'll have you spread-eagled on a wagon wheel. [CUT TO TROOPER YORKE] If you desert you'll be found, tracked down and broken into bits. That is all.

The recruits are taken by the sergeants for training, except for Trooper Yorke, who is escorted to his father's tent. Yorke establishes how long it is since he last saw his son, and yet how displeased he is that he failed at West Point. He makes it clear that there is to be no nepotism on his post:

YORKE: Well, on the official record, you're my son. But on this post you're just another trooper. You heard me tell the recruits what I need from them. Twice that I will expect from you. At Chapultepec my father, your grandfather, shot for cowardice the son of a United States senator. That was his duty. I will do mine. You've chosen my way of life. I hope you have the guts to… endure it. But put out of your mind any romantic ideas that it's a way of glory. It's a life of suffering and hardship and uncompromising devotion to your oath and your duty.

But Ford doesn't allow the scene to end on such a hard statement of arid duty. Trooper Yorke refuses to dismiss until his salute is properly returned, according to 'Army regulations', and, when he leaves the tent, Col. Yorke measures his son's height against the tent's roof, as the extradiegetic music modulates from a martial flourish into a more domestic theme.

We can see two things from this sequence. First, to be a true leader (and Yorke is a true leader in the eyes of the film) there is no apparent distinction, on the surface, from being an unsympathetic martinet: Yorke's speech to the recruits is as uncompromising as Thursday's speech to his officers. However, second, we see that the true leader tempers his severity with both an overwhelming sense of duty (Yorke's willingness to shoot a senator's son if duty calls for it) and a private, unexpressed, affection for those in his care.

Even though Thursday ultimately succeeded as the symbol of a leader, he failed as a man because he was isolated from his community, represented by his daughter, his domestic accommodation, and his relationship with his fellow officers. Yorke is a more sympathetic character but even he cannot escape the inevitable consequences of being a leader. He is alone and isolated; his family is removed from him by his sense of duty. Even when his estranged wife comes to the Fort to buy out their son, she acknowledges that she can never overcome her rival, the American Cavalry. She describes Yorke as 'that ramrod, wrecked ruin. The same old Kirby'. To be a leader is to be cast off from society and all that makes us human.

But, as we have already seen, to be cast off from society does not mean being cast-off from the Organization. The immortality which accrues to true members of the Marines, the Cavalry, the Regiment, the Organization, is the feudal *fief* which derives from surrendering to the power of *MythL*. The importance of this idea to Ford and *MythL* is seen in the way an encomium to the past and future men of the regiment is repeated in the closing narration of *She Wore A Yellow Ribbon*:

> So here they are, the dog-faced soldiers, the regulars, the fifty-cents-a-day professionals, riding the outposts of a nation. From Fort Reno to Fort Apache, from Sheridan to Stark, they were all the same: men in dirty shirt blue and only a cold page in the history books to mark their passing. But wherever they rode, and whatever they fought for, that place became the United States.

This is the means by which the American Adam and the isolated, heroic individual *MythL*, has survived its apparent repudiation in the films of the previous chapter. The American Adam may remain the heroic, isolated leader, just so long as he leads citizen soldiers.

'...an ordinary man doing the best he can'[47]

In 1998 Hollywood returned to this theme, in the most spectacular, impressive, and profitable means imaginable. Steven Spielberg's *Saving Private Ryan* received near, but not universal, adulation. It earned $440 million worldwide in its first three years of release, and received five Academy Awards, including Best Director for Spielberg. It is a film which 'radiates grace, gravitas, and good intentions'.[48]

'Sheer massed authenticity'

Part of Steven Spielberg's 'good intentions' was to present an 'authentic' record of the Normandy invasion of 1944. In his many interviews to publicise the film Spielberg repeated, again and again, his desire 'to recreate the Omaha Beach landing the way the veterans experienced it, not the way Hollywood producers and directors have imagined it'. He was 'trying to show something the war film really hadn't dared to show'[49]. This was an issue of morality, setting aside any aesthetic considerations. Spielberg told media representatives in Los Angeles:

> You know, in this age of disclosure, it would have been irrespon-
> sible for me to undercut the truth of what that war was like...
> There have been 84 World War II films that showed something
> else. This would have been the 85th slap in the face to the men
> who died knowing the truth.[50]

In order to do this, Spielberg and his team assembled (and publi-cized their assembling) the greatest number of authentic World

---

[47] John Wrathall's description of Captain Miller in a review for *Sight and Sound* (1998).
[48] Thomas Doherty, *Cineaste* (15 December 1998): 68.
[49] In an interview quoted by Suid, *Guts and Glory*, 626.
[50] Judith I. Brennan, 'Rating the Big One', *The Los Angeles Times*, 15 July 1998.

War Two weapons, uniforms, insignia and regulations since, if
not the Normandy landings then certainly, the filming of *The
Longest Day*,[51] the film which most critics took as the baseline
measure of Spielberg's achievement. The filmmakers' dedication
was recognized by the critics: 'Like monks bent over an illuminated
manuscript', Spielberg and his crew paid 'attention to martial
detail'.[52] The film crew refought the Normandy landings 'with a
degree of hard detail unprecedented in fictional Cinema'.[53] As Neal
Ascherson put it, 'Spielberg's method is to smash through all the
philosophical problems [in the depiction of war] by sheer massed
"authenticity"'.[54] Despite his ambivalence about the film's political
intentions, Ascherson concludes 'at the end, almost anyone must
feel: "Yes, that is what it must have been like."'[55]

This meant, for some critics, that *Ryan* was unlike any other war
film ever made. James Wolcott referred to the 'cornball, recruiting
poster legend of John Wayne'[56]; Derek Malcolm tells us *Ryan* 'is
not a John Wayne movie. It is trying desperately hard to say that
war is an obscenity'.[57] They believed that Spielberg was attempting
to make something 'authentic' (whatever that might mean). The
paradox is the attempt at authenticity required a huge degree of
artistic manipulation. As Spielberg acknowledged:

[We] stripped all the glossy filters and filaments from the lenses
so they were just like the kind of lenses they actually used in the
Second World War. We shot a lot of the war sequences with the
shutter speed used by those Bell and Howell cameras of the
1940s for making newsreels.[58]

---

[51] John Wayne played Lt Col. Benjamin Vandervoort, commanding officer of 2nd
Battalion, 505th Parachute Infantry Regiment (82nd Airborne). In 1944 Vandervoort
was 27 years old; when Wayne made the film he was 55.

[52] Doherty, 'Ryan [review]', 68.

[53] Geoff Brown, *The Times* (10 September 1998).

[54] Neal Ascherson, 'Missing In Action', *The Observer*, 6 September 1998. Note the
distancing quotation marks used by Ascherson.

[55] Ascherson, 'Missing In Action'.

[56] James Wolcott, 'Tanks For The Memories', *Vanity Fair*, August 1998.

[57] Derek Malcolm, 'Saving the director's bacon', *The Guardian*, 6 August 1998.

[58] Linda Sunshine (ed.), *Saving Private Ryan: the men, the mission, the movie*
(1998), 79.

The colour palate was deliberately manipulated in post-production, with 'about sixty per cent of the color... extracted from the final negative'.[59] Spielberg and his cinematographer Janusz Kaminski included and created camera movement, such as shaking and wild, uncontrolled pans. The (unfiltered) camera lenses were allowed to become contaminated by sea-water and 'blood'. We viewed the beach, aware that we were viewing it through a cameraman's lens. Rather than using cuts between shots to provide the cinematic rhythm for the landings on Dog Green sector, for example, Spielberg and his editor (Michael Kahn) punctuate the sequence with camera *movement*, thus 'maintaining a greater sense of the substance of the pro-filmic event'.[60] To make the film seem more authentic, Spielberg and Kaminski, perhaps counter-intuitively, made the audience more aware that they were watching a created artefact. It is only by drawing attention to its constructed nature that its authentic qualities are simultaneously asserted.

We can see this in the film's most celebrated sequence, the landing on Omaha beach. Throughout the 20-odd minutes, Spielberg moves the camera and privileges its point of view inconsistently. First it functions as a conventional omniscient 'point of view': we see one Higgins boat from above and to the front, and then cut to an unsteady side view of at least six boats, bow to bow, from slightly above, again, what was possible if the camera were part of the scene. The camera then shifts to point of view shots for both the attacking Rangers and the Wehrmacht defenders, before moving back to the position of the omniscient external viewer: Rangers fall into the sea, drowning as the near-silent, balletic, bullets scythe through sea and bodies filmed from a fixed, submerged, viewpoint. It then specifically assumes the point of view of Captain Miller (Tom Hanks) on the beach, and the sound design reinforces the individualisation of this point of view, with Miller's deafness replicated in the murmuring and subsonic frequencies on the soundtrack.[61] Lastly, it becomes the point of view of an otherwise unacknowledged solider following Captain Miller up the beach: we

---

[59] Janusz Kaminski in Sunshine, *Men, Mission, Movie*, 81.
[60] King, *Spectacular Narratives*, 121.
[61] Identified by Wrathall as a reference to Klimov's harrowing *Come and See*.

hear the Ranger's panting – *our* panting? – on the soundtrack. As Toby Haggith says, with the faux-documentary aesthetic assumed by Spielberg this is, to say the least, 'perplexing': 'only a suicidal cameraman flying around the battlefield in an armoured micro-light could have covered the battle at Omaha as comprehensively as Spielberg's camera-team'.[62]

Even so, *Saving Private Ryan* is an aesthetic success. We believe that this is what it must have been like, even if the data against which we measure that judgement are actually the series of combat films we have already seen: 'A viewer thinks, "This is true, I am seeing truth", but the source of visual belief comes from the nontruth of movies'.[63] And so we bracket out the historical and cinematic inconsistencies in the presentation of the film.

Spielberg's intention was clear: '…if we've done our jobs, [the audience] will think we were actually on the beach on D-Day'.[64] In the words of one critic, he aimed to 'prescriptively guide the audience's eye and understanding, as if screaming to us "This is exactly like WWII footage" or "Now you understand what the main protagonist experiences." But it is not, and we don't'.[65] As Sam Fuller put it 'You can never do it. The only way… is to fire live ammo over the heads of the people in the movie theatre'.[66]

There are theological inconsistencies in the way *Ryan* is made as well. Tom Carson, in an entertainingly dyspeptic essay, argues that Matt Damon (marvellously) plays the 'guileless farm boy' Ryan as a Jesus figure, and this means that the movie becomes a manifestation of 'what must be the ultimate American fantasy – one in which our guns and courage prevent the crucifixion, letting Jesus move to the suburbs and, in old age, take the kids on sentimental journeys back to Golgotha'.[67] *The Last Temptation of Christ* is actually the Veterans' trip to Normandy.

---

[62] Haggith, 'D-Day Filming', 348.

[63] Basinger, *Anatomy of a Genre* (2003), 177.

[64] Sunshine, *Men, Mission, Movie*, 79.

[65] Laurent Ditmann, 'Made You Look', *Film & History* (December 1998): 67–8.

[66] Lee Server, *Sam Fuller* (1994), 22, 52.

[67] Tom Carson, 'Rabid Nationalism', *Esquire*, 1 March 1999.

But those who object to the 'unauthentic' nature of *Ryan* have misunderstood the nature of the film. They have (perhaps deliberately?) taken the filmmaker at his word, and assessed the film as if it were a 'just-as-it-was' record of the events of June 1944. But *Saving Private Ryan* is neither a descriptive, nor an historical artefact. It is *normative mythology*. The 'realism' which it uses as its medium and as its goal, is a realism that 'feels real', or what we can believe might have been real, if we had been there: hence the surrendering approval of an astute critic like Ascherson. In effect, Spielberg is using 'realism' as just another cinematic technique to present an unrealistic, programmatic film.

> *Saving Private Ryan* has much less to do with what veterans or historians want us to know, and much more with what Spielberg wants us to see.[68]

An example, again from the opening sequence: Miller, shocked into stupor on the water's edge, views the horrors of the landing (flamethrowers exploding, men on fire running from a landing craft, a soldier searching for his severed arm). Then

> ...[he] reaches for his helmet, which has fallen into the sand. It remains on camera just long enough for viewers to catch its ironic significance; the helmet is in exactly the same position as the one which can be found behind the title credits and in the advertising photos of Darryl Zanuck's relentlessly heroic *The Longest Day*.[69]

Thus, even in the Omaha sequence, the part of the film most lauded for its innovative vision and moral honesty, 'Spielberg used virtually every cliché in the genre in a way that seems fresh only

---

[68] Ditmann, 'Made You Look', 66.
[69] Phil Landon, 'Realism, Genre, and "Saving Private Ryan"', *Film & History* (December 1998), 61. Later we meet a captain called 'Hamill', and Private Reiben says, of the attack on the radar station, 'I don't have a good feeling about this one'; both are references to Lucas's *Star Wars* cycle.

because of the camera work and editing'.[70] It is 'a generic war movie about a generic war'.[71]

We have measured and appreciated Ryan, not against the history of the War, but against the history of the war film. In short, the more faked it is, the more authentic it is assumed to be. Umberto Eco and John Wayne's career concur.

Saving Private genre

We can see how important the *genre* of the war film is in understanding *Ryan* if we examine the opening moments. The film begins in darkness, with a bare minimum of production titles displayed. John Williams's soundtrack is playing: a solo French horn, over a martial rhythm tapped out on snares and lower strings. As the title disappears, we hear, crackling and snapping, a flag in the wind. The solo horn is swiftly joined by others, playing in the open fifths and glissandos which, since Aaron Copland's 'western' works, have been a musical metonym for 'America'. The image of the flag fades in, but not completely. Like *Patton*, *Saving Private Ryan* begins with a full-frame image of the flag of the United States. Unlike *Patton*, this flag is the 50-star flag of the present day,[72] in movement (not pinned to the flats of a theatre wall). And, most noticeably, whereas the flag in *Patton* is pristine and depicted in its full colour range, the flag in *Ryan* is faded, washed out, almost translucent: 'Old Glory' is something less than glorious.[73]

This seems uncannily like a cinematic version of Jeanine Basinger's influential taxonomy of the War Combat film. Basinger

---

[70] Suid, *Guts and Glory*, 630.

[71] Suid, *Guts and Glory*, 634.

[72] It is intriguing how many commentators are unable to recognize which flag is portrayed when. For example, Hallet constructs his review partially around the 'fact' that this is the 48-star flag of the World War Two period: Hallet, 'Ryan [review]', 69. The 48-star flag has the stars arranged in a perfect rectangle.

[73] Curiously, in Leni Riefenstahl's *Tag der Freiheit* the first shot after the titles, fading in from black, is of the German *Nationalflagge* filmed against the sun, with a soundtrack of solo brass and timpani. The shot is strikingly similar to Spielberg's image.

presents a 'summary of the genre,'[74] made up of the 'primary units' of genre film making. Through references to the units the narrative of the film is presented. The genre begins the film's credits, which 'unfold against a *military reference*'[75] – a map, or a flag, or a regimental insignia. The credits will include the name of a *military advisor*, and a *dedication* ('to the memory of the men who…'; a quotation from a great national war leader). We are introduced to the '*group of men*, led by a *hero*' who will undertake the *mission*, necessary to achieve a significant strategic *objective* ('this mission will shorten the war by six months…'). The group will contain an outsider, 'an *observer* or *commentator*'. The hero is not the original leader, but has had 'leadership forced upon him in dire circumstances'. The group undertake the military objective, and in the undertaking, the story unfolds, and a 'series of episodes occur which alternates in uneven patterns'[76] of antitheses between action and rest, danger and safety, humour and heartbreak. We encounter the *enemy* (although it may only be through suggestion and a faceless presence). In these narrative episodes, *military iconography* (by which she means hardware and systems) is presented and demonstrated, using the medium of the group's observer as a stand-in for the civilian audience. The group is subject to internal *conflict*, which is resolved when they encounter *external conflict*. *Rituals* are enacted, both from past and the present (for example, a recreation of a Christmas celebration or discussions of post-war plans, usually whilst weapons are cleaned). Members of the group *die* ('The minorities almost always die, and die most horribly'[77]). A *climactic battle* takes place, during which 'a learning or growth process' happens. The 'situation is resolved', although it sometimes has required the death of the entire group. 'THE END appears on the screen', sometimes accompanied by a posthumous rollcall of those killed.

---

[74] Basinger, *Anatomy of a Genre*, 67–9. Basinger prints the 'primary units' of the genre in bold, which I have substituted, outside direct quotation, with italics.

[75] Basinger, *Anatomy of a Genre*, 67.

[76] Basinger, *Anatomy of a Genre*, 68.

[77] Basinger, *Anatomy of a Genre*, 69.

During the telling of the story, 'tools of cinema are employed': tension and release are indicated through cutting and camera movement; composition, lighting, art direction, and the use of documentary footage (or, indeed mock-documentary footage) all contribute to an audience's sense of 'intimacy and alienation' and its judgement about the authenticity of the story.

Ultimately, the 'audience is ennobled for having shared their combat experience, as they are ennobled for having undergone it. We are all comrades in arms'.[78]

Toplin believes that Robert Rodat, the screenwriter for *Ryan*, must surely have 'honed his skills' by reading Basinger's 'magnificent primer'.[79] He notes how Basinger's unit of the 'group' is represented by *Ryan*'s squad: 'a small U.S. military unit made up of diverse ethnic types. There is a smart aleck from Brooklyn, a Jew, a religiously inclined southern sharpshooter (who resembles Sergeant York)',[80] and so on – what Doherty called a 'multi-ethnic sampling of homo americanus'.[81] This conforms absolutely to Basinger's prescription for the 'group':

> …a mixture of unrelated types, with varying ethnic and socioeconomic backgrounds. They may be men from different military forces and/or different countries. They are of different ages. Some have never fought in combat before, and others are experienced. Some are intellectual and well-educated, others are not. They are both married and single, shy and bold, urban and rural, comic and tragic.[82]

The diversity of the group is reinforced by the symbolic nature of their geographical origins. The Mid West represents 'stability', the Southerner is naïve, but has 'good shooting ability', the New Englander is educated and the New Yorker sophisticated. Specific

---

[78] Basinger, *Anatomy of a Genre*, 69.
[79] Robert Brent Toplin, 'Hollywood's D-Day' in *Why We Fought*, Rollins and O'Connor (ed.) (2008), 310.
[80] Toplin, 'Hollywood's D-Day', 310.
[81] Doherty, 'Ryan [review]', 70.
[82] Basinger, *Anatomy of a Genre*, 69.

states are favoured, and amusingly, an area of a city: 'in the war film, Brooklyn is a state unto itself, and is almost always present one way or another'.[83] Private Reiben (Edward Burns), the soldier who articulates the internal conflict in the group, is from Brooklyn (his combat blouse is inscribed with 'Brooklyn, NY, USA'). James Ryan and his brothers are all from Iowa. By placing the Ryan brothers in Iowa,

> Spielberg equates them with archetypal Americans who live in the heartland and embody quintessential American values [in] so many Hollywood films.[84]

Within the group, the audience is represented by Corporal Timothy E. Upham (Jeremy Davies), a translator and mapmaker of 29th Infantry Regiment. Upham, whom we meet in a rear signals area in neat uniform and equipped with a typewriter, has not fired a weapon since basic training. His attempts to ingratiate himself with the group are met with hostility: basic field security has to be explained to him (do not salute the captain); he is writing a book on the 'bond of brotherhood'; he doesn't understand what 'FUBAR' means. There are strong parallels, Landon suggests, in the function of Upham as the external observer and Stovall (Dean Jagger) in *Twelve O'Clock High*: he 'mediates between the military unit and the audience'.[85] Unlike Stovall, Upham is a coward. He is 'our entry into the reality [of total war] because he sees it clearly as a vast system designed to humiliate and destroy him. And so it is. His survival depends on his doing the very best he can, yes, but even more on chance'.[86] Thus, when the group assault the radar station, Upham is left on the start line, and observes the skirmish through a sniper scope left by crack-shot Jackson (Barry Pepper). The group disappear over the skyline, and the audience sees only

---

[83] Basinger, *Anatomy of a Genre*, 69.
[84] Landon, 'Realism, Genre', 59.
[85] Landon, 'Realism, Genre', 61. 'Interestingly, the director saw himself in Upham, and screenwriter Rodat intended him "as a stand-in for the audience"'. (Quoted in Landon).
[86] Roger Ebert, review in *Chicago Sun-Times*, 24 July 1998.

Upham's point of view. The sound of the battle is overlaid with his – our? – heavy breathing.

Upham presents the vocal argument for 'decency' by not summarily executing the German POW captured at the radar station. The rest of the group realise that the needs of the mission and the realities of war and revenge require 'Steamboat Willie' (Joerg Stadler) to be shot. Upham attempts to intervene on the side of clemency: 'This isn't right. He's a prisoner. He surrendered. He *surrendered*, sir!'.

Only at the very end does Upham take action. He kills the killer of Captain Miller, the same German soldier for whom he effected a release. Upham leaps out of a shell hole and confronts six German soldiers. One is Steamboat Willie: 'I know this soldier', the German says. 'Shut your mouth', Upham responds (literally 'hold your snout!'). Willie appeals – 'Upham!' – upon which Upham shoots him dead. Willie was a prisoner. He had surrendered. To the rest of the prisoners Upham screams, 'Scram! Vanish!' as the film stock flares with light in the same way we saw in the Omaha sequence. As Roger Ebert says of Upham, '[e]ventually he arrives at his personal turning point, and his action writes the closing words of Spielberg's unspoken philosophical argument'.

The question then is, what is Spielberg's philosophical argument?

Captain Miller's message

The original advertising for *Ryan* told us that 'The Mission is a Man'. Similarly, the message of the film is also a man: Captain Miller. Miller is the only character to be given dying words about more than his own pain and suffering: he is the only character 'allowed to die imparting some sort of "message" upon us'.[87] Miller's last words, before his shaking right hand finally stops shaking, are to

---

[87] Ditmann, 'Made You Look', 65. Carpazo dies in silence in the rain; Wade dies crying for his mama; Jackson dies sniping from the bell tower, reciting Psalm 144; Mellish dies asking his killer to stop, to listen to him; Horvath (Tom Sizemore) dies, saying he just got the wind knocked out of him – no messages there.

Ryan: an emphatic 'Earn this'. Ditmann thinks this is both 'a curse or a peace offering'.[88] Doherty thinks is something more pointed: 'a reminder,'[89] directed not at Ryan but at the 'callow inheritors' of Ryan's posterity, children of the post-war generation.[90] This was recognized by one viewer:

> The message was not just for Ryan, but for everyone in the audience as well, who benefit from the sacrifices made during the Second World War.[91]

In this way, the framing of the war sequences, with the present-day visit to the cemetery, when Ryan as an old man asks his wife if he has been a good man, has he lived a decent life, is not 'blubbery'[92], or 'dully ceremonial'[93], or 'confused chauvinism'[94]: 'Better than any of the violence Spielberg thought he needed, the quiet thanks that Ryan offers at Miller's burial spot serves as the film's *raison d'être*'.[95]

In this way *Ryan* is a traditional World War Two combat film, in which the possibility of decency is a perennial theme. As Captain MacDonald says to his troops in *Beach Red*: 'This isn't the end of everything out here. Some of us are going back home, and we can't leave all that's decent on this battlefield'.[96] *Ryan* demonstrates for us that, in the brutality of war, we can know that the American GI was not brutal:

> ...the common American soldier was fundamentally a good man who loved his country and his family. He went to war out

---

[88] Ditmann, 'Made You Look', 65.

[89] Doherty, 'Ryan [review]', 71.

[90] Doherty, 'Ryan [review]', 71.

[91] Reported in 'An Internet Discussion' *Film & History* (December 1998): 73–4.

[92] Carson, 'Rabid Nationalism'.

[93] David Denby, 'Heroic Proportions', *New York*, 27 July 1998.

[94] Hallet, 'Ryan [review]', 69.

[95] Suid, *Guts and Glory*, 637.

[96] Wilde's film is a clear ancestor of the Omaha beach landing in *Ryan*, opening as it does with a 30-minute sequence of a beach invasion on a Japanese-held island: 'its present-tense story is almost nothing but combat'. Basinger, *Anatomy of a Genre*, 257.

of a sense of duty to both, and he wanted to get it over with as quickly as possible. Rather than being a natural-born killer, he was a loving family man who abhorred the use of extreme force but could inflict it when necessary.[97]

The loving family man is exemplified by John Miller, a school teacher[98] who coaches baseball, and whose wife has rose bushes in her garden. He is traumatized by battle, yet still able to rouse himself to continue doing the necessary job. Miller is the hero of the film, and as Basinger tells us, 'the hero has leadership forced upon him in dire circumstances'.[99] For Miller those circumstances could not be more dire, in a firehole on Dog Green: 'Who's in command here?'. 'You are sir!'.

Miller rises to the task. He is tough ('they assembled him at OCS [Officer Candidate School] out of spare body parts from dead GIs', Reiben teases Upham), but he keeps a count of the men who have died under his leadership. He has assimilated to the needs and demands of the military structure. When Carpazo (Vin Diesel) wants to take the little girl from Neuville to the next town, because it is 'the decent thing to do', Miller tells him 'We're not here to do the decent thing. We're here to follow fucking orders'.

Miller separates himself from his men. He doesn't share their griping: 'I don't gripe to you, Reiben. I'm a captain. There's a chain of command. Gripes go up, not down. Always up'. He gently satirizes them, by inverting Rieben's complaints, and playing up to the fact that the company have a pool on his origins and civilian life: 'What's the pool on me up to right now?'. As played by Hanks, Miller 'realizes that maintaining his distance is crucial to military discipline, and thus survival'.[100] Miller accepts the mission to find Ryan because that will earn him the right to get back to his wife.

---

[97] John Bodnar, 'Postwar Memory in America', *American Historical Review* (June 2001): 805.
[98] 'Their occupations vary: farmer: cab driver, teacher'. Basinger, *Anatomy of a Genre*, 69.
[99] Basinger, *Anatomy of a Genre*, 68.
[100] Basinger, *Anatomy of a Genre*, 259.

Following Carpazo's death the squad shelter in a ruined church, and Miller speaks to Upham, who finds that combat experience is good for him. When Miller expresses surprise, Upham recites: 'War educates the senses, calls into action the will, perfects the physical constitution, brings men into such swift and close collision in critical moments that man measures man'.[101] Upham, in his neediness to be part of the squad, with his comically inappropriate attempts to connect his experiences with war as described by Tennyson and Shakespeare, is the man denounced by Emerson in 'The American Scholar', 'the bookish man who relies on the past'.[102] Upham is the scholar, 'in the degenerate state', who has become 'a mere thinker, or, still worse, the parrot of other men's thinking'.[103] Miller is the opposite of Upham. He is not thrown by Upham's scholarliness: 'Yeah, well I guess that's Emerson's way of finding the bright side'. But the whole of Miller's demeanour and deportment shows that he would have won Emerson's approval. Indeed, he has almost been constructed according to Emerson's specifications. Miller is the model of 'the great man... who in the midst of the crowd keeps with perfect sweetness the independence of solitude'.[104]

It is significant that, in a moment of transition for John Miller, between his roles of anonymous warrior and compassionate leader, it is Emerson, of all the possible writers on war, who is quoted by the filmmakers.[105] The sequence was placed into the shooting script to offer the audience 'glints of a higher sensibility'[106] in Miller. He is, we are assured, a scholar-warrior, that 'most generic

---

[101] The quotation is from Ralph Waldo Emerson's lecture 'On War', delivered to the Boston Peace Society, March 1838. Printed in *Miscellanies*, vol. 11, Complete Works (1911), 152.

[102] Auster, 'Triumphalism', 102.

[103] Emerson, 'The American Scholar (1837), 53.

[104] Emerson, 'Self-Reliance (1841), 31. See the way, later in the film, Miller mentions to Ryan his contextual memory of his wife, with her rose garden, but refuses to divulge any more: 'That one I save just for me'.

[105] This is yet more evidence, according to Auster, of the film's sensibility of 'American triumphalism': Auster, 'Triumphalism', 102–3.

[106] Bart, *The Gross*, 157. The Emerson quotation was added by Scott Frank as scriptdoctor.

of all Hollywood heroes, "the uncommon common man"',[107] the very definition of Emersonian individualism.

When Miller is required to suppress the mutiny within the squad following the death of Wade (Giovanni Ribisi) at the radar station, he does so by finally breaking the cover of his closely guarded privacy. He tells the men where he is from (Addley, Penn); he tells them his job (he teaches English composition); he tells them about his fears for his relationship with his wife ('Sometimes I wonder whether I've changed so much my wife will even recognise me whenever it is I get back to her'). He tells them that the missions of the war are subservient to his desire to return home, and resume his life and be subsumed by it:

> I don't know anything about Ryan. I don't care. The man means nothing to me, it's just a name. But if – you know, if going to Ramelle, and finding him so he can go home, if that earns me the right to get back to my wife – well, then… then that's my mission.

It is dramatically unclear why Miller's revelations should stop the mutiny. Cohen calls it a 'deus ex machina', although, remembering Spielberg and Emerson's humanism, it could be more properly labelled a *homo ex machina*. It is the true humanity of Miller which allows the mission to continue: Miller's confession represents for Spielberg 'the mystical citizen-soldier theme: the disgruntled soldiers are somehow supposed to feel this'.[108] The speech as originally scripted was even more revealing. Hanks in performance removed much of the excess: 'It seemed to compromise the integrity of my character for him suddenly to explain himself'.[109] Hanks is able then to walk the narrow line between a believable Emersonian individual and a believable officer in the American Rangers. His

> …brilliant performance allows a viewer to see that beneath Miller's weary stoicism and despite the battlefield experiences which

---

[107] Auster, 'Triumphalism', 102.
[108] Cohen, 'Ryan [review]', 324.
[109] Quoted in Bart, *The Gross*, 157.

have driven him to the verge of collapse, the high school English teacher turned citizen soldier never questions the reasons for which the War is being fought or abandons his sense of duty.[110]

Miller is the personification of the pride taken by liberal, individualistic democracies in their armies. The war, and the strategy of the generals, meant that the 'citizen soldiers were attempting to fulfil tasks which ran profoundly against the grain of their societies' culture'. The (western) Allied armies were manned by 'conscientious but never fanatical civilian soldiers'.[111] Miller is the 'antithesis of the *Wehrmacht* automaton'.[112] He is mortal. We see his hand shake, presumably through battle trauma (although the scriptwriters tell us that the shaking began in Portsmouth, *before* embarkation, so it cannot be the result of cowardice). We smile sympathetically when he explains to Ryan that the shake is his attempt to keep the rhythm of the Piaf record playing in Ramelle. We are shaken ourselves when Miller's hand finally comes to rest. All the way through the film Miller's mortality and humanity is signified with this 'physical tic and visual symbol that will have a wrenching emotional payoff in his last seconds of animation'.[113]

It is not coincidental that Miller's squad finally discover Ryan in a 'small, *leaderless* group of paratroopers'.[114] Miller offers Ryan two things, the 'ticket home', and then, when that is rejected, leadership: this encompasses the original squad, Ryan, and his remaining 'brothers', guarding a small bridge on the Mederet river from falling back into German hands. Miller is 'a natural leader who might have sprung from a Walter Mitty daydream'.[115]

If Spielberg's 'message' to the audience is a reminder to 'earn' the results of the death of Miller and his men, his message comes via the medium of Emersonian individualism. As they prepare to receive the counter-attack of the SS Panzer Division in Ramelle,

---

[110]Landon, 'Realism, Genre', 62.
[111]Max Hastings, *Armageddon* (2004), 105.
[112]Doherty, 'Ryan [review]', 70.
[113]Doherty, 'Ryan [review]', 70.
[114]Landon, 'Realism, Genre', 59. [Emphasis added].
[115]Doherty, 'Ryan [review]', 70.

Miller and Horvath muse on the challenge challenge and the injustice against which Private Reiben has struggled all through the mission: 'You want to explain the math of this to me? I mean, where's the sense in risking the lives of the eight of us to save one guy?'. Horvath inches towards an answer:

> HORVATH: ...what if by some miracle we stay, and actually make it out of here. Someday we might look back on this and decide that – saving Private Ryan was the one decent thing we were able to pull out of this whole – godawful, shitty mess. That's what I was thinking, sir. Like you said, Captain, we do that, we all earn the right to go home.

By the end of the final battle, only Reiben and Upham remain alive, and Upham was not a member of the original squad: this truly is 'all for one'. Miller does not fight his war to extinguish evil, or to uphold freedom, or to prepare the world for the furtherance of liberal democracy. He fights his war to go home. When it is clear that he will never go home, he tells Ryan (and through him, Ryan's progeny) to earn the deaths of the individual soldiers of his squad: the post-war generation are to 'rehabilitate traditions of good fathers, patriotic men, and self-sacrifice'.[116] Thus, *Ryan* itself rehabilitates the mythologizing leadership of Colonel Thursday and Captain York. The nation is made great through its survival of the testing times, whether it is the Indian Wars of the South-West or the liberation of Normandy. It will only survive through the heroism, detachment and moral decency of the American Adam, reluctantly putting down his baseball bat, and picking up his rifle. In short, as Bodnar says:

> Past, present, and future are now contingent on standards of individual behavior rather than on democratic ideals. [117]

Emerson's ideals have reached their perfect avatar in Captains Miller and York, through the personifications of Tom Hanks and John Wayne.

---

[116] Bodnar, 'Postwar Memory', 816.
[117] Bodnar, 'Postwar Memory', 817.

Chapter 7
The Duke of deception

To the people of the world, John Wayne is not just an actor and a very fine actor. John Wayne is the United States of America. He is what they believe it to be. He is what they hope it to be. And he is what they hope it will always be.

MAUREEN O'HARA (1979)

In a ruminative piece written shortly after the death of John Wayne, Terry Curtis Fox noted a parallel between the life, career and old age of the actor and the dream of the American West. In Wayne's life we saw at work the same processes at work in the romanticization of the West, the interchange between the dream of the West, the 'free man living greatly' and the 'reverie of adolescents'.[1] Because the America West was a greater and wider land than the European settlers had ever known, the myths of the American West, and especially the myth of the one who settled in the West, the American Adam, also needed to bigger, better, 'more real', than those from which they originated.

We understand the American West, just as we understand John Wayne, through a dialogue between 'authenticity' and 'realism'. The two things, although often confused, aren't the same. Mistaking them is root cause for such errors as watching *Fort Apache* to

---

[1] Bernard De Voto, 'Plundered province', 4.

understand the socio-economic development of the American south-west through the actions of the Indian Affairs agent; thinking that *Shane* will teach us the economics of subsistence farming in Wyoming territory; believing that *Saving Private Ryan* is the filmed version of the *Ranger Handbook*, and we can learn how to disable an SS-Regiment by watching Captain Miller at work.

To ask if we can rely on the representation of the Westerner, the Cavalry Trooper, the Gunfighter, the Citizen Soldier (all properly capitalised) in popular Hollywood film, is to misunderstand the role these archetypes play in our society.

Rather we watch these films (in profitable quantities) because they reflect something back to us—something of the pain, wonder and complexity of being a human being. We fall, like Thurber's Walter Mitty, into dreams of what we wish to be, but, unlike Mitty, we know that we could never achieve our dreams. So we project our dreaming need upon the iconic representatives of that very need. We require of Wayne, and Ladd, and Hanks, a degree of common humanity: we need to see enough of ourselves in them to feel connected. But we also require them to be essentially unknown. As McBride and Wilmington say, the most powerful quality of Wayne's acting ability was not his horseriding, or his masculinity, or his ability with a gun or his fists, but simply 'his mysteriousness'.

> The audience is never quite sure what he is going to do next, and every shift in mood is a revelation of something which, at the end of the film, will still remain partly inexplicable.[2]

The mysteriousness gave Wayne his status. Similarly, would Shane have been such a powerful representative of salvation to his unnamed community if they had known who he was and where he was going? Status, in Wayne's case, both built up, and derived from, 'an authoritarian manner'.[3] His postwar film roles, in a time in which American society was so uncertain about where it was

---

[2]McBride and Wilmington, 'Prisoner of the Desert', *Sight and Sound* (Autumn 1971): 212.

[3]Terry Curtis Fox, 'The Duke of Deception', *Film Comment* (October 1979), 70.

going, what it needed to be, and where its new frontier was to be found, gave Wayne the opportunity to play his part removed from the petty requirements and values of other characters in the narratives. Instead:

> ...Wayne depicted moral authority, a knowledge of what was right, which superseded any of the squabbling beneath him.[4]

The personal qualities of the actor were reflected in the parts he was given, by directors (like John Ford, and Howard Hawks) sensitive enough to detect his lightning rod qualities. Wayne's personal 'intransigence, his innate authority, his ability to suggest an inordinate sorrow beneath a heroic exterior', made him a star and a 'political symbol'. He became identified 'with a mythical America of moral certainty and individual power. The older Wayne got, the more he could embody the American Past'.[5] John Wayne (the person) became 'John Wayne' (the avatar).[6] Fox concludes his meditative piece with this description:

> Wayne fused two apparently contradictory qualities: those of a man who is thoroughly a part of society, who is more than willing to put himself second to society's demands... and those of a man who is thoroughly outside society, a loner who cannot be reconciled with 'civilization'.[7]

This is almost exactly a description of the character of Captain John Miller, hero of *Saving Private Ryan*, and the (fictional) hero to whom a grateful generation paid US$500 million of thanks? Just as myths are the stories we tell time after time, mythic actors, the ones whose films we watch time after time, are the ones who are successful at portraying the power of the avatar, time after time.

---

[4] Fox, 'Duke of Deception', 68.
[5] Fox, 'Duke of Deception', 70.
[6] We can see this happening with the transformation Marion Morrison, the person, into John Wayne, the actor— director Raoul Walsh and producer Winfield Sheehan decided to rename him without Morrison/Wayne even being present: see Roberts and Olson, *John Wayne, American* (1997), 84.
[7] Fox, 'Duke of Deception', 70.

We saw in previous chapters how the model and symbol of John Wayne was repudiated. Paradoxically, the repudiation was based upon the same mythic-structures of thinking which created Wayne as an icon of American society: a free man, living greatly had no need of 'John Wayne', but at the same time, 'John Wayne' was the cause and guarantor for every man to be transformed into the free man, living greatly. Both the construction *and* the denunciation of the mythic figure are products of the same, deeper, structural, cultural dynamics. We hate 'John Wayne' for the same reasons we need 'John Wayne'. And we need 'John Wayne', even without realising our need. As the theatre critic John Simon put it:

> Oh, hell: the last century had its Iron Duke, Wellington; this century has its Granite Duke, Wayne. Every era gets the leader it deserves; John Wayne is ours.[8]

The mysteriously attractive man[9]

Which makes is all the more peculiar that the classic example of this American icon, living freely in the American West, was not played by John Wayne, but by Alan Ladd, in the title role of *Shane*. This film exhibits 'with remarkable purity all the basic components of the classical Western'.[10] The story is 'simple and moralistic, undeviating in its imagery and utterly without irony, but precisely for those reasons it allows its images to work as myth powerfully and directly upon the audience'.[11] The mysterious stranger rides into the nameless and characterless town of pig farmers, with a past and a gun. When the homesteaders face extinction from the

---

[8]Writing in 1975. Cited by Roberts and Olson, *John Wayne, American*, 645.
[9]Lloyd Baugh's description of Shane, along with 'friend, helper, confidante...moral support and encouragement...educator, protector, defender...[with] goodness and natural grace...' in *Imaging the Divine (*1997), 162–3.
[10]Will Wright, *Sixguns and Society* (1975), 33.
[11]David Jasper, 'Systematizing the Unsystematic', in *Explorations in Theology and Film* (1997), 241.

cattle ranchers Shane takes up his gun again ('It's only a tool. It's men who are good or evil'), and makes the township safe for the domesticity represented by Joey (Brandon De Wilde), his father Joe Starrett (Van Heflin), and his mother Marian (Jean Arthur). The film deals with the interplay between history and mythology, content and style, the 'aestheticizing tendency', as its 'highest expression': the *mythos* of the West is 'virtually reduced to its essentials and then fixed in the dreamy clarity of a fairy tale'.[12]

Shane is the personification of the Western hero, hardly a man at all, 'but something like the Spirit of the West'.[13] He is 'the man-in-the-middle who mediates the forces of civilization and savagery'.[14] His mediation comes through the use of his gun, or, more properly, his willingness to embody the emotions and actions by which the force and meaning of the gun is enacted:

> Shane is purified violence. He is celibate but he loves. He is not from the valley but from the mountain.[15]

In the end, Shane returns to the mountains, mortally wounded, having entrusted Joe and Marian to the care of Joey. David Jasper recognizes the religious dimensions of this narrative arc: 'as a drama of salvation in the "holy land" of the American West [the film] fulfils the viewer's fantasies without disturbing the longings which underpin them'.[16] Shane is Moses, unable to reach the Promised Land; he is Jesus, establishing the Church by giving his Mother and St John each into the care of the other. But, more importantly, he does not belong in the homesteaders' town; he came from elsewhere, and he will die elsewhere, after having served and led the people of whom he is not a part: 'the hero who saves the family cannot remain within it without disrupting it further'.[17] He must leave the community he saved in order to free it of his (violent)

---

[12] Robert Warshow, 'Movie Chronicle: The Westerner', in *The Immediate Experience* (2001), 120.
[13] Warshow, 'Westerner', 120.
[14] Thomas Schatz, *Old Hollywood/New Hollywood* (1983), 105.
[15] Bernard Brandon Scott, *Hollywood Dreams and Biblical Stories* (1994), 52.
[16] Jasper, 'Systematizing', 241.
[17] Lyden, *Film as Religion*, 142.

taint; 'he becomes the [expelled] scapegoat to which we transfer our own violent sins'.[18]

In this way the American Adam has become the American Cain; exercising heroic individual leadership results in being expelled from the community and marked, not with the curse of the restless wanderer [Gen. 4.10–12], but with the status of hero and leader. As Shane tells Joey, 'there's no living with a killing... there's no going back from one. Right or wrong, it's a brand. A brand that sticks'.

The leadership we deserve

We saw in Chapter 2 how modern management operates within this mythic structure. The most powerful 'myth-kitty' called upon by Business Process Re-engineering is not rational management, or 'just-in-time' logistics, or 'Quality Control Supervision', but, simply and triumphantly, 'The Code of the West'.[19] This Code, which has cultural and legal existence, meant that, in the face of assault or violence, there was no 'duty to retreat'.[20] Violence could, in fact *should*, be met with violence. Even such a civilized man as President Eisenhower in a televised address in 1953 advocated the Code of the West by saying American society allows you to 'meet anyone face to face with whom you disagree'. The Code meant 'you could not sneak up on him from behind, do any damage without suffering the penalty of an outraged citizenry', but 'if you met him face to face and took the same risk as he did, you could get away with almost anything, as long as the bullet was in front'.[21]

The myth of the West, and its heroic, pioneering inhabitants, is not a whimsical piece of cultural history. Its effects are felt directly

---

[18] Lyden, *Film as Religion*, 142 (and similarly 92–3); see also Lyden, 'To Commend or To Critique?' *Journal of Religion and Film* (October 1997).

[19] Grint and Case, 'Violent Rhetoric', 566–8.

[20] Grint and Case, 'Violent Rhetoric', 558.

[21] 'Eisenhower Scores Character Attack', *The New York Times*, 24 November 1953; cited by Grint and Case, 'Violent Rhetoric', 567, but there mistakenly attributed to Wild Bill Hickcock and not the President.

in our society today, and in no more a pernicious way, as BPR
exemplifies, through the continuing cult of violence.

The monomythic cult

It is impossible, says Rowan Williams, in *The Truce of God*, to
understand any ethical project (in his particular instance, the
Christian imperative to peace-making) without first examining the
fantasies of violence which appear to haunt our society. 'Violence'
must mean something more than the 'level of realism' by which
'physical struggle and physical injury'[22] are depicted—although
popular concerns about society's exposure to dramatic violence
do not seem to move much beyond concerns about 'realism'.[23]
Williams gives us four different ways to categorize our cultural fears
and fantasies.

First, there is the violence of *catastrophe*, through which we
experience the destruction or irreparable damage of our sophisticated technologies and/or systems. Catastrophe is unpredictable
and utterly overwhelming: 'uncontrollable force has been unleashed
against us, and we are helpless victims'.[24] Recent examples of this
genus might be eco-catastrophe films such as *Volcano*, *Dante's
Peak*, *2012* and *Armageddon*.

Second, there is the violence of *occult terror*, in which force is
unleashed against us, but this time from unseen, unknown and
unknowable powers: *Poltergeist* and *The Fog* would be good
examples of this genus.[25] Williams notes the popularity of the
possessed child trope in this genus, part of the delight of cinema
in expressing paedophobia:[26] *The Others* might be an example.

Third, there is violence that is the result of human *insanity*.
We see the actions of the psychopathic mass murderer working

---

[22] Rowan Williams, *The Truce of God* (2005), 3.
[23] See the way in which *Saving Private Ryan* was received and its perceived
'authenticity'.
[24] Williams, *Truce of God*, 4.
[25] Or indeed, almost any film directed by Hooper and Carpenter.
[26] See Kendall R. Phillips, *Projected Fears* (2005), 109–12.

against the 'vulnerable and marginal'.[27] Very often, and tellingly, this violence is enacted by males against females. As Williams says, the violence has a 'curiously amoral quality, it is done by an agent outside the ordinary range of social control and reasoned decision'.[28] Carpenter's *Halloween* is a good example.

Fourth, the final category we might call the *revenge of nature*. Films which include animal attacks, whether the animals are fictional, factual, conceivable, or just plain fantastic, are all evidence of our fears about uncontrollable violence: *The Birds*, *Cujo*, and even *The Thing* would be included. This sub-genus includes many films within the science-fiction genre. The alien in *Alien* is natural: we just don't understand it.

Although the forms of, and audiences for, these genres may be different, they have a close 'family resemblance', as Williams calls it. They are all fantasies originating in the 'source and nature of violence'. They share in the implicit, helpless assumption that 'violence is something done *to* us by agencies over which we have no control'. There is very little sense of moral judgement in these fantasies, according to Williams: 'the agents of [the violence] are beyond or below moral assessment. Violence "happens."' Williams laments that this inability or refusal to see that violence has a moral component means that our society is incapable of recognizing the involvement of our own members in the commissioning and tolerating of violence. We pretend that 'violence is never something ordinary human beings *decide to do*', ignoring that the commissioning of violence is 'something to do with power, vision, understanding and choice, with the ways in which we make sense of our lives'.[29]

Paul Ricoeur made the connection between the origins of violence and our fears. There is a human-shaped hole in the centre of our morality of violence. Ricoeur says that we admit to 'a very limited and very reassuring idea of violence' by reducing it to two extremes; on the one hand murder, on the other hand, the 'strength of nature'.

---

[27] Williams, *Truce of God*, 5.
[28] Williams, *Truce of God*, 6.
[29] Williams, *Truce of God*, 7, 9. [emphasis in original.]

Between a murder and an avalanche, however, there is the whole realm of the intermediate, which is perhaps violence itself: human violence, the individual as violence. His violence has aspects of the hurricane and of the murder: on the side of the hurricane, it is the violence of desire, of fear, and of hate; on the side of murder, it is the will to dominate the other man, the attempt to deprive him of freedom or of expression, it is racism and imperialism.[30]

According to Ricoeur we cannot understand the power and persistence of violence without understanding the role and responsibility of the individual in violence. This is the reason why human society deals with the 'problem' and the 'contradictions' of violence mythologically, to bridge the epistemological and moral gaps between what exists and what is permitted, between what we can admit about, and what is the reality of, ourselves.[31] Three authors (two working collaboratively) have produced significant works on this mythic overcoming of the contradictions of violence: Lawrence and Jewett's 'American Monomyth'[32] and Wink's 'myth of redemptive violence'.[33]

Walter Wink's myth is simple enough to summarize: 'Violence is the ethos of our times. It is the spirituality of the modern world'.[34] It is an ultra-successful mythology because it is not recognized as such.[35] The myth, according to Wink (following Ricoeur[36]), has its beginnings in and derives its power from the Babylonian creation/destruction myth of *Enûma Eliš*, from which comes the moral propositions that 'violence inheres in the godhead… [and that evil]

---

[30] Paul Ricoeur, 'Violence and Language', *Journal of French and Francophone Philosophy* (2011): 32. Originally written in 1967.
[31] As Lévi-Strauss put it in 'Structural Study of Myth', 229.
[32] Originally published as Robert Jewett and John Shelton Lawrence, *The American Monomyth* (1977); subsequently updated and extended as *The Myth of the American Superhero* (2002). Quotations will be from the latter volume.
[33] Originally published in Walter Wink, *Engaging the Powers* (1992).
[34] Wink, *Engaging the Powers*, 13.
[35] '…precisely because it does not seem to be mythic in the least'. Wink, *Engaging the Powers*, 13. Lévi-Strauss concurs.
[36] Ricoeur, *The Symbolism of Evil* (1969), 175–210.

is an ineradicable constituent of ultimate reality, and possesses ontological priority over good'.[37] In the beginning was chaos, and order only triumphed over chaos by means of violence: Tiâmat (female and symbolizing chaos) was killed and dismembered by Marduk (male and representing order). Thus, we see a pre-history version of Williams's male-on-female psychopathic violence. Therefore, 'might is right', the gods 'favour those who conquer', religion exists only 'to legitimate power and privilege', life is 'a theatre of perpetual conflict in which the prize goes to the strong'.[38]

'Peace through strength' continues in popular culture today. The myth of redemptive violence may be expressed thus:

An indestructible good guy is unalterably opposed to an irreformable and equally indestructible bad guy. Nothing can kill the good guy, though… he (rarely she) suffers grievously, appearing hopelessly trapped, until somehow the hero breaks free, vanquishes the villain, and restores order…[39]

Popular cultural expressions of the myth differ from the aetiology of the myth in one significant way: Tiâmat's killing by Marduk was for a *purpose*: political, creative, legitimating. Violence today appears to be violent for its own sake:

Redemptive violence gives way to violence as an end in itself—not a religion that uses violence in the pursuit of order and salvation, but a religion in which violence has become the ultimate concern, an elixir, sheer titillation, an addictive high, a substitute for relationships. Violence is no longer the means to a higher good, namely order; violence itself becomes the goal.[40]

---

[37] Wink, *Engaging the Powers*, 14.
[38] Wink, *Engaging the Powers*, 16,17.
[39] Wink, *Engaging the Powers*, 17. For Wink, the myth is cyclic, and the bad guy escapes to be bad again another day.
[40] Wink, *Engaging the Powers*, 25.

Needing salvation

Wink's myth operates in an entirely mythical mode, proper to its identified origins in *illud tempus* of Babylonian creation. And yet I have argued that *MythL* is rooted in a specific culture and context, the world effected by America. In order to understand this, to comprehend the 'myths of the mighty', we need to understand the nature of American Religion, properly capitalized in Harold Bloom's kaleidoscopic, eccentric and informative study of *the* American Religion.[41]

This religion is driven by a soterological neediness; it is fundamentally a search for salvation. But 'salvation' should be, and cannot be, understood in any narrow doctrinal and creedal terms, even if spoken of by the adherents of various American religions (lower case). Bloom instead argues that before the creeds of the Southern Baptists, the Presbyterians, the Mormons, or whatever, get to work, there is a prior need and a prior belief: American Religion 'manifests itself as an information anxiety': how can the believer *know*? But what is it that the believer needs or wants to know? The question is to do with freedom, but not political freedom. The follower of American Religion (and that is everyone who lives within the American cultural framework, whether Protestant, Catholic, Jew or atheist) is a 'self', searching for itself in the face of the primordial abyss: the goal of American Religion is 'a solitude in which the inner loneliness is at home in an outer loneliness'. In other words, the freedom to be a self comes from knowing itself 'to be free both of other selves and of the created world'. It is this freedom that counts as salvation within the American Religion, a salvation-freedom that, by definition, 'cannot come through the community or the congregation, but is a one-on-one act of confrontation'. The adherent of the American Religion is the hero of his/her own salvation history: he/she is the triumph of the 'Self Asserted'.[42] In this way, Bloom argues, American Religion

---

[41] For more on Bloom's American Religion see the section in Chapter 3.

[42] Bloom, *American Religion*, 31, 32, 33.

is a form of 'Orphism', an 'esoteric mystery cult' centred on 'the potential divinity of the elitist self'.[43]

Here is the connection between Bloom's American Religion and Lawrence and Jewett's American Monomyth. The Monomyth is the 'practical theology' version of the Religion. It is the means by which the elitist self realizes its divinity and how it expresses its connection with the primordial abyss. If American Religion is *lex credendi* (the law of belief), then the American Monomyth is *lex agendi* (the law of acting).

The violent redemptive task

The advantage of Jewett and Lawrence's American Monomyth is that it is firmly rooted in the minutiae of American cultural life. We can see who is responsible for the enacting, and the propagating, of the myth. It is easily summarised, and Jewett and Lawrence have done so on a number of occasions. They based their idea on what they call the 'classical monomyth' of Joseph Campbell,[44] which was itself a version of an initiation-narrative. Lawrence and Jewett adapted Campbell's theory because they sought to account for a specifically American context. So Lawrence and Jewett define the Monomyth in this way:

> A community in harmonious paradise is threatened by evil; normal institutions fail to contend with this threat; a selfless superhero emerges to renounce temptations and carry out the redemptive task; aided by fate, his decisive victory restores the community to its paradisiacal condition; the superhero tends to recede into obscurity.[45]

Jewett and Lawrence later adapted the definition by paying more attention to the moral nature of the hero:

---

[43] Bloom, *American Religion*, 52.
[44] Discussed above on p. 77.
[45] Lawrence and Jewett, *American Superhero*, 6.

...a lone hero is summoned by destiny to a mission of redeeming innocents suffering depredations by evil powers. The hero marks himself as morally fit by renouncing sexual and material temptations, thereby enabling himself to rescue the community whose institutions are too weak to protect it from predators.[46]

See how Jewett and Lawrence take into account Shane's mysterious attractiveness. Shane/the hero is 'lone': he is extra-societal, coming in from the outside, and returning to the place beyond his temporary community: he might have been 'in' the weakened community, but he was not 'of' the weakened community. His asexual and ascetic nature both symbolizes and creates this separation.[47]

Remember also how Shane achieves his 'redemptive task' through the means of what Jewett and Lawrence call 'golden violence',[48] violence enacted by a righteous man for a righteous cause. Extra-legal violence, vigilantism, is an important part of American self-understanding: such films as Michael Winner's *Death Wish,* provide a 'transitional bridge' between 'archaic myth' and 'current needs': the 'ever-recurring fantasy of redemptive violence' on the first part, and violent acts committed by 'virile males' or 'weak male outcasts' on the second.[49] The moral danger of the monomyth therefore arises in the myth being enacted: 'such fantasies lead audiences to follow leaders who act as vigilantes to rid the world of evil. It should not be surprising that this message occasionally comes from some superheroes themselves'.[50] Lawrence and Jewett go so far as to describe this 'message' and 'following' process as 'discipleship':

...popular materials issue a call that seems aimed at courageous viewers. This is what we call the *invitation to emulate*...

---

[46] Jewett and Lawrence, 'Heroes and superheroes' (2009), 390.
[47] Recall the beautifully underplayed scenes between Shane, Marion and Joe Starrett in which Shane renounces the temptation to take Marion as wife and/or lover.
[48] Lawrence and Jewett, *American Superhero*, chapter 6.
[49] Lawrence and Jewett, *American Superhero*, 113.
[50] Jewett and Lawrence, 'Heroes and superheroes', 399.

> Some of those who participated vicariously in the mythic drama
> internalize the behaviour patterns and subsequently follow them
> when they face analogous situations in their lives.[51]

The American Monomyth, therefore, is not a morally neutral cultural
artefact. The Virginian, the Lone Ranger or Paul Kersey[52] have a
real effect on real lives. The actions of the superhero, the extra-
legal, extra-societal Adam, are not cathartic, but invocatory:

> The superhero of the American monomyth does not free us from
> violence, but perpetuates it even as he claims to be a force for
> 'peace' in his own use of rationalized violence.[53]

Tom Wright made the connection between the monomyth of
redemptive violence and *realpolitik* following the killing of Osama
bin Laden in Pakistan as a result of action by American Special
Forces in May 2011. The only difference, he asserted, between
British commandos executing IRA members in a Boston suburb
and the action in Abbottabad is 'American exceptionalism. America
is subject to different rules to the rest of the world'. The reason
for the exceptionalism is the failure of 'proper justice',[54] and the
subsequent right of Americans to take back justice from, what
Owen Wister called, the 'withered hands' of the law, into their own
hands 'where it was once at the beginning of all things'.[55] President
Obama was praised for the action, 'even by his bitter opponents',
for completing a phase in the war against Al-Qaeda, but, more
importantly, because 'he has just enacted one of America's most
powerful myths'.[56]

As Wister puts it, describing the Virginian's famous threat 'when
you call me that, *smile!*', 'The letter means nothing until the spirit

---

[51] Lawrence and Jewett, *American Superhero*, 117. [Emphasis in original.]

[52] Examples given by Lawrence and Jewett: Kersey is the name of the character
played by Charles Bronson in *Death Wish*.

[53] Jewett and Lawrence, 'Heroes and superheroes', 400.

[54] Tom Wright, 'America's Exceptionalist Justice', *The Guardian,* 5 May 2011.

[55] Judge Henry's description of the ineffective law of Wyoming in Owen Wister, *The
Virginian (1902)*, 284.

[56] Wright, 'America's Exceptionalist Justice'.

gives it life'—and for Wister and the Virginian, the spirit gives the letter life by producing a pistol to back up the threat.[57]

Under the American monomyth of redemptive violence, to be a leader/hero means to be prepared to use violence. To be a disciple/follower means to accept, in turn, an invitation to use and be thrilled by violence. But, as Wright asks:

> ...what has any of this to do with something most Americans also believe, that the God of ultimate justice and truth was fully and finally revealed in the crucified Jesus of Nazareth, who taught people to love their enemies, and warned that those who take the sword will perish by the sword?

Wright reminds those within the Church, the 'religious admirers of leadership', to paraphrase Pattison, that there is a basic problem in this admiration of leadership in North Atlantic society. With its roots in the mythic use of violence by the outsider, the extra-societal Adam, what can we find in the Scriptural tradition to counteract, or set aside, this cult of violence? Surely we can find some ways in which the crucified Jesus of Nazareth rescues leadership from both Marduk and John Wayne?

---

[57]Wister, *The Virginian (1902)*, 29.

SECTION THREE

Domination and discipleship

With extreme impatience, many young people today confuse the great nation-forming leader with this or that party leader—only few truly intellectual youth avoid this confusion. These intellectual youths understand with the certainty of God's mercy that only the superior human being is the salvation of the world, that he whose myth is the continuing source of fecundity and fruitfulness for the race, is a true leader of the people... Only a superior human being is leader and ruler: he is utterly radiant, world-encompassing, all-comprehending spirit, a fundamentally sage heart, utterly masculine, all infusing action, utterly suprapersonal, visionary will of Earth, he is creator of the people, the nation; in him the divine spirit and earthly kingdom are one.

JONAS LESSER (1932)

Chapter 8

Leading and leaving the dead

Jesus points his disciples to God and himself walks the way of God, yet it is not possible to substitute another teacher for him; a pupil may move from one philosopher to another and a disciple from one rabbi to another but Christians cannot go to another leader. The disciple of the rabbi, if all goes well, becomes a rabbi; the pupil of the philosopher may equally become a philosopher and have his own pupils; disciples of Christ, however, never become Christs or have their own disciples.

ERNEST BEST, FOLLOWING JESUS (1981)

The praxis of leadership in the Jesus Movement

Leadership as a secular social dynamic is inescapably mired in the violence and individualism of Marduk and John Wayne. Many contemporary Christian thinkers and opinion-formers (see how difficult it is to avoid the word 'leaders'?) either don't see that this is the case, or, think that it is possible to rescue leadership from Marduk for Jesus. It is possible, indeed necessary, to celebrate both the Christian tradition of leadership and the tradition of Christian leadership. Maybe so.

If so, then we will need to undertake two preliminary tasks. First, we need to begin with Jesus: is it possible to say anything about Jesus's intentions and purpose: other than the 'Messiah, the Son of the most High God'[1], what sort of person was Jesus and what sort of purposes did he have? Second, as we have already seen and agreed that leadership is something which only happens in a social context, a community even, we need to work out what sort of social context, community, it was in which Jesus exercised his leadership, and in which he expected leadership to be exercised (if any).

Of course, none of this, despite showing my own presumptions, is a given. The double task is complicated by its relationship to the so-called 'quest for the historical Jesus'. There have been, according to N. T. Wright, at least four different quests,[2] and their conclusions have been complicated: Jesus was a revolutionary; Jesus was an eschatological or an apocalyptic prophet; Jesus was a Galilean holy man, opposed to the religious establishment; Jesus was a sage; Jesus was a Cynic philosopher; Jesus was a magician; Jesus was a myth.[3] Nowhere in all these different images do we find support for George Carey's analysis: it is never asserted that the interpretative key for the person and meaning of Jesus is a first century for a managerial programme for a target-setting and appraisal system.

There are some who argue that it is impossible to say anything coherent or reliable about the historical Jesus: thus, for example, Bultmann's judgement: 'I do indeed think that we can now know

---

[1] A given for me as a Christian priest, and a given for the Christian tradition.
[2] N. T. Wright, *Jesus and the Victory of God* (1996), pt. 1, especially sections 1.3, 2.1 and 3.1.
[3] S. G. F. Brandon, *Jesus and the Zealots* (1967); E. P. Sanders, *Jesus and Judaism* (1985); Bart D. Ehrman, *Jesus, Apocalyptic Prophet* (1999); Geza Vermes, *Jesus the Jew (*1983); Burton L. Mack, *A Myth of Innocence* (1988); Ben Witherington, *Jesus the Sage* (1994); F. Gerald Downing, *Christ and the Cynics* (1988); Morton Smith, *Jesus the Magician* (1978); George A. Wells, *The Jesus Myth* (1999).

almost nothing concerning the life and personality of Jesus'.[4] For Bultmann, the meaning of Jesus (an *existential* meaning for present-day students, rather than the *historical* meaning of Jesus or the *personal* meaning of Jesus for himself) is to be found in the words of Jesus, but he doubts that the very words can be accurately recovered. However, Bultmann was unnecessarily fixed on one aspect of Scripture, the words; he overlooked the significance of Jesus's actions, actions that are expressive of his purpose. As Ben Meyer puts it, 'the principle public actions of Jesus were symbolic and these symbolic actions were correlative to his proclamation'.[5]

In other words, it ain't just what he said – it was also what he did. There is a close identity between Jesus's *words* about the kingdom of God and his *enacting* of the kingdom of God: the flock of Israel is gathered [Mt. 15.24; 10.6; Lk. 19.9; cf. 13.6], and lost sheep are found [Lk. 19.10; Lk. 15.3–7; par. Mt. 18.10–14]; the sick are cured [Mk 2.17; par. Mt. 9.12; Lk. 5.31], the possessed are cleansed [Lk. 13.32], and the dead are brought to life [Mt. 11.5; par. Lk. 7.22. Mt. 8.22; par. Lk. 9.60; Lk. 13.3; 15.32]; the Law is completed [Mt. 5.17]; and the banquet of salvation is brought into being [Mk 2.17; par. Mt. 9.12; Lk. 5.31. Lk. 19.9–10].[6] Thus, according to Meyer, Jesus was the 'bearer of the supreme mission to Israel', which began as a circle of the baptized gathered around a holy man, and culminated in the ultimate 'act of faith-recognition' in the responses of the baptized circle to Jesus's passion.[7]

The 'purpose' of Jesus

Actions and words form a whole to show Jesus's 'self-understanding', another way of describing Jesus's 'purpose'. There is a danger in using such terminology. Much post-Bultmann scholarship

---

[4]Rudolf Bultmann, *Jesus and the Word (1934)*, 8.
[5]Ben F. Meyer, 'Jesus Christ', *The Anchor Bible Dictionary* (1992), 780–1.
[6]See the summary in Ben F. Meyer, 'Jesus' Ministry and Self-Understanding', in *Studying the Historical Jesus* (1994), 351–2.
[7]Meyer, 'Jesus' Ministry and Self-Understanding', 351.

says that it is wrong to attempt to shoehorn a picture of Jesus into something which is *"'psychologically comprehensible.'"*[8] But this doesn't mean that we should be content with descriptions which are psychologically *in*comprehensible. To say that Jesus had *no* self-understanding or purpose would be just that: 'He must have had some self-understanding. He must have reflected on his own relationship to the major proclamation... He must have wrestled with the implications of his words and actions for his self-understanding'.[9] We can approximate to a description of Jesus's 'self-understanding', what N. T. Wright has called a 'heuristically functioning label', if we answer Paul Rhodes Eddy's question: 'What beliefs about himself would Jesus have held in order to most plausibly explain what he said and did?'.[10] Wright himself is, correctly, unabashed by attempting this question: trying to answer it shows that we are not attempting psychoanalysis, nor romantic fiction, but history:

> History seeks, among other things, to answer the question: why did this character act in this way? And among the characteristic answers such questions receive: he believed, at the core of his being, that it was his duty, his destiny, his vocation, to do so.[11]

And what was that vocation? Jesus was to be the 'mediator of God's final controversy with his people'.[12] In this way, he was the 'the climactic and definitive fulfiller of the hopes of Israel'[13], and the fulfiller who was, necessarily, to be rejected. The Kingdom of God was come among His people, and the exile, which continued despite the physical return from Babylon, and which included the person of the Lord (YHWH)[14], was now to be overcome in the person

---

[8] Bultmann, *Jesus and the Word*, 5. [Emphasis in original.]

[9] Charlesworth, *Jesus Within Judaism*, 135.

[10] Paul Rhodes Eddy, 'Remembering Jesus' Self-Understanding', in *Memories of Jesus* (2010), n. 2, p. 227.

[11] Wright, 'Jesus' Self-Understanding', 53.

[12] Amos Wilder, 'Eschatology and the Speech-Modes of the Gospel', (1964), 29.

[13] Meyer, 'Jesus' Ministry and Self-Understanding', 353.

[14] Wright, *Jesus and the Victory of God*, chapter 13.

of Jesus, in whom we find the 'tabernacled' presence of YHWH.[15] 'And the Word became flesh and lived among us...' [Jn 1.14] is better translated as 'and tabernacled [εσκηνωσεν] in our midst'. This tabernacled presence was that as found in the Temple in Jerusalem (not in the sense of an image or metaphor, but exactly). The work of the Temple (forgiveness of sins and restoration of fellowship with God), was also the work of Jesus: 'He was acting as a one-man Temple-substitute... [and when he] came to Jerusalem the place wasn't big enough for both of them, himself and the Temple side by side'.[16] Jesus's major proclamation was 'the dawning of God's Kingdom in his presence and through his words and miracles'.[17]

We need to bear in mind the dangers of docetism, in which Jesus is removed from his historical roots and becomes a cipher, or a 'moderately pale Galilean'.[18] To do this we should examine the social / political / religious or economic context in which the 'Jesus movement' recorded in the Christian scriptures found itself.[19] But before we can do that we need to see if the Jesus Movement is just that, a movement which looks like a social organization, with structures in common with every other social organization, whether from the period of Second Temple Judaism or North Atlantic society. If we can find parallels between the Jesus Movement in particular and 'social organizations' in general, then we might be able to identify any 'timelessness' within the patterns of social structure, leadership and followership expressed by the Jesus Movement. In other words, if the Jesus Movement is a 'social organization' like those we see around us today, are we able then to see something 'timeless' and 'enduring' in the community, leadership and followership of that movement which we can emulate?

---

[15]Wright, 'Jesus' Self-Understanding', 56–8.
[16]Wright, 'Jesus' Self-Understanding', 57.
[17]Charlesworth, *Jesus Within Judaism*, 135.
[18]N. T. Wright's caricature of A. N. Wilson's biography of Jesus: N. T. Wright, *Who Was Jesus?* (1992), chapter 3; A. N. Wilson, *Jesus* (1992).
[19]The phrase is taken from Gerd Theissen, *The First Followers of Jesus* (1978), 1. Theissen defines the Jesus movement as 'the renewal movement within Judaism brought into being through Jesus and existing in the area of Syria and Palestine between about AD 30 and AD 70'. The appropriateness of this nomenclature has been disputed: see Richard A. Horsley, *Sociology and the Jesus Movement* (1989), 30–42.

The Jesus movement as a social organization

For a social organization to be a social organization Marvin Olsen says three interlocking factors must be present: the organization must have *boundaries* (to distinguish it from its social environment); *structural stability* (which comes from 'fundamental patterns of social order' often preserved by superficial change); and *a unique culture* (expressed by 'values, goals, norms, rules and other ideas'). In short, 'a social organization is a relatively bounded and stable occurrence of social order, together with an associated culture'.[20] Other scholars have built upon this concept of 'organizational culture', relating it to leadership, and back again. Schein says that culture is a 'pattern of shared basic assumptions that the group learned as it solved its problems of external adaptation and internal integration, that has worked well enough to be considered valid and therefore, to be taught to new members as the correct way to perceive, think and feel in relation to those problems'.[21] This is unavoidably a dialogue, between 'culture' and 'leadership':

> Culture and leadership are two sides of the same coin in that leaders first create cultures when they create groups and organizations. Once cultures exist, they determine who will or will not be a leader.[22]

Immediately we see the importance of the founder/leader to the creation, definition and sustaining of the organization and its culture. Aitken concurs, and says that leadership is so important that it has its own culture. 'Leadership culture' is 'that amalgam of primary purpose, critical behaviours and essential personal values, identified and agreed by the leaders as authentic and functional for their distinctive organisation culture (whole or part), which the

---

[20] Marvin E. Olsen, *The Process of Social Organization* (1968), 66–9.
[21] Edgar H. Schein, *Organizational Culture and Leadership* (1992), 12.
[22] Schein, *Organizational Culture and Leadership*, 15.

leaders (formal and emergent) role model through their everyday communications and actions'.[23]

Social Organizations have an Organizational Culture, which is largely determined by their relationship to the Leadership Culture. Every social organization (including, we are testing, the Jesus Movement?) is focused largely upon 'leadership, the allocation of power, the differentiation of roles, and the management of conflict'.[24]

Let's examine how Olsen's three fundamental factors might apply to the Jesus Movement.

Bounded

In what ways might we describe the Jesus Movement as being 'bounded', with a clear delineation of roles within and without? We might be able to see boundaries of the Jesus Movement by looking at the oft-mentioned parallels between it and the rabbinical movement.[25]

At first glance the parallels seem promising. Jesus is frequently called or referred to as 'rabbi' – twice in Matthew, four times in Mark, none in Luke, and eight in John, although, in comparison, and perhaps equivalently, he is referred to as 'teacher' διδάσκαλος (*didaskalos*) 44 times, and mentioned as having pupils [Mt. 9.11; 17.24; Mk 12.32; Lk. 19.39; and so on].

However, Hengel is not convinced that the Jesus Movement was rabbinical: he entitles a section of his classic study on the Movement 'Jesus was not a "rabbi"'.[26] Theissen and Merz agree with Hengel: all three think the best sociological match to Jesus is

---

[23]Paul Aitken, "Walking the talk", *Journal of General Management* (Summer 2007): 18–19.

[24]Wayne A. Meeks, *The First Urban Christians* (1983), 84. Meeks is discussing the *ekklēsia* of the apostolic period, but, following Olsen's third criteria, stability over time, these factors must surely apply to the earlier expression of the same entity in the period of Jesus's ministry.

[25]The most frequently made parallel, according to James D. G. Dunn, *Unity and Diversity in the New Testament* (1977), 104.

[26]Martin Hengel, *The Charismatic Leader and His Followers* (1981), 42–50.

the wandering charismatics[27]). They produce a table of contrasts between traditional understandings of rabbinic-pupil relationships and what seems to be at work within the Jesus movement:[28]

Rabbinic teacher-pupil relationship	Relationship of Jesus to his disciples
Stable abode in a house of study	Itinerant life in Galilee and its environs
Limited period of time: a change of teacher is possible	Discipleship is a permanent relationship
Conscious forming of traditions by memories	Free formation of traditions
Discipleship is reserved for men	There are also women among the followers and hearers

The parallel between the Jesus and rabbinical movements also breaks down when we think of the thresholds of the Jesus Movement: it is unclear, according to Dunn, whether we should 'recognize the distinction between "disciples" and "followers" as significant'. (And a clear distinction between those within and those without a social organization is necessary for Olsen's model to apply.) Jesus appeared to have expressed and practised a concern to include those who were regularly excluded from the grace of the covenantal relationship with Israel's God by the 'main opinion-formers' of Second Temple Judaism: the poor (a familiar favoured group in prophetic Judaism), but also 'sinners', whose status as objects of disapproval was clear to all and among whom could be included 'many practitioners of "common Judaism"'. The way in which Jesus's inclusive vision differed from his 'prophetic predecessors' was in his expectation that the inclusion would be

---

[27] Although, as Mark Edwards warns 'Cynics were free itinerants without a creed or social organization, while [Christians] were avowedly the people of a book'. Mark Edwards, 'The Development of Office in the Early Church' (2000), 325.

[28] Based on the table in section 5.2, Theissen and Merz, *The Historical Jesus* (1998), 214.

fulfilled in the near future, and would be fulfilled within and because of him. This is why, as a symbolic prophetic action, he anticipated the inclusion through 'the circle of discipleship which he drew around him'.[29]

The circle is more accurately described as 'circles'. We can see a series of overlapping relationships and obligations in the groupings centred around Jesus: the inner circle of the Twelve; the women followers; 'secret' followers; those who hear Jesus gladly [Mk 3.35]; those who live out his teaching [Mt. 7.24–25]; sinners who repented [Lk. 18.13–14; 19.1–10]; Gentiles [Mt. 8.10]; even sympathetic Pharisees [Lk. 7.36; 11.37; 14.1].[30] In the end, Dunn says, we need to live with the ambiguity of *circles* of discipleship: 'What is striking about these circles of discipleship is the way they overlap and intertwine, forbidding us to make any hard and fast distinction between disciples and followers, or to designate different grades of discipleship'.[31] And those who attempted to make distinctions were severely rebuked by Jesus himself [Mk 9.38–41/Lk. 9.49–50]. As Schweizer says: Jesus 'founds no new Church; for there is no salvation even by entering a religious society, however radically transformed. Even the best reform of Church order still does not achieve conversion to God'.[32] According to this approach, Christ's mission was to no greater, or more complex form, of social organization than the individual. This was not necessarily the case. It is possible that Schweizer is here describing what he thinks Jesus ought to have done. Other theologians disagree with his confusion between 'church' and 'religious society':

> ...in essence Jesus Christ was no more the founder of the Christian religious community than the founder of a religion. ... He brought, established, and proclaimed the reality of a new

---

[29] Dunn, *Jesus Remembered*, 1:540.

[30] See especially the clear elucidation of the audiences and circles surrounding Jesus in John P. Meier, *A Marginal Jew* (2001), chapters 24–7.

[31] Dunn, *Jesus Remembered*, 1:540–1.

[32] Eduard Schweizer, *Church Order in the New Testament* (1961), 24 (§ 2c). Cited by Dunn, *Unity and Diversity*, 105.

humanity. ...It is not a new religion recruiting followers... Rather,
God established the reality of the church, of humanity pardoned
in Jesus Christ – not religion, but revelation, *not religious
community, but church.*[33]

The boundary between being, and not being, a follower of Jesus
is permeable: '...many of his disciples turned back and no longer
went about with him'. [Jn 6.66]. Bruce Chilton notes that Jesus
had allowed for this 'theology of failure, the recognition that the
word of the kingdom would not always prove productive after
sowing'.[34] But a permeable boundary is still a boundary, even if
it is an invisible one: 'most people in the crowds never crossed
the invisible line separating curious or sympathetic audiences
from deeply committed adherents'.[35] This permeable, invisible,
boundary was made all the stronger by the way in which the Jesus
Movement conforms to the two other criteria of Olsen's model.

Stable

For any grouping to exist as a social entity, Olsen requires a second
constituent factor, 'structural stability'.[36] Is it possible to say that the
Jesus Movement constitutes an enduring community?

To begin with the answer seems 'Yes'. Dunn gives us six
reasons[37] why it may be fairly thought that Jesus and his disciples
constitute an enduring community.

First, we see the repeated use of the word ἐκκλησία (*ekklēsia*),
the assembly of God's people [Mt. 16.8; 18.17]. Does an assembly
count as a community? Curiously, other than three instances in two
verses of Matthew's Gospel, the New Testament use of *ekklēsia* is

---

[33] Dietrich Bonhoeffer, *Sanctorum Communio* (DBWE 1) (1998), 152–3.
[34] Bruce Chilton, 'Friends and enemies', in *The Cambridge Companion to Jesus* (2001), 79.
[35] Meier, *Marginal Jew 3*, 30.
[36] Olsen, *Social Organization*, 69, 44–50.
[37] Dunn, *Unity and Diversity*, 104–5.

non-Gospel: 19 times in Acts, five times in Romans, 30 times in 1 and 2 Corinthians, 20 times in Revelation, and so on.

Second, we can see the programmatic way in which Jesus selects and uses the twelve disciples of the inner circle. He regarded, in some way, the twelve as representatives of Israel's past and Israel's future [Mt. 19.28; par. Lk. 22.28–30], and the way in which the number is symbolically reused in the tradition of the feeding of the five thousand [Mt. 14.15–21; par. Mk 6.34–44, Lk. 9.12–17, Jn 6.5–13]. This is an important point: Jesus was not, in Lohfink's memorable formulation, instituting 'disciples in an *eschatological office of witness*'[38]; rather this was a 'symbolic prophetic action', which was both 'an exemplification or demonstration', and also, more importantly, 'the initiation of something future, something which was already present in an anticipatory manner in the prophetically performed sign'.[39] The symbol was the sign and the sign was the thing itself!

Third, Jesus made use of the well-established imagery of Israel as God's flock and God as the good shepherd. Dunn points out the dependence of Lk. 12.32 and Mt. 10.6; 15.24 [par. Mk 14.27] on the Old Testament use [in Isa. 40.11, Ezek. 34.11–24, Mic. 4.6–8 and so on].[40] The 'good shepherd' is to be recalibrated as Jesus: if you want to see what Scripture meant by 'the good shepherd', Jesus says, then look at me.

Fourth, Jesus made an explicit contrast between his disciples' status as a family and the status of his biological family [Mk 3.31–35], in which the former has a greater status, and a greater claim on his attention and presence because of their explicit acceptance of fulfilling the will of God. Furthermore, it is implied that it is impossible to fulfil the will of God without accepting the conflict with the disciple's biological family: 'Whoever comes to me and does not hate father and mother, wife and children, brothers and sisters, yes, and even life itself, cannot be my disciple' [Lk. 14.26]. 'Hate' here functions hyperbolically, as a form of μετάνοια, the 'turning away' required by followers of Christ, which includes family and

---

[38] Gerhard Lohfink, *Jesus and Community* (1984), 9–10. [Emphasis in original.]
[39] Lohfink, *Jesus and Community*, 10.
[40] Dunn, *Unity and Diversity*, 105.

all previous ties.[41] Jesus also reinforced the disciples' status *within* the new family: they were to be as little children, [Mt. 18:3] with the privileges and restrictions of little children.

Fifth, at the Last Supper Jesus changes the status of the disciples through introducing the new Covenant: 'And he did the same with the cup after supper, saying, "This cup that is poured out for you is the new covenant in my blood"'. [Lk. 22.20 and par.]. The disciples are to be '"founder members" of the new covenant, as the new Israel'.[42] A new covenant requires a new covenant community.

Sixth, any community worth the name will have some form of recognizable organization. Can this organization be read from the hints in Lk. 8.2–3 and Jn 12.6? – a common purse was kept, and there was a means by which sympathetic outsiders, Mary, Joanna, and Susanna, could support the work of the disciples.

Ultimately, Dunn decides against the possibility of talking about a community of Jesus for three reasons. First, there was no ritualized ceremony which marked the joining or the leaving of this community. Jesus seems to have swiftly dropped the 'baptism of John' as a requirement to follow him, 'presumably because he did not want any cultic or ritual act which might become a barrier to be surmounted'.[43] This, of course, assumes that a boundary is only made or expressed by ritual ceremonies. As Olsen notes, participants need not be 'self-consciously aware of what they are doing when they create these boundaries'.[44] Often the means of identifying boundaries will exist in 'the underlying patterns of social organization',[45] such as attendance, the sharing of values or participation. The ambiguity in these 'shared-value boundaries' was acted upon by the disciples, when they attempted to forbid exorcisms in the name of Jesus [Mk 9.38–41, and par.], and the

---

[41] Lohfink, *Jesus and Community*, 32–5.

[42] Dunn, *Unity and Diversity*, 105.

[43] Dunn, *Unity and Diversity*, 105. Although that 'presumably' does cover a great deal of assumption into the possible motivations for Jesus's actions.

[44] Olsen, *Social Organization*, n. 2 on p. 66.

[45] Olsen, *Social Organization*, 66.

evangelists, when Jesus's own attitude to inclusion was inverted ('against me', Mt. 12.30, Lk. 11.23; versus 'with me', Mk 9.40).

Second, the role of the disciples as members of the new covenant and in the emblematic number of twelve seems to be something reserved for the future, rather than something to be acted out in Jesus's present:

> There is no evidence that they were regarded or acted as functionaries, far less a hierarchy, constituting a community gathered around Jesus in Palestine...What power and authority they did exercise was not within a community of discipleship for its upbuilding, but was given to them to share in Jesus' mission.[46]

In other words, the Twelve 'exemplified the gathering [of Israel] simply through the fact they were created as *Twelve*, but they also exemplified through being sent out to all of Israel'.[47] Institution and mission were inseparable.

Third, Dunn correctly points out the complete dependence of the disciples and their community upon Jesus himself. The word used most often to designate the followers of Jesus ('that is, for one who accepted his teachings and sought to be identified with him'[48]) is 'disciple': μαθητής (*mathētēs*), meaning 'a pupil' or 'a learner'. Discipleship, fellowship with Jesus, meant 'following' him. 'Following Jesus' meant doing the will of God: 'Whoever does the will of God is my brother and sister and mother' [Mk 3.35]. It would be wrong to think that during his teaching ministry Jesus was 'empowering' his disciples to undertake their own missionary work. When he sent out the Twelve [Matt; Mark] or the Seventy [Luke], he was 'pursuing his ministry by proxy'.[49] This was not collaborative ministry, and it is not sustainable ministry: it was only 'larger or smaller groups of disciples either observing his mission

---

[46] Dunn, *Unity and Diversity*, 106.
[47] Lohfink, *Jesus and Community*, 10. [Emphasis in original.]
[48] From the Introduction to Richard N. Longenecker, *Patterns of Discipleship in the New Testament*, (1996), 2.
[49] Dunn, *Unity and Diversity*, 106.

or hindering his mission or participating in some small part in his mission'.[50] Here, the mission of the Twelve, or the Seventy, is naturally overshadowed by the importance of Jesus's passion for salvation: 'The person and activity of the disciples as they followed their Master had... no "soteriological" dignity, and could not but fall into the background, for the community wished to be informed not about the "words and deeds" of the first disciples, but purely and solely about the activities of their Lord'.[51] In other words, there is no salvation to be found in following Peter, James or John, but only in so much that Peter, James or John are able, authentically, to connect their listeners to the person and actions of Christ.

Dunn finds these three objections convincing, giving them greater weight than the six factors which might demonstrate a community centred on Jesus. He provides a warning against speaking of the disciples as the 'church': if they are the church, then they are a church of a particular character: 'a group or groups of disciples gathered around Jesus with each individually and together *directly* dependent on Jesus *alone* for all ministry and teaching'.[52]

Culturally distinguishable

We need to place the Jesus Movement within its context of Second Temple Judaism, the social / religious / political and economic context in which the ministry of the Jesus Movement was exercised.[53]

The religious community within which the Jesus Movement lived and moved and had its being was Judaism; the political community was the Roman province of Judea (and the client kingdoms of

---

[50] Dunn, *Unity and Diversity*, 106.
[51] Hengel, *Charismatic Leader*, 79. Hengel exaggerates his case here: if the early Christian community had only wished or needed to hear 'purely and simply' about the activities of their Lord, there would have been no need for the Acts of the Apostles and some of the details of the early Pauline epistles.
[52] Dunn, *Unity and Diversity*, 106. [Emphasis in the original.]
[53] We should remember however that these words are neatly anachronistic.

the Herodians); the economic community was that of tenanted farming, prosperous enough to support a taxation economy and large estates owned by absentee landlords.[54]

Each of these three overlapping communities had some influence on the characteristics of the Jesus movement. However, as James Dunn, among others, has pointed out, it is more useful to note the overlap than to fix on the differences between the three. During the twentieth century scholarship moved from describing a single, pre-Rabbinic 'normative' Judaism to recognizing the huge variance of practices and doctrines – this as a direct result of the discovery of the Dead Sea Scrolls.[55] Thus Kraft and Nickelsburg say that 'early Judaism appears to encompass almost unlimited diversity and variety – indeed it may be more appropriate to speak of early Judaisms'.[56]

This fashion has declined in recent years as scholars recognized the essential unity of Judaism[57], focused on the religion, political and social life of the people and the land. Dunn speaks of the 'four pillars'[58] of Second Temple Judaism, the 'axiomatic convictions round which the diverse interpretations and practices of the different groups within Judaism revolved'.[59] The pillars were the

---

[54] See Hanson and Oakman, *Palestine in the Time of Jesus* (1998), chapter 4, '"The Denarius Stops Here": political economy in Roman Palestine'.

[55] Dunn gives five factors in this change: the Dead Sea Scrolls, a general resurgence in interest in 'intertestamental Judaism', the beginnings of a tradition-historical analysis of Rabbinc Judaism, a re-examination of the nature of 'Pharisaic' Judaism and the recognition of Christian anti-semitism after World War Two: James D. G. Dunn, *The Partings of the Ways* (2006), 15–21.

[56] Introduction, in Kraft and Nickelsburg, (eds), *Early Judaism and its Modern Interpreters* (1986), 2.

[57] James Dunn underlines the importance in getting the terminology right: 'Judaism' originated as a self-defining term by and for those who were 'worshippers of the God whose Temple was in Jerusalem' *over and against* the 'rest of the world' (for example, 'Greeks' or 'Gentiles'). The preferred term for describing the person in his relationship with his own people is 'Israelite' (see for example Paul in Rom. 11.1 or 2 Cor. 11.22). In other words, '"Jew" betokens the perspective of the spectator (Jewish included), 'Israel' that of the participant. See Dunn, *Jesus Remembered*, 1:263, 264.

[58] First described in Dunn, *Partings*, chapter 2.

[59] Dunn, *Partings*, 47. The passage is italicized in the original as a summary definition.

Temple; belief in God; belief in Israel as an elected nation; and the place of the Torah in Judaism's self-understanding.[60]

Broadly, therefore, first century Judea and Galilee was a Temple-based religious and political entity, and the intensity of the differences between each of the groupings (Pharisees, Essenes, and Zealots, the brigands, Herodians, and 'troublemakers') was a result of exactly how much each group shared: internal to Judaism (what Dunn calls 'Judaism from within'); and external, as a result of the social and political circumstances of the time.

The most important common feature from within was the unquestioned importance for each of the groups of the four pillars of Second Temple Judaism. Differences arose only because each grouping felt, according to Dunn, that the importance of one or other of the pillars was not sufficiently taken into account by their rivals.[61] In this respect, variations in belief and practice were an expression of what Freud would dismissively and misleadingly have referred to as the narcissism of minor differences.

The most important common feature from without was the fact of Roman rule and economic oppression: 'the pressing needs of most Jews of the period had to do with liberation – from oppression, from debt, from Rome'.[62]

Bearing this in mind, it is still reasonable to say that the differences between the Jesus Movement and the other movements within Judaisim were 'fundamental'. The legitimacy of the Zealots was 'demolished' by the punch-line to one of Jesus's enacted parables [Mk 12.17; par. Mt. 22.21; Lk. 20.25; *Gos. Thom.* 100]. The teaching of the Pharisees was condemned as 'a perversion of the will of God' [Mk 7.8], which wickedly 'frustrated the command of love' [Mk 3.4] by its rigour and connived with 'the will to disobey' [Mk 7.10–12] through its leniency. Against the Sadducees, 'whose

---

[60] Dunn, *Jesus Remembered*, 1:286–92.

[61] Dunn, *Jesus Remembered*, 1:1, 285–6.

[62] N. T. Wright, *The New Testament and the People of God*, (1992), 169. For Wright, the implication of this is to begin the sociology of Second-Temple with the 'special interest' groups of the period, those which explicitly described the need for revolutionary liberation: the Maccabees, the brigands under Hezekiah, Judas 'the Galilean' and so on (Wright, *New Testament and the People of God*, 170–81.)

very selfhood was peculiarly bound up with the temple',[63] Jesus prophesies the destruction of the Temple and its replacement, in his own person, in three days [Jn 2.19].

The differences between the Jesus Movement and the three schools have two consequences. First, there is no point in trying to decide which one of the three is most closely related to the Jesus Movement. Second, and at the same, the difference means that it is possible, following Olsen's third criterion, to say that the Jesus Movement is culturally distinct within the life of Second Temple Judaism.

We have examined three of Olsen's fundamental factors for any social grouping in their application to the Jesus Movement. How does 'leadership', so important to 'organizational culture', apply to the Jesus Movement?

The Jesus Movement as a leadership community

We saw in the first chapter the way in which the ministry of Jesus has frequently been used as an exemplar for patterns of leadership in today's church, corporations and society. John Adair, for one, expresses this clearly. He says there are four aspects to the leadership expressed by Jesus. First, it was expressed on a journey. The proclamation of the coming of the kingdom of God was, for Jesus, a journey which led from his baptism, through his teaching ministry in Galilee and Jerusalem, to the passion. The journey is (part of) the message: a leader, therefore, 'is the person who, in one form or other, shows the way on that common journey'.[64] Second, Adair notes that Jesus's leadership was expressed through what we now call teamwork. Some disciples were called, some disciples chose him. Jesus chose to yoke them into a team (Adair notes the origin of the English word 'team' in the Old English *team*, the rope which hitches draft animals together). Hence the appropriateness

---

[63]Ben F. Meyer, *The Aims of Jesus* (1979), 239.
[64]John Adair, *The Leadership of Jesus* (2001), 91.

of Jesus's metaphor and promise: 'Take my yoke upon you, and learn from me; for I am gentle and humble in heart, and you will find rest for your souls' [Mt. 11.29]. This team is not hierarchical but is based on friendship:

> There is no trace of hierarchy or inequality in the relation of friendship. Arguably, to be a friend stresses freedom more than to be a brother or sister, where there is a tie of 'blood'. 'My friends' suggests the companionship, camaraderie of those who work together in a common cause.[65]

Third, says Adair, Jesus's leadership is articulated and invigorated by a clear statement of a vision: 'The time is fulfilled, and the kingdom of God has come near' [Mk 1.14]. This made the greatest possible difference to the lives of Jesus and his followers:

> Jesus' own vision was about the clarity of his purpose and the necessity of his early death. He had a vision about his followers; he sends them very explicitly into the world to preach the gospel. Jesus was visionary for his followers because he looked at the world and the way people live in a very different way. Achievements were not based on keeping the law but on demonstrating love.[66]

Fourth, and finally, Jesus's leadership was expressed through service, and a form of service in which the values and hierarchies of the kingdom are the inverse of the world's values and hierarchies. Those who seek places of honour will lose them [Lk. 11.7–14]; expectations of honour within the Twelve are subverted [Mt. 20.20–28/Mk 10.35–40/Lk. 22.24–27]; those who seek public status and respect are condemned [Mt. 23.5–12]. Jesus's servant leadership is distinguished by an 'unqualified availability'.[67]

---

[65] Adair, *Leadership of Jesus*, 117.
[66] Peter Shaw, *Mirroring Jesus as Leader* (2004), 6.
[67] Adair, *Leadership of Jesus*, 139.

Adair's work in the leadership of Jesus has been very influential. Shaw among others, acknowledges his debt to Adair.[68] However, in Adair's own work and those who have followed him, we can identify a fatal discrepancy. All discussions of 'leadership' supposedly based upon a firm New Testament foundation are actually **second-order formulations**: we *infer* from the text that this is the way a leader behaves, or ought to behave, even if the text of text is actually focused upon a different matter entirely.

We can see this fallacy working on leadership in the New Testament by examining three representative passages which are often cited as examples of the 'New Testament's teaching on leadership'. The examples are not exhaustive, but other passages we might have chosen will also be susceptible to the second-order inference. The passages are the 'leadership discourse' of Jn 21, the role of the 'supervisor' in 1 Tim., and the 'presider' in Rom. 12.

Leading and feeding sheep – John 21

Jesus's post-resurrection appearance to the disciples and Peter in Jn 21.15–23 is very often glossed as a discourse on 'leadership'. This is especially true in recent popular scholarship. Thus, for example, Andrew Dawswell says that Jesus prepares the ministry of the Church for the post-Ascension experience by envisioning 'a distinctive individual leadership role for Peter',[69] and cites Mt. 16.13–19 and Jn 21.15ff in support. Jn 21 can be read, alternatively, as a masterclass on the 'three critical elements of leadership', the 'conduct', 'context' and 'complications' of Christian leadership.[70]

Popular presentations are reinforced by more scholarly exegesis. Thus Randy Poon characterizes Jesus's interaction with Peter as,

---

[68] Shaw, *Mirroring Jesus*, 9–10.

[69] Andrew Dawswell, *Ministry leadership teams* (2003), 14.

[70] Tom Frame, 'Jesus's checklist for good leadership', *The Church Times* (8 August 2008). 'Context' requires us to note that this article was published in the church press just before the 2008 meeting of the Lambeth Conference. Presumably the author saw a direct contemporary resonance for his interpretation.

among other things, an exercise in capacity-building for previously weak followers:

> [Peter] has to know for himself that he is ready to take on the responsibilities that Jesus sets before him and that he is indeed ready to obey his Lord as a sign of his love for Him [Jn 14.15]. ...Jesus' encounter with Peter that day engages the headstrong disciple and helps him decide intrinsically whether he is committed and willing to follow Jesus.[71]

Similarly, Wilson, using socio–rhetorical criticism and the secular leadership theory of leader–member exchange, determines that on one level the passages display a 'development path' devised by Jesus for Peter, which is, 'in a fashion consistent with active management-by-exception and clear directives consistent with contingent reinforcement, forms of transactional leadership'.[72] Other scholars, operating without the benefit of such advanced management concepts, come to similar conclusions.

Peter is questioned with a three-fold pattern about the care of the 'sheep' of the 'flock'. His answers, even if unsatisfactory, are enough for him to be entrusted with the role of the shepherd, one previously reserved for Christ himself [Jn 10]. Jesus's questioning demonstrates that Peter has the devoted love that is the essence of leadership (to paraphrase Brown[73]). This, then, is the justification for Peter's unique apostolate: 'the command to feed the sheep includes two activities which we have shown to be the successive expressions of Peter's apostolate: leadership of the Primitive Church in Jerusalem and missionary preaching'.[74] At the very least, it is the Johannine equivalent of 'the apostolic mission conferred on the other disciples in the post-resurrectional appearances'.[75]

---

[71] Randy Poon, 'A Johannine model of leadership', *Journal of Biblical Perspectives in Leadership* (2006): 66.

[72] John H. Wilson, 'Jesus as Agent of Change', *Emerging Leadership Journeys* (2010): 19.

[73] Raymond E. Brown, *The Gospel According to John (XIII–XXI)*, (2008), 1111. Brown considers it to demonstrate the 'essence of *discipleship*'.

[74] Oscar Cullmann, *Peter, Disciple, Apostle, Martyr* (1962), 65.

[75] Brown, *John XIII–XXI*, 1113.

There are two objections to this interpretation.

First, does Peter's assumed role of shepherd involve an assumption of leadership? The ministry of the shepherd, especially in John, is *not* a ministry of leadership, but rather of protection. Granted, according to John, the model shepherd is admitted by the gatekeeper to the sheepfold, is recognized by the sheep, and leads the sheep out from the fold [Jn 10.3 4]; but this is not the ultimate purpose, the *telos*, of the ideal shepherd. Thus Schnackenburg overstates his argument when he says Peter 'is to lead the 'lambs' to the pasture of life and guard them in union with Jesus'.[76] The *telos* of the ideal shepherd is to lay down his life for the sheep as a direct result of receiving the commandment to do so from the Father [Jn 10.18]. Peter's qualification to share in this commandment does not come from his love for the sheep, but rather from his love for Jesus ('do you love me?'. Jn 21.15,16,17). And that love is comparative: because Peter loves Jesus more than he loves the other disciples (or, alternatively, because he loves Jesus more than the other disciples do?), he is permitted to follow the example of *the* good shepherd. The example is a willing and obedient acceptance of death: 'for among all the NT uses of shepherd imagery, only John x specifies that one of the functions of the model shepherd is to lay down his life for his sheep'.[77]

This is reinforced by the second objection, which takes seriously the context of Jesus's conversation with Peter. Immediately following the injunctions to 'feed my sheep' is the prophecy of Peter's martyrdom:

> Very truly, I tell you, when you were younger, you used to fasten your own belt and to go wherever you wished. But when you grow old, you will stretch out your hands, and someone else will fasten a belt around you and take you where you do not wish to go. [Jn 21.18]

---

[76] Rudolf Schnackenburg, *The Gospel According to St John* (1982), 373.
[77] Brown, *John XIII–XXI*, 1114.

There is a parallelism here with the description of discipleship in Mk 8. Mark requires (1) denial of self, (2) a taking up of the cross, and (3) following Jesus. John requires (1) the surrendering of the fisherman to the role of shepherd [vv. 15–17], (2) the loss of personal autonomy which is expressed through being girded and led by others, and (3) an explicit command to 'Follow me!' [v. 19, repeated at v. 22], which means 'follow me to death' – '(He said this to indicate the kind of death by which he would glorify God.)' [v. 19].[78] In reality, all three parts are a surrendering to death; the death of the ideal shepherd, the destination of death that no one wishes to reach, and the explicit following of Jesus to death.

Bacon made an explicit connection between this discourse and our second passage from 1 Tim.: Peter is assigned 'the functions of a faithful shepherd', but these functions are limited to 'the *administrative* activity of a 'ruling overseer' in the classification of 1 Tim. 3.1–7'.[79] How does the leadership of a model shepherd compare with the leadership of a ruling overseer?

Supervising and managing households – 1 Timothy

It does not matter, for our task, the questions about the 'authenticity' of 1 Tim. Even if 1 Tim. is not authentically Pauline, then we can at least say that it indicates the way in which the early Christian community *thought* a first century Christian community should be organised. In 1 Tim. 3.1–7 we see the first, and only, mention of *episkopē* in the New Testament in relation to a position within the community. It is a difficult word to translate linguistically and conceptually, 'not because the Greek is unclear, but because English equivalents can be misleading'. 'Bishop' has accumulated

---

[78]The parallels noted by Tomas Arvedson, in 'Some notes on two New Testament pericopes' (1958): 77.

[79]B. W. Bacon, 'The Motivation of Jn 21.15–5', *Journal of Biblical Literature* (1931): 74. Bacon contrasts this assignment with the role of the 'teaching' elder from 1 Tim. 5.17 given to the Beloved Disciple.

later meanings, and it is difficult to read that 'without associating aspects of pomp and ceremony (and authority)' which are neither historically nor ecclesiologically appropriate 'in the case of the supervisor of a relatively small *collegium* in the first-century Roman Empire'.[80] Johnson here notes the appearance of *episkopos* alone, separated from its companions in the rest of the New Testament: *diakonoi* in Phil 1.1, *presbyteros/presbyterion* in Tit. 1.7, Acts 20:28. 'Supervisor' is the best translation for the word, idea, and role, says Johnson, as it is 'a remarkably simple structure of leadership, and [has a] complete lack of theological legitimation'.[81] Or, as Raymond Brown emphatically puts it: 'No cultic or liturgical role is assigned to the presbyter-bishops in the Pastorals'.[82]

The lack of a cultic locus is developed in the chapter: the supervisor 'must manage [προ-ϊστάμενον] his own household well, keeping his children submissive and respectful in every way – for if someone does not know how to manage his own household, how can he take care of God's church?'. [1 Tim. 3.4–5]. *Prohistēmi* means 'to govern or administer', but its root meaning is 'to stand-before, to be in the one in such a position'. It is the verb or participle usually translated as exercising leadership within the ecclesial community [see Rom. 12.8 and 1 Thess. 5.12] and 1 Tim. uses it to mean supervision over deacons [3.12] and elders [5.17] as well as the ministry particular to the *episkopos*. But before whom is one 'before-standing'? In what forum in this 'ruling well' exercised? The supervisor must keep 'his children *submissive* and respectful in every way' / 'with his children in *subordination* with complete reverence'.[83] *Hypotagē* is the same noun used to describe the position of women in the ecclesial assembly in 2.11. The supervisor is to maintain order in his household, and by analogical extension, within the ecclesial community. This is leadership modelled uncritically on the cultural norm of Greco-Roman culture, particularly in the absolute rule of the *pater familas*. As Johnson points out, for

---

[80] Johnson, *1 & 2 Timothy* (2001), 212.
[81] Johnson, *1 & 2 Timothy*, 213. The choice of 'supervisor' is Johnson's own, and somewhat begs the translation.
[82] Raymond E. Brown, 'Episkopē and Episkopos', *Theological Studies* (1980): 336.
[83] Johnson's translation: *1 & 2 Timothy*, 212.

Paul the question in verse 5 is rhetorical: 'the ability to rule the church [as *paterfamilias*] presupposes at least the ability to govern one's own household' in the same, culturally determined, manner.[84]

Deacons [in 1 Tim. 3.12] and elders [in 5.17] are expected to supervise the blend of household and ecclesial community in a similar manner. After all, the *ekklēsia* (the church) is itself the *oikos tou theou* (the household of God) [1 Tim. 3.15].

> Clearly, leadership here is envisaged as a much more directive and controlling role than is comfortable for contemporary readers who at best consider leaders as 'enablers' or 'facilitators'.[85]

Before-standing and gifts – Romans 12

Paul's description of leadership in 1 Tim. does seem to assume that it replicates the conventional hierarchies of his society. What about his description in Romans, where 'before-standing' is much more closely connected to the gifts of the Holy Spirit?

The *charisma* of Rom. 12 are 'the specific participation of individual Christians in grace'.[86] That participation is 'the special gift for service',[87] and the service is the edification of the church. Paul therefore gives us a (non-exclusive but symbolic) list, in which the gifts are accompanied by the serving gerund-participle (in other words, the gift is dependent on the way and the extent to which it is expressed): prophecy, in proportion to faith, ministry and ministering; teacher, teaching and so on. An exception is the leader; he is to be *diligent* in his 'before-standing' (ο προισταμενος εν σπουδη) [Rom. 12.8]. But as Ziesler points out, *proïstamenos* is placed, sixth in the list, between 'contributing liberally' and 'performing acts of mercy'. The context is the 'social-service aspect of the primitive church's

---

[84] Johnson, *1 & 2 Timothy*, 216.
[85] Johnson, *1 & 2 Timothy*, 223–4.
[86] Joseph A. Fitzmyer, *Romans* (1992), 646.
[87] Johnson, *1 & 2 Timothy*, 253.

life',[88] not its organization. The reference, surely, is to the person in charge of the church's financial support, and therefore a more reasonable translation would be 'he who gives let him do so with simplicity, he who cares with zeal, he who does good with cheerfulness'.[89] This 'leader' role is dependent, not on theology, but on the social circumstances of the Roman church: as Cranfield puts it, the phrase seems to conjure an image of the charitable administrator who by 'virtue of his social status' was able to act as friend, advocate and protector 'for those members of the community who were not in a position to defend themselves'.[90] This is first century *noblesse oblige*. However, there is a theological depth to this teaching, which moves beyond mere charity: 'the task of the προϊστάμενοι is in large measure that of pastoral care, and the emphasis is not on their rank or authority but on their efforts for the eternal salvation of believers'.[91]

'Leadership' here is not heroic. It is to administer diligently the pastoral care of the *ekklēsia*. To do so will require the disqualification of those who love money [1 Tim. 3.3], among other examples of bourgeois morality. And yet, as Johnson points out, 'to ask for a leader who has moral probity and is known by outsiders as having such virtue is to make a legitimate request at any time, but, above all, when the reputation of the community is threatened by leaders who lack such qualities'.[92] Paul wants discretion, care and diligence on the part of those who hold any kind of financial or social power in the community. The one who 'before-stands' might be a leader, but he is one who serves [Lk. 22.26].[93]

The bounded, stable, and culturally distinguishable characteristics of the Jesus movement do not seem to have placed a great weight on the quest for 'leadership'. At least, the sort of leadership we have found in the Jesus Movement and its scriptures does not seem to be the sort of leadership looked for and desired by the secular scholars of the twentieth century and their ecclesiastical

---

[88] John Ziesler, *Paul's Letter to the Romans* (1989), 300.
[89] Bo Reicke, 'προϊστημι', *Theological Dictionary of the New Testament* (1968), 701. Compare with 'he who gives aid, [to do so] with zeal' in Ziesler, *Romans*, 290.
[90] C. E. B. Cranfield, *Romans* (1979) 2:626–7.
[91] Reicke, 'προϊστημι', 701.
[92] Johnson, *1 & 2 Timothy*, 225.
[93] Reicke, 'προϊστημι', 702.

admirers. If the Jesus Movement was not a leadership movement, what, therefore, can we say its nature more exactly was?

The Jesus Movement as a discipleship community

Simply put, the Jesus Movement was a *Discipleship Community* (DC), in which the primary purpose of the community was to instil in its (loosely defined) members, a sense of what it means to be a disciple ('one who accepted [Jesus's] teachings and sought to be identified with him'[94]).

Thus, following Dunn, the proclamation of Jesus's Gospel was based on the three-fold message of: 'Repent'; 'Believe'; 'Follow Me'.[95] This last part shows the irreducibly personal nature of the Jesus Movement. Within the DC, the most important relationships were personal: everything was focused through and around Jesus. Dunn's emphasis on personal relationships with Jesus is borne out by the insight of Dietrich Bonhoeffer, in which Christian discipleship should only be, *can* only be, mediated through the person of Jesus Christ, through the process which Bonhoeffer called *Christus als Gemeinde existierend*, Christ existing as community.[96]

Which scriptural passages show most clearly the outworking of this DC? In what ways did the community of the Jesus Movement, swiftly, come to understand its vocation and its relationship with its founder?

Discipleship and the cross

Jesus was judicially executed through the Roman punishment of crucifixion. This was a major evangelistic and theological handicap

---

[94]From the Introduction to Longenecker, *Patterns of Discipleship in the New Testament*, 2.
[95]Dunn, *Jesus Remembered*, 1:13.2.
[96]See, for example, Bonhoeffer, *DBWE 1*, 121.

for the early Church. Paul recognised it as such when he referred to the 'stumbling-block' for the Jews and 'foolishness' for the Gentiles to hear the message of a crucified Christ [1 Cor. 1.23]. The stumbling block did not recede for later Christian apologists. Thus Justin acknowledges that the pagans regard the crucified Christ as evidence of Christian 'madness' (μανία), in that 'we give to a crucified man a place second to the unchangeable and eternal God'.[97]

Pagan observers were no less damning. For Tacitus, Christianity as a whole was a 'pernicious superstition';[98] for Pliny the Younger it was also 'extravagant'.[99] Even popular authors were able to mock the public role of the cross: Plautus connected the outstretching of arms with the weight of the cross-piece of the cross:

> You'll soon have to trudge out beyond the gate in that attitude, I take it – arms outstretched, with your gibbet on your shoulders.[100]

Minucius Felix, a Christian apologist (fl. c. AD 210), shows how such scorn was sustained in pagan Roman culture:

> ...he who explains their ceremonies by reference to a man punished by extreme suffering for his wickedness, and to the deadly wood of the cross, appropriates fitting altars for reprobate and wicked men, that they may worship what they deserve.[101]

As Hengel, who collated many more examples of Greco-Roman attitudes to the cross and crucifixion, puts it:

> A crucified messiah, son of God or God [himself] must have seemed a contradiction in terms to anyone Jew, Greek, Roman

---

[97] Justin Martyr, 'First Apology', 13.4. See also *Dialogue with Trypho* 8.3; 10.3; 90.1; 137.1ff.
[98] Cornelius Tacitus, *The Annals*, 15.44.3.
[99] Pliny the Younger, *Letters* 10.96.4–8.
[100] Plautus, *Miles Gloriosus*, 2.4.7.
[101] Minucius Felix, *Octavius* 9.4.

or barbarian, asked to believe such a claim, and it will certainly have been thought offensive and foolish.[102]

And yet we have it on good authority that Christ was crucified. And, more than that, the fact of his crucifixion was a central part of Christian preaching from the beginning, as we can see from its incorporation in Paul's letters, and the way Jesus's own teaching about crucifixion was retained. Why was the fact of crucifixion so important for the proclamation of the Gospel? What does the cross have to teach those who seek to follow Christ?

Taking up – Mark 8

He called the crowd with his disciples, and said to them, 'If any want to become my followers, let them deny themselves and take up their cross and follow me'. [Mk 8.34]

This passage comes within the long exploration of discipleship in Mk 8.22–10.52. According to Ernest Best it marks the transition in Jesus's ministry from public to private, where the focus is no longer teaching *to* the crowd but teaching *for* the disciples. The crowds might be present, they might overhear, or even be addressed by Jesus, but from this central section of the gospel onwards, the content of Jesus's message is intended for the inner circle, those who have chosen to follow him: it is 'the centre of Mark's instruction to his readers on the meaning for them of Christ and their own discipleship'.[103]

The section begins and ends with the healing of a blind man, the man from Bethsaida and the separate healing of Bartimaeus. The healings function as catalysts for Jesus's true nature and purpose to be both demonstrated and explained. The blindness of the man at Bethsaida is contrasted explicitly with the blindness of Peter in refusing to see the nature of the Messiah's vocation [Mk 8.32].

---

[102] Martin Hengel, *Crucifixion* (1977), 10.
[103] Ernest Best, *Following Jesus* (1981), 15.

Mark does not give us the terms of Peter's rebuke, but Matthew presents it as an attempt to preserve Jesus from such a fate: 'God forbid it, Lord! This must never happen to you' [Mt. 16.22]. Jesus's response is just as direct as before: 'Get behind me, Satan! For you are setting your mind not on divine things but on human things' [Mk 8.33].

Now it is time to set the disciples' minds (and the minds of the accompanying crowd) upon divine things, to instruct the listeners into the true nature of the discipleship they seem to have so blithely accepted. Jesus turns to the assembled crowd and instructs them on the nature of the relationship into which they have entered.

Ernest Best points out the significance of Mark's Greek in vv. 34–38. The commands 'deny' and 'take up' are in the aorist tense: the action is past and complete. But the verb translated 'follow' as in 'take up their cross and follow me', ἀκολουθείω, is in the present active imperative singular: its meaning is 'to be in the same way with'. The action, the *following*, with a cross that has been once and for all taken up, continues.

In the social and religious world of first century Palestine, a disciple would often expect to 'follow' his rabbi. 'Following' meant something particular and practical: in Rabbinic literature, to follow was 'the act of the disciple who walks at a respectful distance behind their master'.[104] However, for Jesus and his disciples, 'coming after' means something new and innovative:

> The call is not one to accept a certain system of teaching, live by it, continue faithfully to interpret it and pass it on, which was in essence the call of a rabbi to his disciples; nor was it a call to accept a certain philosophical position which will express itself in a certain type of behaviour, as in stoicism; nor is it the call to devote the alleviation of suffering for others; nor is it the call to pass through certain rites as in the Mysteries so as to become an initiate of the God, his companion – the carrying of the cross is no rite! It is a call to fall in behind Jesus and go with him.[105]

---

[104] Eduard Schweizer, *Lordship and Discipleship* (1960), 12.
[105] Best, *Disciples and discipleship* (1986), 7f.

For Mark, the taking-up of the cross is neither wholly metaphorical, as it is with Luke ['If any want to become my followers, let them deny themselves and take up their cross *daily* and follow me'. Lk. 9.23: emphasis added]; nor is it wholly literal. Even though Mark was probably written in the time of the Neronian persecution (AD 63),[106] Mark expected some of the disciples to survive physically to the time of the Second Coming of Christ and the vindication of the persecuted church: 'Truly I tell you, there are some standing here who will not taste death until they see that the kingdom of God has come with power' [Mk 9.1]. The 'cross' must mean, therefore, the 'ever present possibility' of persecution in the early church.[107] As Daniel Berrigan said, 'If you want to follow Jesus, you had better look good on wood'.[108] It should be noted that Berrigan does not mean by this that the means of Jesus's passion should be literally and physically emulated; rather he affirms that to be a true disciple of Jesus will require an intimate and costly acquaintance with persecution and suffering. Hurtado describes this as a 'cross-emphasis' in Mark's Christology and the scheme of his Gospel, which 'coheres with his emphasis on Jesus's crucifixion as the paradigm of faithful discipleship'.[109]

In the instruction to take up the cross Mark makes no distinction between two potential audiences: the crowds and the disciples. He is happy to differentiate between the two in other passages; for example showing Jesus physically or rhetorically withdrawing to give his disciples a hidden teaching; in Mk 9.9 'he ordered them to tell no one about what they had seen, until after the Son of Man had risen from the dead'; in Mk 10.45 'For the Son of Man came not to be served but to serve, and to give his life a ransom for many' [see further Mk 4.10ff; 6.31; 7.17; 10.10]. In this passage the significance of the cross and its connection to Jesus's own resurrection is described to the inner circle alone. But in Mk 8 it is both

---

[106] Best, *Disciples and discipleship*, 8.
[107] Best, *Disciples and discipleship*, 9.
[108] This aphorism is widely attributed to Berrigan, but never with a source. Even Ross Labrie, the editor of a collection of his writings, was unable to confirm the accuracy of the attribution to me.
[109] Larry W. Hurtado, 'Following Jesus', in *Patterns of Discipleship*, 25.

crowd and disciples who are presented with the *consequences* of discipleship: it is only later that the disciples are presented with the *rewards* of discipleship. This is, Best says lightly:

> ...the reverse of the modern evangelist's practice: to preach Christ crucified and then explain to converts the nature of discipleship and the activities involved therein. Does this mean that it was the custom in Mark's community to challenge the uncommitted with the hard call to dedicated service and leave the difficult matter of the cross until they had accepted the call to committal?[110]

Best thinks that this would be unfair to Mark: the intention of the evangelist is to question the commitment of those who claim to be Christian but whose expression of faith was feeble and half-hearted. For Mark and his community there was

> ...essentially no difference in the meaning of Christianity for the new Christian and the experienced convert of long-standing: for each it is as simple and as difficult as taking the cross and denying the self.[111]

These two aspects for discipleship in the early Church are equally important and we should treat them separately.

Discipleship and denial

There is a practicality to discipleship of the early church: it is not 'mere' intellectual assent, or ritual action. It is an encompassing attitude, which finds its expression through continuing action. And the encompassing attitude is to be summed up in the word 'denial': ἀπαρνέομαι (*aparnéomai*).

---

[110] Best, *Following Jesus*, 31. The whole section on Mark 8.34–9:1 on pp. 28–54 is relevant to this discussion.
[111] Best, *Following Jesus*, 32.

This is the important word to understand if we are to understand Christianity's earliest concepts of leadership and followership. *Self*-denial is the royal road to discipleship. Often, however, inquiries are so fixated on the question of the destination, discipleship, that the place of origin is neglected: *what* or *who* is it that is being denied?

In modern Western culture the answer is so apparent as to be axiomatic: the self being denied is simply and completely the autonomous individual. We see a fine, and perhaps defining, expression of this idea in the work of Adolf Harnack. In the third of his sixteen lectures on 'What is Christianity?' delivered in the University of Berlin in 1899–1900, Harnack explored the meaning of the 'kingdom of God'. For Harnack the metaphor was only explicable as a kingdom of individuals:

> The kingdom of God comes by coming to the individual, by entering into his soul and laying hold of it. True, the kingdom of God is the rule of God; but it is the rule of the holy God in the hearts of individuals; it is *God Himself in His power*. From this point of view everything that is dramatic in the external and historical sense has vanished; and gone, too, are all the external hopes for the future.[112]

Harnack justified his position by reference to Jesus's teaching through parables:

> Take whatever parable you will, the parable of the sower, of the pearl of great price, of the treasure buried in the field – the word of God, God himself, is the kingdom. It is not a question of angels and devils, thrones and principalities, but of God and the soul, the soul and its God.[113]

Harnack was not alone in this belief: almost everyone in his

---

[112]Lecture III, in Adolf Harnack, *What Is Christianity?* (1904), 57. [Emphasis in original.]

[113]Harnack, *What Is Christianity?*, 57–8. Of course this is only true if one ignores the parable of the tares, the net, the talents, sheep and goats, and so on.

time and culture thought the same way. So, for example, Paul Wernle believed that 'the most certain characteristic of Jesus' thought [was] a decisive stern religious individualism'.[114] Ernst Troeltsch, in a polemical attack on social democratic sociology, makes it clear that the Christian faith is not a social organization concerned with social justice (the Christian church was not 'a social movement', neither was it 'the product of a class struggle', nor was it concerned with the 'social upheavals of the ancient world'). Rather the root idea was religious individualism: '...in the whole range of Early Christian literature...there is no hint of any formulation of the "Social" question'; the central problem is always purely religious...' For Troeltsch, 'purely religious' problems are to do with 'the salvation of the soul, monotheism, life after death, purity of worship, the right kind of congregational organization, the application of Christian ideals to daily life, and the need for severe self-discipline in the interests of personal holiness'.[115] Jesus has nothing to say about social injustice. He 'was too lofty a figure to be addressing workaday concerns of social reform... Above all, he was concerned to help the individual prepare the soul for an imminent Kingdom that was not of this world'.[116]

This may have been so for nineteenth- and twentieth-century Germany, in which a Romantic and heroic individual was the proper seat for the 'self'. It certainly is so for North Atlantic society, as we have seen, where a separated and lonely individual, separated out from the rest of society, is given the highest social status. We cannot say the same for the culture of the Palestine of Jesus's day.

We might say that 'self' is the arena in which 'self-interest' might be expressed, and the values of self-interest protected: in 'individualistic cultures' like our own, 'self-interests are proper to single persons'. In ancient Mediterranean culture, the 'self' was to be understood properly as a 'collective' entity.[117] What we call the 'self' is limited to the autonomous actions of an individual:

---

[114]Paul Wernle, *Jesus* (1917); quoted in Martin Dibelius, 'Jesus in contemporary German theology', *The Journal of Religion* (April 1931): 191.

[115]Ernst Troeltsch, *The Social Teaching of the Christian Churches* (1931), 1:39.

[116]Constance L. Benson, *God and Caesar* (1998), 159.

[117]Bruce J. Malina in *The Social World of Jesus and the Gospels* (1996), 73–4.

within a collectivist culture, the lines of the self are drawn, paradoxically to our way of thinking, further out, incorporating the needs and identities of other individuals and groups, what Malina calls 'ingroups'. This wider self finds security, identity and meaning within something called a 'fictive kin group'.[118] These are the groups we choose, or by whom we are chosen, in order to be something bigger than ourselves. There is a striking parallel with the Southern African concept of *ubuntu,* under which an individual is only human inasmuch as s/he is in connection with a wider community.

We see remnants of this process, even in the virulently individualistic nature of North Atlantic society, when we see the appeal of football supporting, or the army, or following a particular music group or style ('Emos against the world!'). The same thing is at work, on a much more important level (because it is to do with ultimate questions of salvation and redemption) in the world of the Jesus Movement. There 'adherence to a fictive kin group centred on God and adhering to the teaching of Jesus was to characterize true Israel'.[119] In short, denying the self in Jesus's world meant something more (something greater) than refusing oneself little treats.

Davis notes how this works in Mark's Gospel. The calling of the Twelve [Mk 3.13–35] is followed by 'a group of stories set in a house which show Jesus at odds with his blood kin and forming a "new family" including only those who do the will of God'. The leaving of 'one's literal family' is both the cause of persecution and the means by which one 'embrace[s] a new Christian family'. [120] One theologian, despite teaching in Harnack's university, was able to affirm this collectivist teaching: 'Human existence has continuity only through the other person. We are imaginable only as bound to our neighbour'.[121]

We can examine in more detail the how a fictive kin group is created in the teaching of Lk. 9.57–62.

---

[118] Malina, *Social World of Jesus*, 87.

[119] Malina, *Social World of Jesus*, 94.

[120] Philip G. Davis, 'Self-understanding in Mark' (1990), 112.

[121] Dietrich Bonhoeffer, 'Dogmatic Exercises' in *DBWE* 12 (2009), 222.

Leaving the dead – Luke 9

> To another Jesus said: 'Follow me'. But he said, 'Lord, first
> let me go and bury my father'. But Jesus said to him, 'Let the
> dead bury their own dead; but as for you, go and proclaim the
> kingdom of God'. [Lk. 9.59–60]

As Sanders points out, this teaching has a double impact.[122] The
first, a positive one, is widely recognised: to be a disciple of Jesus
is a response to an urgent call, and trumps all other responsibilities.
So, for example, Schweizer argues that this shows 'discipleship
excludes all other ties'. The disciples of Jesus 'should be prepared
to deny everything, including their lives'.[123] But, as Sanders notes,
the refusal to bury one's parents is not just disobeying filial obligations; it is also disobedience to God in the Torah.[124] Caring for the
dead bodies of one's family superseded all other commandments
of the Torah:

> He who is confronted by a dead relative is freed from reciting
> the *Shema*, from the Eighteen Benedictions, and from all the
> commandments stated in the Torah.[125]

It is not enough to set this refusal to obey the Torah to one side, as
if Jesus were referring to a different situation from that envisaged
in the Law: it is hard, says Sanders, 'to believe that Jesus saw the
requirement to bury dead parents as only "domestic responsibility"
and did not know that it was a commandment from God'.[126] In this
circumstance at least, it appears Jesus believed that the call to
follow him would require clear disobedience of the Law of Moses.
Discipleship, here, sets the disciple beyond the conventions and
requirements of society. The 'fictive kin group' has first call.

---

[122] Sanders, *Jesus and Judaism*, 253.
[123] Schweizer, *Lordship and Discipleship*, 16, 21.
[124] Sanders, *Jesus and Judaism*, 253.
[125] Berakoth 3.1, quoted in Hengel, *Charismatic Leader*, 9. There is a significant
transgression of this commandment in the work of Emerson: 'I shun father and
mother and wife and brother, when my genius calls me'. *Self-Reliance* (1841), 30.
[126] Sanders, *Jesus and Judaism*, 254.

Five things to say about leadership in the New Testament

We have seen in the scriptural witness what Hengel has called the 'almost inseparable fusion of the "Jesus tradition" and "community formations" in the Gospel traditions'.[127] In other words, from the very beginning, from the earliest scriptural traditions, the Christian community behaved as if there was a continuity between what it understood discipleship to be, and what was taught and modelled by its founder. What they wrote is what they understood Jesus to have taught. It is what Gerhard Lohfink has called the 'confirmation of truth through praxis'.[128] That confirmation goes backwards, from the writing of the Scripture to the memory of who Jesus was. That confirmation also has to go forward, from the witness of Scripture to the practices of the Christian community in our own days and times. In order to make that forward connection, we can say five things about 'leadership' and discipleship in the New Testament.[129]

First and foremost, whatever else we say, we should acknowledge that Jesus called people to follow him, in a way in which a direct allegiance to his person and authority was expected. Schweizer calls this 'decisive, indeed as *the* decisive act'.[130] To be a disciple meant *following* Jesus.

Second, Jesus's calling begins something new, in which everything will be changed. Even the oldest, most instinctive, requirements of the Law and the function of grace through the Law, are subject to change, if not overthrowal (as we saw with the injunction to bury the dead in the previous section). This calling assumes 'the character of an act of divine grace'.[131]

Third, 'following Jesus' means sharing an intimacy with Jesus, and performing acts of service with and to him. As Hurtado puts

---

[127] Hengel, *Charismatic Leader*, 83.
[128] Lohfink, *Jesus and Community*, 176.
[129] Following, and expanding upon, Schweizer, *Lordship and Discipleship*, chapter 1.
[130] Schweizer, *Lordship and Discipleship*, 20.
[131] Schweizer, *Lordship and Discipleship*, 20.

it, it means following *Jesus,* 'with no rival, no distraction and no competition for the allegiance of his disciples'.[132]

Fourth, it requires self-denial, which, as we have seen in the cultural world of first-century Palestine, is not limited solely to (modern) understandings of the self as an individuated person; the self was identified and located within a complex network of relationships, responsibilities and obligations. These are all to be given up.

Fifth, and not unexpectedly, denying the self, whether collectivist or individualist, in order to follow Jesus will lead to rejection, suffering and death, just as Jesus himself experienced all those things. But rejection, suffering and death is also the path to redemptive glory, for the Teacher and disciple alike.

If there is a continuing connection between the Jesus Movement and the witness of Scripture and the Christian community today, then we shall see these five factors at work in the world in which we inhabit, confirming truth through praxis.

Where shall we see this confirmation?

---

[132] Hurtado, 'Following Jesus', 25.

Chapter 9
Mythos and anti-mythos

A society's mass fantasies are anything but trivial, and I do not think we have anything to gain by underrating or simply mocking them... Societies give themselves away in their favourite fantasies; they betray their assumptions of what the world is really like.

ROWAN WILLIAMS, 'THE TRUCE OF GOD'

'...True, adventurous and uninhibited...'

As we learnt in the foreword, when the Foundation for Church Leadership was launched, Bishop Michael Turnbull described the situation faced by church leaders, and questions that haunt them:

> A question never far from the mind of a church leader is 'How can I break out of institutional shackles and be the true, adventurous, uninhibited leader I want to be?'.[1]

---

[1] Michael Turnbull, 'Introduction', 4.

The Bishop is famous for have authored a report which restructured and reformed the secretariat of the Church of England, but this question makes me think that he was actually ambitious to be Aragorn, true King of the West:

> Hold your ground! Hold your ground! Sons of Gondor, of Rohan, my brothers, I see in your eyes the same fear that would take the heart of me. A day may come when the courage of men fails, when we forsake our friends and break all bonds of fellowship, but it is not this day. An hour of wolves and shattered shields, when the age of men comes crashing down, but it is not this day! This day we fight! By all that you hold dear on this good Earth, I bid you stand, Men of the West![2]

Thus we can see the triumph of *Mythological-Leadership*. In an organization which sought to connect the best of business praxis with the depths of Christian theological *doxis*, the assumed model of leadership which is at work is leadership as self-expression, self-reliant individuation. To be a true leader is to disconnect oneself from community ('institutional shackles') and to launch out on a journey ('adventurous') of personal growth ('I want to be'). Church Leadership is thus, finally, completely and definitively, Emersonian.

We have sketched out one possible way of reading the mythography of our time, with its constant yearning for the leadership of the heroic individual and the constant flowing between assertion, repudiation, and resurgence of this yearning. We have seen there is a relationship dynamic between leader and follower, the individual and his community, the will to power and the lack of will to passivity. But is this important? What difference does it make? Leadership may function mythologically, but so what? In other words, is there a moral importance attached to this question? I believe there is,

---

[2] Aragorn's speech before the Black Gate, from Peter Jackson's *The Return of the King*, (2003). The speech was the creation of Jackson and his fellow scriptwriters, Fran Walsh and Philippa Boyens. It doesn't exist in Tolkien's original: there we are told only 'Little time was left to Aragorn for the ordering of his battle'. (J. R. R. Tolkien, *The Lord of the Rings*, (2002), 891.) More evidence of the mythologizing power of movies!

and the nature of this moral question can be usefully, and properly, summarised under the heading of 'heresy'.

Expecting the inquisition

'Heresy', like 'myth', 'leadership', 'art' or 'religion' is another one of those 'essentially contested concepts'. It is difficult to use the word without images of the Inquisition (Spanish or Monty Python) crossing our imagination. It was and remains a politically and socially charged word, often being used as a means of social control, determining what ideas and actions can be counted within and without the Pale (look, for example, at the frequency with which the expression 'political heresy' is used in the news media).

But what is heresy? Most works treat the subject by giving a history of the various beliefs condemned as heretical, a combination of the social sciences / Justice Stewart method of definition: we trace instances of the idea through history and then we'll know it when we see it. See, for example, Alister McGrath's excellent history of heresy where the author gets to Chapter 5 before attempting to define an 'essence' of heresy: the remainder of the book is a (very readable) account of different forms of Christian heresy.[3] E. D. McShane's article on 'The History of Heresy' is another good example: we read of Arianism, Donatism, Monothelitism, and the Albigenses (in the pre-Modern period alone).[4] This demonstrates the pragmatism of medieval theologians: they were not concerned as much with 'abstract heresy as with guilty heretics', in other words, 'persons within the community who were defined as a threat to the faith and to the institution'.[5]

One problem with this approach is that we limit heresy to matters of belief: Orthodox Christians believe *this* about the nature

---

[3] Alister E. McGrath, *Heresy* (2009).
[4] E. D. McShane, 'Heresy (History of)', *New Catholic Encyclopedia* (1967).
[5] Lester R. Kurtz, 'The Politics of Heresy', *American Journal of Sociology* (1983): 1087.

of Jesus Christ; Nestorians (condemned as heretics) believe *that* about the nature of Jesus Christ. Both states, orthodoxy and heresy, begin and end in belief and belief only: heresy, in this way of thinking, is just that – a way of thinking. To encounter this wrong way of thinking was to encounter, literally, 'bad faith'. The heretic was wilfully a heretic, guilty not just of wrong thinking, but also the wrong attitude to their thinking: heresy possessed an 'obdurate posture', turned its 'face against the whole Church' and swarmed 'to form its own conventicle'. It was marked by a 'stubborn inflexible will' and 'intractability and pertinacity'.[6]

This implies that heresy has its origins in the actions and the will of the individual (a congenial thought for Brian Cohen, perhaps?[7]). But as Kurtz and McGarth have noted, heresy cannot exist without a social dimension. Kurtz give five dimensions to heresy, which shows how it exists somewhere more than inside an individual's thinking.[8]

First, a heretic has to be 'close enough to be threatening but distant enough to be considered in error'. It is developed from within orthodoxy, and, indeed, claims orthodoxy for itself. It is the narcissism of the small (but crucial) difference. The heretic, therefore, is 'a deviant insider'.

Second, heresy develops out of social conflict, and is built out of the issues raised in that social conflict. Heresy addresses the issues which make people anxious in any given time or culture:

> As social groups find an 'affinity' between their status interests on the one hand and a particular configuration of ideas or worldview on the other, they identify with that definition of the situation and use it to legitimate or enhance their social status.

Because of this, every heresy necessarily 'implies a political stance' (i.e. one which has something to say about the present political

---

[6]F. X. Lawlor, 'Heresy', *New Catholic Encyclopedia* (1967), 1063.
[7]'You've got to think for yourselves. You're all individuals!' says Brian to the crowds.
[8]In both the article already cited and his book *The Politics of Heresy* (1986), chapter 1.

settlement), and so 'every heretic leads an insurrection, implicitly or explicitly'.[9]

Third, because heresy has social origins, it also has 'social consequences'. The problem of heresy, is, 'at its root, a problem of authority': how elites maintain social control, and how subordinates challenge social statuses. Every heretic will get 'something out' of the heresy, even if it is only the status of being an authentic teacher of the faith: this does not mean that heretics and their opponents are 'necessarily malicious or self-serving',[10] but neither does it exclude the possibility.

Fourth, the process of defining and labelling a heresy will have doctrinal consequences: parties take sides and 'it becomes increasingly difficult to mix positions and beliefs'. What you believe, and more powerfully, what you are able to believe, are all affected by heresy and the fight against heresy. This is not necessarily a bad thing: defining one's own beliefs, even if in opposition to another's, at least allows your beliefs to have been tested. The morality of this depends on the, previously mentioned, social and political consequences of engaging with heresy.

Fifth, the process of defining and labelling heresy is best understood as a ritual. By this Kurtz does not mean, simply, 'bell, book and candle' and liturgies of anathema. Rather, he means a process by which changes in status and condition are negotiated to minimize stress and anxiety, in either the individual or a larger group such as a clan, tribe or society. In this respect, defining heresy has the same social function that myth fulfils in Lévi-Strauss's definition, 'to provide a logical model capable of overcoming' the contradictions between life as experienced and life as idealised.[11] In other words, rituals of heresy (and myth) 'relieve social and psychological tensions and to focus anxiety on that which is controllable'.[12]

This is heresy. This is the danger faced by the Church. A temptation to believe harmful things, to organize in damaging

---

[9] Kurtz, *Politics of Heresy*, 4.
[10] Kurtz, *Politics of Heresy*, 5.
[11] Lévi-Strauss, 'Structural Study of Myth', 229.
[12] Kurtz, *Politics of Heresy*, 6.

social ways, to tolerate abusive political relationships: *all for very good reasons.*

The baptism of mythological-leadership

We can see how harmful, damaging and abusive the heresy of 'leadership' might be when we come to a final description of the true model of leadership, *MythL*, operating within the Church today. It is at work within the Church because it is the way our culture, North Atlantic society, understands leadership to be, and understands it in such an unconscious way that we don't even realize that *MythL* has this power and influence upon us.

We have seen the antecedents of *MythL*: Carlyle's 'great man' obsession; Emerson's construction of an 'American Adam' religion of solipsism, in which the true object of veneration is the heroic, lone, rugged, individual; the power of the West, and the place of the Frontier; the nineteenth-century fear of the crowd and the twentieth-century oppression of those in the crowd who were different; the elevation of Hitler, and the enfolding of that elevation into American culture.

At the same time the secular world attempted to sell *ManL* as the solution for our entire political, social and resource conflicts. If you don't have leaders, you won't be successful. *ManL* spoke to the profound, existential, anxiety following World War Two, that our familiar, if flawed, world, was threatened by external powers, outside our control: 'them', 'those', 'it'. The only solution was to have someone who could make us nimble, responsive, creative, effective, successful: a leader!

Living between these two powerful forces, the Church, inevitably, attempted to discover its own flavour, its own theme of leadership, *MissL*, which could stand in distinction to the 'johnny-come-lately' strictures of the business school.[13] It has produced

---

[13]What is Steven Croft's attempt to co-opt Moses for leadership but an attempt

papers, reports, syllabuses and quality assurance documents all designed to foster, encourage and express the leadership (innate or developed) it finds in its ordinands and ministers. It believes that this is a useful and necessary project; otherwise, why would it devote so much time, money and effort to the promulgation of its varying definitions?

But underneath the ostensible goals of *MissL* and *ManL* lies the mythic sub-strata of *MythL*. Building on the important definitional work of Jewett, Lawrence, and Wink, we can finally describe the outline of *Mythological-Leadership*, adapting Jewett and Lawrence's many definitions of the American Monomyth. When we talk about leadership, this is what we are talking about:

> The Leader originates outside the community he is called to lead. The structures of the community have failed to deal with an existential threat, but the rise of the threat has coincided with, or even called up, the arrival of the idealistic Leader, who is selfless, ascetic, asexual and alone. The community, as a collective and as individuals, dissolve into the dominance of the Leader, who swiftly assumes an authority that is less to do with his office and more to do with the power ascribed to his personality. The Leader will find himself faced by violent opponents, and their implacability, and the violence they offer, demonstrates the sincerity and the righteousness of the Leader's actions. He remains patient and controlled in the face of provocations, 'utterly cool and thus divinely competent'[14]. The leadership of the Leader is exercised on behalf of the community, and thus must be directed outwards: to be successful, leadership is something that is exercised *against* the 'Other'.[15] The community is finally saved through a violent confrontation, in which only the guilty and unrighteous are hurt, with the sole exception of

---

to claim chronological priority? See 'Advocating Creative Church Leadership' in chapter 1.

[14] Lawrence and Jewett, *American Superhero*, 47.

[15] 'People want religious leaders to tell them that *they're* right', and thus, by extension, that the 'Others' are wrong. Rowan Williams, 'The stable door is open', *The Times* (December 2007).

the Leader, who is mortally wounded. However, by his stripes the community has been redeemed: the 'siege of paradise'[16] is lifted, and the community has thrilled by the exercise of vicarious violence, focused away from the community. The Leader is removed from the community, and his exit demonstrates both the costliness of his sacrifice and his disconnection with the community in the first place. Very few recognize his leaving, and, if he is remembered, it is in a distorted and hypocritical way – those from within the community who were most opposed to his presence are now the greatest advocates of his memory.

Inescapably within this model of *MythL* we come across the need (unexpressed and unacknowledged) that the Leader is required to be violent, on behalf of 'Us' against 'Them'. This 'violence' may be moral or symbolic or figurative or metaphorical, but it is still violence. There is no situation that cannot be redeemed by the death of Tiâmat.

As McGrath says of heresy it represents 'certain ways of formulating the core themes of the Christian faith – ways that are sooner or later recognized by the church to be dangerously inadequate or even destructive'.[17] Heresy develops from within the community of faith, as an 'alternative belief system within its host', which, like a virus, uses 'its host's replication system to achieve dominance'.[18]

Martyn Percy said something similar about the willingness of the Church to engage with 'spirituality' rather than the Gospel, in an attempt to be evangelistically successful. He imagined the conversation with contemporary culture as if it was happening in Babylon at the time of the Exile:

> You can imagine the Israelites in, say, Babylon, and those wonderful, whispering voices of Anglican accommodation that would've been around even then, turning round to the leaders and to the prophets saying, "Now look. We're not really saying that we want to dump Jehovah. All we are saying is that the

---

[16] Lawrence and Jewett, *American Superhero*, 47.
[17] McGrath, *Heresy*, 12.
[18] McGrath, *Heresy*, 34.

Babylonians have done really rather well for themselves. They have nice gardens. They seem to be running rather good water-systems. The roads are excellent; health-care provision is good. So, we're really saying how about a bit of a mixed economy here? How about giving these gods a bit of a run, and keeping on with Jehovah, and let's see how it goes?"

Percy warns against this entirely reasonable, results-oriented strategy: 'The things you might want to do, to bring success, and growth, may ultimately do more harm than good'. It is analogous, he says, to putting the Body of Christ on steroids: 'it gives you plenty of critical mass, for just a little bit of effort, and it looks great. But the medium- and the long-term-consequences can be disastrous'.[19]

'Leadership' is an alien virus, ingested by the Christian host. It seems to be reasonable (reflecting our wider society's anxiety about direction, effectiveness, and coherence), and appears to synthesize many Scriptural discussions of influence, witness, pastoral care and oversight. But 'leadership' in our society is fatally flawed by its roots in violence, the will to power and destruction. It doesn't matter how many hyphens we tack on to the front of it ('*servant*-leadership', '*compassionate*-leadership', '*collaborative*-leadership')[20], it is still leadership, and therefore antithetical to the model, ministry and challenge of being a disciple of Jesus Christ.

Where can we find another model, an *anti-mythos*, which stands against this primordial and ineluctable Domination System, and might conform more closely to Jesus's rejection of the violence of the rule of men?[21]

---

[19]Martyn Percy, 'Challenges of Contemporary Culture' (2012).

[20]Imagine hyphenating totalitarianism to see how incoherent this strategy really is: 'ecological-Nazism', 'compassionate-Fascism', 'synergistic-autocracy'!

[21]The 'Domination System' is an epithet of Wink's coining. *Engaging the Powers*, 110–11.

Refuting the dominion of some over others[22]

By May 1934 the Nazi government had been in power for 14 months. The process of *Gleichschaltung* was beginning to impinge upon the practice of Christianity and the polity of the Church. Churchmen opposed to such 'Co-ordination' met in Barmen, in North Rhine-Westphalia. Under the guidance of Karl Barth, the synod issued the Barmen Declaration, which reminded the Church that it was not the world, and the world that it was not the Church.[23] The Third Article of the Declaration makes clear that the Evangelical Church of Germany,

> ...as a church of pardoned sinners, has to witness in the midst of a sinful world, with its faith as with its obedience, with its message as with its order, that it belongs solely to him [Jesus Christ, its Lord] and that it lives and wants to live solely from his comfort and from his direction in the expectations of his appearance.[24]

The fire, the brilliance, the pathos of the leader[25]

The issues in German society which led to the Barmen Declaration had already been publicly addressed by a young Lutheran theologian, Dietrich Bonhoeffer. In the year before Barmen he gave

---

[22] From the Fourth Thesis of the Barmen Declaration (1934) in John H. Leith (ed.), *Creeds of the Churches* (1982), 521.
[23] See Sam Wells's introduction to the Declaration in Samuel Wells, *Christian Ethics* (2010), 186. For a further, excellent, discussion of the historical context and content of the Declaration, see Eberhard Busch, *The Barmen Theses Then and Now* (2010).
[24] Busch, *Barmen Theses*, 49.
[25] Bonhoeffer's epithets for the younger generation's concept of 'leader' in an essay published as 'The Younger Generation's Altered View of the Concept of Führer', (1933) in *DBWE* 12 (2009), 266–8.

an address on 'The Führer and the Individual' as part of a series of lectures on 'The Younger Generation' broadcast by Berliner Rundfunk. Bonhoeffer's lecture was broadcast on February 1, 1933, two days after Hitler was appointed Reich Chancellor. The lecture was well received by the radio critics, but the lecture was curtailed before he addressed the specific political and religious critiques of the Führer cult.[26]

Bonhoeffer identifies the contrast between the younger and older generations, the former born since the turn of the century (*DBWE 12*, 269) and who have experienced the crisis in which 'the previously well-established Western world came apart at the seams' (*DBWE 12*, 271). As a result of this crisis they have issued an 'impassioned call...for new authority' (*DBWE 12*, 272), which, through opposition to the 'unreal individualism' of the older generation, could only imagined 'in terms of a new human being' (*DBWE 12*, 272), one in whom the search for community and authority could be combined and found. This is a natural process: there have always been leaders, and '[w]here there is community there is leadership' (*DBWE 12*, 274). But before the leader was embedded within a 'given social structure', and was dependent upon a specific context: we had 'teachers, statesmen, fathers'. Now the demand is for a leader divorced from this social structure, 'totally divorced from an office... essentially and only leader' (*DBWE 12*, 274). We have *solo dux*.

Because of the deracination of the leader, we have the deracination of the follower: the 'individual is totally dissolved; he becomes a tool in the hands of the leader' (*DBWE 12*, 277). The individual submits, and is disconnected (Bonhoeffer provocatively calls this process *Ausschaltung*, deliberately recalling the *Gleichschaltung* of the new government). The leader, assuming the 'collective power of the people', is 'transformed into the political–messianic idea of leader that we see today' (*DBWE 12*, 278). This the leader must refuse. He is morally obliged to 'lead the led from the authority of the leader's person to a recognition of the true

---

[26] Part of Bonhoeffer's intention was to address the influential work of Jonas Lesser, quoted as the epigraph to this section: Jonas Lesser, *Von deutscher Jugend* (Berlin: Neff, 1932).

authority of order and office' (*DBWE 12*, 280). He must 'radically reject the temptation to become an idol' (*DBWE 12*, 280). If the leader accepts this idolization, if he refuses the true, limited nature of leadership ('this clear restriction of authority' *DBWE 12*, 280), then 'the image of the leader shifts to one of misleader' (*DBWE 12*, 280).

The irony is that if there was anyone who could have embodied the German ideal of the Leader it would have been Bonhoeffer. As emerges from his letters, and the impressions of family and friends in the many biographies, Bonhoeffer possessed a 'magnetic personality':

> He had the rugged build of a strong hiker and aggressive tennis player… He liked folk music as well as Bach and he was a fine amateur pianist. He was also a poet of grace and imagination.[27]

Even at 17, in his first year at university, he impressed his fellow students: he was 'a companionable, physically agile and tough young man', who excelled his friends with his 'stormy temperament and self-confidence'.[28]

Paul Lehmann, his friend from Union Theological Seminary in New York, said of him:

> His impressive physique lent support to a resolute bearing and firmness of purpose that simply took command, uncalculated command, of every situation in which he was present. It was apparent that he was destined for leadership, for which he was equipped by national and cultural habit.[29]

With these gifts of intellect and character, and in a culture which valued and sought out the 'great man' and the 'leader',

---

[27] John T. Elson, 'A Man for Others', *Life*, 7 May 1965, 111. Ironically, the cover story on this issue of *Life* is 'After a Bout of Cancer, John Wayne is Back in Action'.
[28] W. Dreier and H. U. Esche in postwar correspondence with Eberhard Bethge. Quoted in *Dietrich Bonhoeffer: a biography*, Barnett and Robertson (eds) (2000), 50.
[29] Paul Lehmann, 'Paradox of Discipleship', in *I Knew Dietrich Bonhoeffer*, (1966), 42.

what prevented Bonhoeffer from becoming another instance of the *Führerprinzip*? He had the great advantage of becoming a theologian and then a Christian (his own description of his career), and then being willing to spend his energy and his intellect in environments in which a critique of the German cult of the leader could be expressed and lived. For, as Lehmann also said, Bonhoeffer 'was without a trace of status-seeking or of pretence', and manifested an 'openness and integrity in relating to all sorts and conditions of men'. Through his deep-seated desire to be in the service of Jesus Christ 'he found the freedom and the power to be truly and contagiously human'.[30]

Calling and following

We can see this most clearly, when, as an indirect result of the Barmen Declaration, Bonhoeffer taught in an illegal seminary of the Confessing Church based in Finkenwalde, Pomerania from 1935 to 1937. It was an immensely productive time for his theological thinking and writing, and three books were the result: *Life Together, The Prayerbook of the Bible* (an introduction to the Psalms)[31] and, most pertinently for our purposes, *Discipleship.*[32] It is possible to regard *Discipleship* as an extended commentary on the third thesis of the Barmen Declaration, for, as Bonhoeffer's editors say in their afterword to *Discipleship*, here he 'expounded [the thesis] in such a way that its truth became undeniable, even beyond the historical context of the Church Struggle in the Third Reich'.[33]

He addresses the deracination of leader and followers head-on, by refusing to engage with the concept on its own terms. Rather, he asserts a new paradigm: 'Discipleship is a commitment to Christ. Because Christ exists, he must be followed' (*DBWE 4*, 59). There is no programme or abstraction which can be substituted for the

---

[30]Lehmann, 'Paradox of Discipleship', 45.
[31]Published together as *DBWE* 5 (1996).
[32]*DBWE* 4 (2003).
[33]Kuske and Tödt, 'Editors' Afterword', in *DBWE 4*, 298.

person of Jesus Christ: 'the dogmatic systems then in vogue were, in fact, mere ideas about Jesus unrelated to the personal obediential relationship to which Jesus calls his followers'.[34] Nothing can be substituted for this absolute, unconditional and personal imperative: 'the call to discipleship is a commitment solely to the person of Jesus Christ, a breaking through of all legalisms by the grace of him who calls' (*DBWE 4*, 59). And it is Jesus Christ himself, in his concrete individuality, which is the measure and completeness of the call: 'No further content is possible because Jesus is the only content. There is no other content beside Jesus. He himself is it' (*DBWE 4*, 59). Jesus is the means by which disciples are called, and the content of that call. Jesus says, 'Follow me', not 'Assent to a series of programmatic strategies', and certainly not 'Submit yourself to an idolizing Disconnection'.

The focus of the call must not and cannot be upon those who respond. This is perhaps one reason why the Gospels make no attempt at a psychologically satisfying explanation of the reason why the disciples responded to Jesus. There is no 'back-story' for the disciples, so that attention is not deflected from the 'front-story' of the one who is calling. And there can be no implicit assumptions about the one who calls: 'this creative Word has no presuppositions whatsoever. ...The Word of God addressed to these particular concrete persons has no presupposition but Itself'.[35]

The Word of God, in the person of Jesus, is *self*-supposition, and that self-supposition is encountered not 'through speculation but through the concrete demands and addresses of others in concrete situations'.[36] Jesus's disciples did not come to him as if he were a Rabbi, in order to 'debate with a learned and wise man and so increase their knowledge'.[37] Rather, a radical separation between old and new is expected; old man and new disciple, old and new life, old sin and new grace. The first step, after hearing the call, is to renounce the self: 'Allegiance to Christ displaces (by

---

[34] Geffrey B. Kelly and F. Burton Nelson, *The Cost of Moral Leadership* (2003), 135.
[35] A. I. McFadyen, 'The Call to Discipleship' *Scottish Journal of Theology* (1990): 463.
[36] McFadyen, 'Call to Discipleship', 475.
[37] McFadyen, 'Call to Discipleship', 469.

transforming) that to self. The command is to "follow me", not to choose a way of life for oneself'.[38] In other words, 'discipleship is not an addition to the old life'.[39] The first thing which must be lost is the 'illusion of independent self-sufficiency',[40] and that can only be achieved by recognising the confrontation with a demand, to which there were (and are!) only two possible responses: obedience or disobedience.

Obedience and grace

The context for the disciples in the Scriptures is the same as the context for Christians in Bonhoeffer's own day: the disciple is called. There is nothing between him and the one who does the calling. However, immediately interposed between the disciple and the caller are the 'forces' of the world: 'reason… conscience, responsibility, piety, even the law and the principle of Scripture' intervene (*DBWE 4*, 77). The human soul can call upon a myriad of rationalizations to refuse the call, or not to hear the call in the first place. None of those rationalizations are acceptable: 'Jesus' call broke through all of this and mandated obedience. It was God's own word. Simple obedience was required' (*DBWE 4*, 77; see the whole of Chapter 3, 'Simple Obedience').

It might seem, therefore, that obedience engenders within the disciple the faith which responds to the call. Or does faith allow the disciple to hear the call in the first place? Bonhoeffer refutes the premise of the question: 'only the believers obey' and 'only the obedient believe' (*DBWE 4*, 64). He neither believes that first there is belief and then there is obedience, nor first there is obedience followed by belief (*DBWE 4*, 63–4): more exactly, there can never be some 'invariable chronological sequence'.[41] The one does not exist without the other.

---

[38] McFadyen, 'Call to Discipleship', 468.
[39] McFadyen, 'Call to Discipleship', 469.
[40] McFadyen, 'Call to Discipleship', 470.
[41] Stephen Plant, *Bonhoeffer* (2004), 100.

Faith and obedience are linked together in a dialectical and indissoluble unity in which willingness to serve God by obeying the Gospel mandates is the natural and spontaneous note of Christian life governed by the person and mission of Jesus Christ.[42]

Bonhoeffer explicates the consequences of this understanding of obedience by his treatment of the encounter between Jesus and the rich young man as a parable (*DBWE 4*, 69–72). The fault of the rich young man lies, first, in seeking the opinion of a wise religious teacher, rather than recognizing his encounter with 'a divine order with unconditional authority' (*DBWE 4*, 70). The rich young man then attempts to sift and prioritize the commandments of God through 'ethical conflict': 'Which commandments should I obey?' [Mt. 19.18]. This is nothing less than 'the human revolt against God'. The young man does not recognize Satan hiding in the question, for, to 'invoke ethical conflict is to terminate obedience. It is a retreat from God's reality to human possibility, from faith to doubt' (*DBWE 4*, 71). And in this instance 'doubt' means the devil's solution to ethical conflicts: 'keep asking questions, so that you are free from having to obey' (*DBWE 4*, 72). The rich young man, in refusing to recognize his encounter with God, is unable to 'affirm' God: instead 'he affirms himself in a distorted form of individuality (isolation and self-interest)'.[43]

The rich young man is the exemplar of Bonhoeffer's attack on 'cheap grace' (*DBWE 4*, Chapter 1). Discipleship is not and cannot be based on any faithfulness which may belong to the disciple. Discipleship, if it comes from an assertion of the power of 'individuals to constitute themselves through their decisions', would then be 'identified with the power of believers individually to achieve heaven on their own resources and therefore for themselves'.[44] That way leads to 'cheap grace'.

Bonhoeffer's autobiographical and ecclesiastical context had made him realize that the 'Protestant principles of faith alone,

---

[42] Kelly and Nelson, *Cost of Moral Leadership*, 134.
[43] McFadyen, 'Call to Discipleship', 466.
[44] McFadyen, 'Call to Discipleship', 466–7.

Scripture alone, and giving glory to God alone now had deteriorated into mere boorish churchgoing, easy procurement of sacramentalized grace, and [the] reduction of the Bible to legalisms and routine rituals'.[45] The task was now to state the condemnation as clearly as possible.

'Cheap grace is the mortal enemy of our church... [it] means grace as bargain-basement goods, cut-rate forgiveness, cut-rate comfort, cut-rate sacrament...' (*DBWE 4*, 43). The German Church had been knowingly complicit in peddling this forgery: 'Like ravens we have gathered around the carcass of cheap grace. From it we have imbibed the poison which has killed the following of Jesus among us' (*DBWE 4*, 53). The only solution is to seek 'costly grace': costly, 'because it calls to discipleship', 'costs people their lives' and thus 'condemns sin'; grace, 'because it calls us to follow *Jesus Christ*', 'thereby makes [us] live', and 'justifies the sinner' (*DBWE 4*, 45: emphasis in original). Above all, it is costly grace because it was costly to God, 'because it costs God the life of God's Son' (*DBWE 4*, 45). The fact of the Incarnation and Passion of Jesus Christ means that grace can be nothing other than costly.

Individual are removed from 'their surroundings and present context', a context of self-infatuation, and then, through renunciation of self (which is different from *self*-renunciation), is recreated through 'an incorporation into a different relation and relational context'.[46] That relation is solely directed towards Christ: 'his call to discipleship dissolved all ties for the sake of the unique commitment to Jesus Christ' (*DBWE 4*, 62). It cannot be the result of an individual's recreation through an act of individualistic will: it is 'not an act of self-constitution though an internally generated and self-directed decision but a response to an external address'.[47] This recreation is what McFadyen calls a 'recontextualization', this time within the 'God-context':

The God-context in which these called persons now find themselves is not, however, primarily individual. Such individual

---

[45] Kelly and Nelson, *Cost of Moral Leadership*, 131.
[46] McFadyen, 'Call to Discipleship', 462, 462–3.
[47] McFadyen, 'Call to Discipleship', 463.

confrontations take place within a history of salvation which is not principally individual but corporate. [48]

The individual experiences grace, but grace is not contingent upon the individual. Rather, grace is experienced by the individual, through 'intersubjectively valid structures of meaning which belong to the social context' in which 'events of grace' take place.[49] In short, grace happens *to* you, not *because* of you.

Community and service[50]

In locating grace within community we see how Bonhoeffer's theology of discipleship and sociality was radically variant to the prevailing Harnackian individualism of his day.[51] It is true that the operation of grace acknowledges the importance of individual obedience:

> Christ makes everyone he calls into an individual. Each is called alone. Each must follow alone. (*DBWE 4*, 92)

But this 'aloneness' is emphatically *not* the same thing as the heroic individualism of nineteenth- and twentieth-century German Protestantism and the American Frontier. Then the individual was defined by his own, autonomous, authority.[52] Rather, Bonhoeffer means that the obedient disciple, through a radical dislocation, is called out of, away from, 'immediate relationships', 'connections with the world' (*DBWE 4*, 98, 93), for this 'immediacy [*Unmittelbarkeit*] is a delusion', and one which is strengthened and deepened by every claim of 'father…, mother…, spouse…, child…, nation…, history' upon the disciple: it is 'the caprice of self-willed

---

[48]McFadyen, 'Call to Discipleship', 472.

[49]McFadyen, 'Call to Discipleship', 472.

[50]For more on the importance of community to Bonhoeffer's thinking see my own *If You Meet George Herbert on the Road, Kill Him* (2009), chapter 9.

[51]See the discussions on pp. 114, 506 above.

[52]For the importance, and misleading nature, of 'authority' in Bohoeffer's thinking, see *DBWE 12*, 279–82.

life' (*DBWE 4*, 95, 92, 93). Instead, in its place is the reality that Bonhoeffer expressed aphoristically when he said '...the Christian concept of the person is really exhibited only in sociality...' (*DBWE 1*, 33). To be placed in the 'God-context' requires an 'external address', which does not, and cannot, occur in 'asocial terms'.[53] Through grace (the process of decontextualization from self-infatuation, and recontextualization within the God-context), the *delusion* of the unmediated *individual* is replaced with the *sociality* of the *person*: for Bonhoeffer 'human beings [are] essentially social persons whose personal and corporate relationships have become self-contradictory through egotism and destructive power'.[54]

The only solution (practical, existential, eternal) is to recognize the transformation of human nature that was effected by self-revelation of God to humanity in the person and saving actions of Jesus Christ: now, because of Christ, our true nature is recovered, to be and to become people in relationship – with each other and with God. In other words, to be human means to be in community,[55] constituted by the call, presence, and judgement of Christ. The Christian community, in this way, is *Christus als Gemeinde exist-ierend*, Christ existing as community (*DBWE 1*, 121).

The only means by which *Christus als Gemeinde* might be true is discipleship. Through discipleship, and within the community of the Body of Christ, 'obedience and faith, works and grace are harmonised in responding to the Lord whose claim upon us is both a total demand and the concrete fullness of grace'.[56]

The confirmation of truth through praxis

But how does this work in practice? Is it just a nice theory, but lacking in empirical data and sociological confirmation? Could

---

[53] McFadyen, 'Call to Discipleship', 463.
[54] Clifford J. Green, *Bonhoeffer: a theology of sociality*, (1999), 156.
[55] See *DBWE 1*, n1, p. 60, and Clifford Green, 'Human sociality and Christian community', in *The Cambridge Companion to Dietrich Bonhoeffer*, (1999), 115.
[56] Haddon Willmer, 'Costly discipleship', in *The Cambridge Companion*, 177.

it be enacted, in a European society in which the power of the *Führerprinzip* dominated?

Bonhoeffer was a realist, but a realist with a particular way of interpreting reality. He knew that there was 'no real Christian existence outside the reality of the world and no real worldliness outside the reality of Jesus Christ'. To deny the ultimate reality of Jesus is to attempt to 'evade the world', which will, in the end, result in 'a sinful surrender to the world'.[57] This wasn't mere theological speculation. It gave Bonhoeffer the means to interpret pragmatically the events of his day. Thus, the worsening international situation in the winter of 1932/33 could be seen as the result of following the world authorities which 'do not constitute absolute authority'. That can only be found in Jesus Christ, who, however, is not concerned to 'bring about security, peace, and quiet', but simply to show that 'we should love God', and thus become disciples and 'witnesses for peace'.[58]

> Bonhoeffer was interested not in merely theologizing about church, but in being part of a church community committed to God's Word in service of others, particularly society's unfortunates, and willing to make the sacrifices embodied in truthfully following Jesus Christ, even though that way might lead to the cross.[59]

The renunciation of mythological-leadership

Any 'leadership' exercised by a Christian must be based, not on personal skills, not on innate traits, not on charismatic authority, not a will to power, not on a willingness to exercise violence, nor on a manipulation of others' fears and fantasies. The end result of all those strategies is to become complicit in the monomyth

---

[57] Dietrich Bonhoeffer, *Ethics*, DBWE 6 (2005), 61.
[58] Lecture, 'Christ and Peace', November/December 1933, *DBWE 12*, 259.
[59] Kelly and Nelson, *Cost of Moral Leadership*, 147.

of redemptive violence. Rather, the 'leadership' exercised by a Christian must be based firmly, wholly and completely under the authority of Christ.

We tease out the renunciation of *MythL* by returning to the five things we could say about leadership and discipleship in the New Testament at the end of the previous chapter.

First, the authority of Christ was primarily expressed by calling people to follow him, in a way in which a direct allegiance to his person and authority was expected. We saw how Schweizer described this as 'decisive, indeed as *the* decisive act'[60] of being a Christian. To acknowledge the authority of Christ means to be a *follower* of Jesus. And to acknowledge the authority of Christ, which, to use the vocabulary of Schweizer and Bonhoeffer, is to be a *disciple* of Christ, is not to choose one authority above other authorities: 'There is only one discipleship, because discipleship is the immediate relation to the one and only Lord'.[61]

Second, to hear Jesus's calling, and to respond to it as a follower, begins something new, in which everything will be changed. As Bonhoeffer said in a letter written from Finkenwalde: 'My calling is quite clear to me. What God will make of it, I do not know'.[62] The best way to describe this, according to Schweizer, is 'an act of divine grace'.[63] Hence, we cannot understand the calling as being *our* possession, under *my* control: 'To hear Jesus' call to discipleship, one needs no personal revelation. Listen to the preaching and receive the sacrament! Listen to the gospel of the crucified and risen Lord!' (*DBWE 4*, 202).

Third, 'following Jesus' means sharing an intimacy with Jesus, and performing acts of service with and to him. As Hurtado says, this means following *Jesus,* 'with no rival, no distraction and no competition for the allegiance of his disciples'.[64] But even within the Discipleship Community of Jesus there were pressures on the

---

[60] Eduard Schweizer, *Lordship and Discipleship* 20.
[61] Willmer, 'Costly discipleship', 177.
[62] 27 January 1936: in *DBW* 14 (1996), 113; Bethge, *Bonhoeffer*, 205.
[63] Schweizer, *Lordship and Discipleship*, 20.
[64] Hurtado, 'Following Jesus', 25.

disciples to behave otherwise: Lk. 9.46 shows us an example.[65] Bonhoeffer noted, realistically, that 'no Christian community ever comes together without this argument appearing as a seed of discord' (*DBWE 5*, 93).

Therefore, fourth, submission to the authority of Jesus requires self-denial, which extends further than the limits of the individual's body and will, and includes the complex network of relationships, responsibilities and obligations in which we deposit our esteem (both self-esteem and social-esteem). These are all to be given up. Willmer again:

> Discipleship was more than an open, indefinite and individual-istic life-quest, because Jesus Christ who called was Lord of the world. Discipleship was not a humanist adventure but a theologically grounded obedience.[66]

That obedience was to be expressed by the requirement of service, which precedes the self and prevents self-actualisation at the cost of others. As Bonhoeffer put it:

> …the church is fellowship, the church-community of the saints, freed by God from isolated existence, each one belonging to the other, giving themselves, accepting responsibility because it was placed on them by God; a community through sacrifice, prayer and forgiveness, shattering the chains of isolation, the reality of being together and for one another, love, fraternity.[67]

Fifth, and finally, to deny this self in order to follow Jesus will lead to rejection, suffering and death, in a world in which the will to power and the will to submit to power are terrifyingly strong. As Bonhoeffer said: 'When Christ calls a man, he bids him come and die' (*DBWE 4*, n. 11, p. 87). But it is not 'suffering as such which defines or exalts the disciple',[68] and neither is it the joy of

---

[65] See the discussion of this passage on p. 225.
[66] Willmer, 'Costly discipleship', 178.
[67] 'What is Church?'. (January 1933) in *DBWE 12*, 263.
[68] Willmer, 'Costly discipleship', 177.

the follower of Christ. Faithfulness to the calling, faithfulness to be a *follower*, as exemplified and achieved by Jesus, is the path to redemptive glory, for the Teacher and disciple alike.

These lessons need to be learnt in a community, a *discipleship* community, as this is the only reality constituted on the only reality of Jesus Christ. As Bonhoeffer later said about the regime he developed in Finkenwalde, the 'brothers' in the seminary need to learn

> ...how to lead a community life in the daily and strict obedience to the will of Christ Jesus, in the practice of the humblest and noblest service one Christian brother can perform for another. They must learn to recognize the strength and liberation to be found in their brotherly service and their life together in a Christian community. For this is something they are going to need.[69]

For any professed Christian community truly to be a Christian community Gerhard Lohfink argues that it needs to demonstrate a 'confirmation of truth through praxis'.[70] We have seen how that truth through praxis was exemplified in the life and ministry of Dietrich Bonhoeffer. In Bonhoeffer we can see the intellectual, theological, and practical rejection of the monomyth of leadership: the *Führerprinzip* and redemptive violence are condemned, through prophetic word and prophetic action. In Bonhoeffer we see, to paraphrase 1 John, no 'darkness of leadership at all'.

Are there any instances of popular film which also share in this Gospel of submission, a willingness to place discipleship before all and any expression of self-individuation? Interestingly, there are two recent examples of just such a thing.

---

[69]Bonhoeffer, *DBW 14*, 175; quoted in Kelly and Nelson, *Cost of Moral Leadership*, 157.
[70]Lohfink, *Jesus and Community*, 176.

The way to powerlessness

Of Gods and Men tells the story of eight French Christian monks who lived in a monastery in the remote Atlas mountains of Algeria. It is closely based on the lives and deaths of the Cistercian monks of Our Lady of Atlas, Tibhirine, and the inspired witness of their Abbot, Dom Christian de Chergé (played in the film by Lambert Wilson). The film was very well received, nominated for a BAFTA, and winning two prizes at Cannes, three Césars, including 'Best Film'.[71]

The film is set in the early 1990s, at the beginning of the civil war which engulfed Algeria following the election success and subsequent suppression of the Islamic Salvation Front (the *Front Islamique du Salut*).[72] We do not realize the time and place to begin with, as the film, deliberately, shows us an almost directionless depiction of the rhythm of the monks' life; praying, singing, working their fields, making honey. The monks read and write letters for their illiterate neighbours, participate in the village's rites of passage. Br Luc (Michel Lonsdale) runs a free medical clinic. Gradually we realize the time, place and danger in which the monks find themselves. Their monastery was founded during the time of French colonialism, and remained in Algeria after the war of independence. They are an unwelcome presence to the Algerian government, and feel threatened by the Islamist terrorists who are at work in the locality: a construction crew of Croatians are brutally murdered nearby. The monks are uncertain about their future and their vocation. Should they leave? What would that say to those who live in the village clustered around the monastery walls? As the village elders say to the monks: 'We're the birds. You're the branch. If you go, we lose our footing'.

The decision to stay is not an easy one. Dom Christian refuses an offer of a military presence in the monastery by the *Wali*, the

---

[71] Interestingly, it was not shortlisted at the Academy Awards that year, the prize going to the Danish thriller *Hævnen*.

[72] A good introduction to the religious and political situation of post-colonial Algeria, as well as an excellent history of the monastery of Notre Dame d'Atlas is found in John W. Kiser, *The Monks of Tibhirine* (2003).

governor. At the subsequent chapter meeting, he is admonished by the brothers. Br Célestin (Phillippe Laudenbach) demands 'How could you decide this without consulting us? All our lives are at stake'. Christian responds 'What would you have done in my place?'.

[Célestin] I'd have let everyone speak and listened to each opinion.
[Christian] To answer what, in the end?

Christian cannot see the problem. A decision had to be made, and the decision he made was in line with the traditions and teachings of his order. Brother Jean-Pierre (Loïc Pichon) intervenes: 'The answer isn't important. The very principle of community is compromised by your attitude'. Christian returns to the question: 'Well then, who wants the army present in the monastery?'. Jean-Pierre, gently, refuses to be deflected: 'You refuse to understand what we are saying'. 'I don't understand!' says Christian, testily. 'None of us chose to live here to be protected by a corrupt government'. There is a pause, and Jean-Pierre continues: 'Christian. We didn't elect you to decide on your own'. Christian is chastened, stops, looks down. He finally realizes that the issue, for the life and security of the community, is not the physical safety provided or not provided by a military complicit in killings and terror. The greater threat to the life of this, Christian, community, is the way in which they make their decisions. The *process* both indicates and determines the content of their life together.

Br Christophe (Olivier Rabourdin) experiences a crisis of faith and vocation. His prayers at night are noisy and violent, like Jacob wrestling with the angel of his fears. He speaks to Dom Christian:

[Christophe] Dying, here and now, does it achieve anything?
[Christian] Remember. You've already given your life. You gave it by following Christ. When you decided to leave everything. Your life, your family, your country. The family you could have raised.
[Christophe] I don't know if it's true anymore. I don't get it. Why be martyrs? For God? To be heroes? To prove we're the best?

There is no easy solution, no argument into conviction or courage. Rather Christophe *and* Christian continue to live in their fears and their uncertainties within the community.

What gives the monks the moral courage to face their death? It was through that deeply unfashionable quality, by being religious, living under a rule and within a creedal order. As (the factual) Dom Christian told a group of Belgian nuns: 'It's magnificent, this order-liness and regularity. One simply continues to do the things one has to do'.[73] Part of that orderliness, which (the fictional) Christian learnt is the surrender of the Abbot to the will of the community. Whereas the Rule of St Benedict describes the Abbot as holding 'the place of Christ in the monastery', responsible for teaching and commanding so as to 'permeate the minds of his disciples' like 'the leaven of divine justice',[74] he is also, in the next chapter injuncted to 'call the whole community together', as 'often anything important is to be done in the monastery'. Just as Célestin advised, the abbot is to hear 'the advice of the brothers, ...ponder it and follow what he judges the wise course'.[75]

There is no 'great man', no 'will to leadership', in a discipleship community: no one is 'to follow his own heart's desire'.[76] The monks abide, in their fears and in danger, but they are transformed through that abiding. Early in the film we are shown a meal in which the lection read as the minks eat in silence prefigures their faith and fate:

> Accepting our powerlessness and our extreme poverty is an invitation, an urgent appeal to create with others relationships not based on power. Recognizing my weaknesses, I accept those of others. I can bear them, make them mine in imitation of Christ. Such an attitude transforms us for our mission. Weakness in itself is not a virtue, but the expression of a

---

[73] Quoted in Kiser, *Tibhirine*, 153.
[74] *RB 1980: The Rule of St. Benedict*, Fry (ed.) OSB (1981), chapter 2:2, 5.
[75] *RB 1980*, chapter 3:1–2.
[76] *RB 1980*, chapter 3:8.

fundamental reality which must constantly be refashioned by faith, hope and love.[77]

The way to community

Emilio Estevez's independently produced film, *The Way,* is on the surface a story of bereavement and mourning. It tells the story of Tom Avery, a settled, conservative, and irascible ophthalmologist from Ventura, California, who travels reluctantly to St-Jean-Pied-de-Port in the French Pyrenees to repatriate the body of his only son. Daniel died in a mountain accident on the first day of walking the Camino, the pilgrimage route which leads through the Pyrenees across northern Spain to the shrine of St James in Santiago de Compostela. Tom and Daniel were estranged; the father's complacency and the son's fecklessness equally to blame. The power of the relationship, which is related through flash-back, and present visions, is strengthened by the casting: Estevez plays Daniel, his real-life father, Martin Sheen, plays Tom. The quality of the acting, script and direction manages to show, movingly, parental grief without succumbing to cloying sentimentality.

At first Tom's only intention is to retrieve his son's body and meagre possessions, and to return to California as soon as he can. However, on a whim, unexplainable to anyone, but especially to himself, he decides to take his son's ashes on the pilgrimage, and to walk the 500 miles to Santiago. He is an unprepared pilgrim. As the film's press kit says: Tom is 'reluctant, uncertain, skeptical, a bit broken and yet, for all his fierce independence, most definitely in need of sustenance from others on his way through'.[78]

Tom is shown to be comfortable in the company of his golfing companions in California, but following his son's death he knows, full well, that there is nothing to be gained from the company of

---

[77] The reading is not identified in the film, but it comes from a sermon preached by Fr Christian Chessel, 'In My Weakness, I Find My Strength'. A longer extract is quoted by Kiser: *Tibhirine*, 199. Chessel was murdered in Tizi-Ouzou, Algeria, in December 1994.

[78] Robyn Leff, 'Press Kit for 'The Way" (2010).

others ('Do you think [Tom] would want to talk to me about it?'. 'I think he'd sooner shove that walking stick down your throat'.) And yet, despite himself, he picks up companions: Joost (Yorick Van Wageningen), the 'fat Dutchman' who is walking to lose weight; Sarah (Deborah Kara Unger) from Canada who only wants to quit cigarettes; Jack (James Nesbitt), a writer from Northern Ireland who is struggling with writer's block – Estevez has admitted the conscious allusion to Dorothy and her three companions in *The Wizard of Oz*.

Tom knew what he would experience before he set off, and none of it would be worthwhile: 'we're all just taking a really long walk, I suppose'. His only aspiration is to walk the Camino, gradually divesting himself of his son's ashes. Tom knows that experience of walking the Camino, and the *peregrinos* he meets, will have nothing that he needs. As Sarah puts it, in exasperation at the speed and business-like nature of Tom's walking, 'Doesn't this guy ever stop to smell the flowers? This isn't a race! So why does it piss me off so much that I haven't seen him stop to take a break? Why does something which should be inspirational make me so... angry?'.

And yet, as Estevez wrote the part and Sheen played it, the key to understanding Tom is the 'chipping away slowly and subtly at the thick slabs of armor [he] has built around himself, as a father and as a man, over the years'. As Sheen says, 'over time, [Tom] begins to see that he's going to have to learn to rely on others – and more than that, he's going to have to let them know that they can rely on him'.[79]

Tom does not set out to find followers. In fact, he does everything he can to avoid 'tag-a-longs'. Even so, the palpable determination he has to reach Santiago conveys itself to people who encounter him, who are each of them, as lost and hurting as he is, even though he is unable to admit it. The kernel of his dispute with his son echoes as a refrain through the film: 'My life might not seem like much to you, but it's the life I choose'. 'You don't choose your life, Dad. You live one'. At the end of the film, Tom has realized

---

[79] Leff, Press Kit for 'The Way', 7.

this truth, through his journey to Santiago, and, more importantly, through the recognition of his connection with humanity, represented by Joost, Sarah and Jack.

The Way To Freedom

Bonhoeffer made no films, but he did express an antidote to *MythL* in the form of a poem. 'Stations on the Way to Freedom' was written in Tegel Prison sometime in early August 1944, and included with a letter of birthday greetings sent to Eberhard Bethge on 14 August.[80] Bonhoeffer realized by this point that the powers of totalitarian violence would achieve his death. And yet he was prepared to celebrate his 'freedom'. Not from confinement, certainly. By 'freedom', Bonhoeffer rather meant the presence of God in his life, accepting his unavoidable calling to live in the presence of God, a 'living with' that meant 'submission, dedicating oneself to God's will and action in any walk of life'.[81] This is 'discipleship', which is both 'the witness of a 'disciple' – that is, 'a human being sanctified by God'[82] – and is also 'being delivered into God's will and plan'.[83] But it would be wrong to think that Bonhoeffer is being programmatic or catechetical in either this poem or his life: 'Stations' is not Bonhoeffer's attempt to teach Christians how they should live. Rather, 'he is examining God's overwhelming presence in a human life'.[84] There is no other way possible, once one accepts the fact and ethical imperative of God's presence in the life of a disciple.

The disciple encounters God in stations,[85] 'places of God's acting',[86] which, because God is 'I AM' [Exod. 3.14], are also

---

[80] See the discussion of the dating, significantly *after* the failure of the 20 July Plot to assassinate Hitler, in Bonhoeffer, *DBWE 8* (2010), n. 1, p. 512.

[81] Hans G. Ulrich, '"Stations on the Way to Freedom": The Presence of God – The Freedom of Disciples', in *Who Am I?*, Wannenwetsch (ed.) (2009), 152.

[82] Ulrich, 'Freedom of Disciples', 151.

[83] Ulrich, 'Freedom of Disciples', 151.

[84] Ulrich, 'Freedom of Disciples', 152.

[85] In German, 'Stationen' has a greater subtlety of meaning than can be translated by 'stages' or 'stations'.

[86] Ulrich, 'Freedom of Disciples', 152.

'places of God's presence'.[87] There are four stations: the disciple encounters God, first, in *discipline* ('Zucht'), secondly in *action* ('Tat'), thirdly in *suffering* ('Leiden'), and finally, in and through *death* ('Tod'). We begin the journey with the search for freedom, but not the self-serving 'freedom' sought by the self-individuating American Adam:

> If you set out to seek freedom, then learn above all things
> to govern your soul and your senses, for fear that your passions
> and longings may lead you away from the path you should follow.[88]

But discipline is not expressed by 'thoughts taking wing' (stanza 2). The disciple is required to 'go out to the storm and the action', trusting in God's goodness and his commandments. Inevitably, to act in a world of storm, the disciple will experience suffering: 'Your hands, so strong and active, / are bound' (stanza 3). Suffering comes in being powerless, but joy and blessed freedom comes from placing that moment of suffering back in God's hands. The token of that perfected glory is completed in death, the 'greatest of feasts', when we finally 'may see that which here remains hidden' (stanza 4). We have sought freedom in 'discipline, action, and suffering'. It is only through dying that we may behold freedom 'revealed in the Lord'.

We can see, through the life and teaching of a man like Dietrich Bonhoeffer, and in occasional glimpses of our culture in films like *The Way* and *Of Gods and Men*, the condemnation of the *mythos* of leadership that is part of, and sustains, the 'system'[89] of violence and oppression. This *mythos* stands condemned, for its worship of power, its pursuit of injustice, its fetishizing of violence, by the silent witness of the mythos of discipleship. Freedom is found, in the hands of God, as we pass through discipline, action and suffering.

---

[87] Ulrich, 'Freedom of Disciples', 154.

[88] Quotations from 'Stations on the Way to Freedom' are all take from John Bowden's translation in Ulrich, 'Freedom of Disciples', 149.

[89] As Wink and Klemperer both call it: Wink, *Engaging the Powers*, 110–11; Klemperer, *The Language of the Third Reich*, chapter 17, 'System' and 'Organisation'.

It is a life that is possible; in reality, it is the only life that is possible if we are to remain, or become, human.

All who either, confessionally, seek to be a disciple of Christ, or those who, morally, seek to resist the 'Domination System' of *MythL*, can find their ethical model in Willmer's summation of the praxis and doxis of Dietrich Bonhoeffer:

> [Bonhoeffer] spoke consistently as a disciple, in a fellowship of disciples. He worked in the world which was mediated to him through the only relation, with Jesus Christ, which he believed could and should be a direct, immediate relation. He rested his whole being, including the worth of his ideas, on the truth of Jesus Christ as the Lord and Son of God. That was a truth he yielded to as a disciple who obeys the call; he explained it with no rational apology but lived it to the end in faith.[90]

---

[90] Willmer, 'Costly discipleship', 188.

Acknowledgements

This book has its origins in a lecture series given more than ten years ago at Christ Church, Oxford, my then place of work. The Dean and Canons of Christ Church had the admirable custom of presenting a Summer Lecture series on some aspect of their current research, gathered under a portmanteau title, to the Cathedral congregation and to any interested auditors from the College or University. In the summer of 2001 the series was on 'Discipleship'. Intimidated by the prospect of contributing to a lecture series given by Regius Professors of Theology, Ethics, Church History and Philosophy I proposed that I speak on the way in which followers were depicted in Hollywood film: it was the one area I knew that my senior colleagues were *not* experts. I prepared and delivered the lecture and it was warmly received. Later, Peter Francis, warden of St Deiniol's Library, Hawarden (now Gladstone's Library), allowed me to deliver another version of the same thesis to the *Film and Theology Colloquy* held in April 2004. With two versions and two deliveries, I remained convinced that there was something more to this idea. In 2007 I was introduced to Dr Chris Deacy, lecturer in Practical Theology at the University of Kent in Canterbury. I had read and enjoyed Dr Deacy's work: his exploration of the dialogue between theology and film exactly addressed my interests and intuitions. I knew that I should pursue the idea in a more rigorous and directed manner, and so began a PhD.

This book grew out of my PhD (the rough difference being the majority of the footnotes taken out, the jokes and prejudices put back in). Dr Deacy was a great encouragement in making sure the thesis was something more than an ecclesiastical rant. Dr David Munchin, a friend, colleague and companion at Gladstone's

Library, shared many of the earliest expressions of my ideas, and honed them with wit and wisdom. Dr Tim Ling was always prepared to exchange ideas and methods, usually over an all-day breakfast. Clergy colleagues in dioceses as disparate as St Albans, Exeter, Chelmsford, London and North Carolina received presentations of work- and ideas-in-progress, and by not reacting with complete incredulity, emboldened me to continue. Occasionally the vehemence of their opposition helped me realise I had hit a nerve (a fine example of confirmation bias on my part).

But colleagues were just there for the ideas: it was my family who lived with the writing. My children have borne the writing of three books and a thesis, with Dad writing another paragraph before the pasta boiled over. My daughters at least, were able to see the point of this work once they learnt that I could include their favourite television programme, *Glee*, in my analysis of Ralph Waldo Emerson (they didn't care for him, but *Glee* made the thesis credible—see page 98). So, to Hannele, Jonas, Rosa, and Arwen, thank you.

The greatest burden was carried by my wife Siân. Undertaking a PhD part-time, whilst working full-time at a job which only allows one day off a week, meant much time that could have been spent doing household chores, supervising children's activities, or even spending time together, was often swallowed by 'just a quick visit to the Library'. Despite this neglect on my part, she was always encouraging, and more than a hundred times expressed her confidence and pride in me and my work.

I am more grateful than I can say to my parents, David and Sheila Anthony, who supported my studies financially, more than 20 years after they might have been reasonably expected to end that support. My father's enthusiasm for the films of World War Two, and his scepticism for their historical accuracy, was probably at the root of my fascination with what war films could tell us about a peacetime society. Even so, from filial respect, I could not face discussing *The Battle of the Bulge* ('Those are never King Tiger tanks, they're post-war American M47 Pattons!'). It is, properly, his teaching at the root of my own explorations, and so, properly, to him this book is dedicated.

A Select Bibliography

A full bibliography and filmography is available at
http://religion.lewisanthony.continuumbooks.com

John Adair and John Nelson (eds), *Creative Church Leadership*
  (Canterbury Press, 2004).
Jeanine Basinger, *The World War II Combat Film: Anatomy of a Genre*
  (Wesleyan University Press, 2003).
Eberhard Bethge, *Dietrich Bonhoeffer: a Biography*, Barnett and
  Robertson (eds), (Fortress Press, 2000).
Harold Bloom, *The American Religion: The Emergence of the
  Post-christian Nation* (Simon & Schuster, 1993).
Dietrich Bonhoeffer, "The Führer and the Individual in the Younger
  Generation," in *Berlin, 1932–1933*, Nicolaisen, Scharffenorth, and
  Rasmussen (eds), DBWE 12 (Fortress Press, 2009), 268–82.
Kelton Cobb, *The Blackwell Guide to Theology and Popular Culture*
  (Blackwell Publishing, 2005).
Steven Croft, "Leadership and the Emerging Church," in *Focus on
  Leadership* (Foundation for Church Leadership, 2005), 7–41.
Philip R. Davies, "'Life of Brian' Research," in *Whose Bible Is It Anyway?*
  (T. & T. Clark, 2004), 142–55.
Keith Grint, *Leadership: Limits and Possibilities* (Palgrave Macmillan,
  2005).
Robert Hewison, *Monty Python: The Case Against* (Methuen, 1981).
John W. Kiser, *The Monks of Tibhirine: Faith, Love, and Terror in Algeria*
  (St. Martin's Griffin, 2003).
Victor Klemperer, *The Language of the Third Reich* (Athlone Press, 2000).
Siegfried Kracauer, *From Caligari to Hitler: a Psychological History of the
  German Film* (Princeton University Press, 1947).
John Shelton Lawrence and Robert Jewett, *The Myth of the American
  Superhero* (Eerdmans, 2002).
Alasdair C. MacIntyre, *After Virtue: a Study in Moral Theory* (Duckworth,
  1985).

Bruce J. Malina, *The Social World of Jesus and the Gospels* (Routledge, 1996).

Antonio Marturano and Jonathan Gosling (eds), *Leadership: The Key Concepts* (Routledge, 2008).

Joseph McBride, *Searching for John Ford* (Faber, 2003).

John P. Meier, *A Marginal Jew: Companions and Competitors* (Yale University Press, 2001).

Gene D. Phillips and Rodney Hill (eds), *The Encyclopedia of Stanley Kubrick* (Facts on File, 2002).

Randy Roberts and James S. Olson, *John Wayne, American* (University of Nebraska Press, 1997).

Richard Slotkin, *Gunfighter Nation: The Myth of the Frontier in Twentieth-century America* (Atheneum, 1992).

Lawrence H. Suid, *Guts and Glory: The Making of the American Military Image in Film* (University Press of Kentucky, 2002).

Jürgen Trimborn, *Leni Riefenstahl: a Life* (I. B. Tauris, 2008).

Robert Warren, "Styles of Leadership," in *A Time for Sharing: Collaborative Ministry in Mission* (Church House Publishing, 1995), 25–8.

Rowan Williams, *The Truce of God: Peacemaking in Troubled Times* (Canterbury Press, 2005).

Garry Wills, *John Wayne: The Politics of Celebrity* (Faber, 1997).

Walter Wink, *Naming the Powers: The Language of Power in the New Testament* (Fortress Press, 1984).

Brian Winston, "Was Hitler There?: Reconsidering 'Triumph of the Will'," *Sight and Sound* 50, no. 2 (March 1981): 102–8.

Index